P9-DXI-013

Literature as Social Discourse

THE PRACTICE OF LINGUISTIC CRITICISM

Literature as Social Discourse

THE PRACTICE OF LINGUISTIC CRITICISM

Roger Fowler

INDIANA UNIVERSITY PRESS

BLOOMINGTON

© Roger Fowler 1981
All rights reserved

No part of this book may be reproduced or utilized
in any form or by any means, electronic or mechanical,
including photocoyping and recording, or by any information
storage and retrieval system, without permission in
writing from the publisher. The Association of
American University Presses' Resolution on
Permissions constitutes the only exception to this prohibiton.

Manufactured in Great Britain

Library of Congress Cataloging in Publication Data

Fowler, Roger.
    Literature as social discourse.
    Bibliography: p.
    Includes index.
    1. Discourse analysis, Literary—Addresses, essays,
lectures.   2. Style, Literary—Addresses, essays, lectures.   3. Language and languages—Style—Addresses,
essays, lectures.   4. Criticism—Addresses, essays,
lectures.   5. Sociolinguistics—Addresses, essays,
lectures.   I. Title.
P302.F63   808'.00141   81-47761

ISBN 0-253-33511-6   AACR2

    1   2   3   4   5   86   85   84   83   82

Contents

Preface

Literature as Social Discourse is a collection of essays on language, literary styles and their social contexts and functions. The essays were written ca. 1973-1978. They thus span a relatively brief period of time and reflect a crystallization in my thinking about linguistics and literature. I argue that, first and foremost, literature is a kind of *discourse*, a language activity within social structure like other forms of discourse. It is as amenable to linguistic study as are all other discourses such as conversations, letters, notices, book-writing, broadcasting, etc. Linguistic analysis of literary discourse aims first of all to specify the formal patterns of texts — poems, plays, novels, etc. — with a degree of precision which is unachievable in conventional literary criticism; avoiding impressionism and permitting clearly articulated debate. But the project goes further than just describing the formal structures which give texts their shape and texture. It is a mistake to regard literary texts as autonomous patterns of linguistic form cut off from social forces. If a linguist such as myself sees them as not simply *texts* but also, or rather, as *discourses*, all kinds of ways are open to interpret and describe them in terms of their vital cultural functions. From this perspective, literature is, like all language, interaction between people and between institutions and people. To regard it as social discourse is to stress its interpersonal and institutional dimensions, concentrating on those parts of textual structure which reflect and which influence relations within society. A study of literary styles which concentrates on such matters requires methodological and theoretical underpinnings which are more sophisticated and more ambitious than those usually presupposed in linguistic stylistics. First, a broad range of techniques of linguistic analysis to cater for the wide range of linguistic constructions which prove to be significant in literary discourse: I have drawn eclectically from a number of linguistic models to provide the requisite coverage. Second, this approach requires a materialist theory of social relations and practices, one which proposes a dialectical relationship between communication and society: the theory of social practice, language and ideology which these essays assume could be described in general terms as Althusserian. Third, a strong sociolinguistic theory is needed: I view the varieties of language found in different literary texts as not simply reflecting the texts' locations in culture (though they do so), but also embodying versions of the world, interpretations or analyses of 'reality'. As Whorf suggested that different languages encode different *Weltanschauungen*, I follow M.A.K. Halliday in proposing that different varieties or registers within one language enshrine variant world-views. Speaking or writing in a variety articulates its own view of the world, and that articulation is a social practice, a conscious or unconscious intervention in the organization of society. Literature's cultural force has its origins in this property of language.

It is a delight to acknowledge the circumstances in which these essays were produced. The literary analyses and the linguistic theory were worked out in seminars and classes with undergraduate and graduate students at the University of East Anglia, Norwich, and at Brown University. To my graduate students at those universities I owe a special debt of thanks for many hours of supervisions during which my own ideas, just as much as my students', were clarified. Several of the papers, at different stages of their composition, were delivered as lectures to university audiences in England, West Germany, Finland, Spain, India and the United States; I am grateful to the people who invited me to those places for the opportunity to bring my arguments into a more formal state and to receive helpful criticism from members of the audiences. I cannot name all the colleagues at the University of East Anglia who have supplied an atmosphere of stimulating debate, so many being involved; among them, I wish particularly to thank Tony Gash for sharing a joint seminar on Literature and Linguistics with me for three years, and finally my co-workers and co-authors in the areas of sociolinguistics and social theory, Gunther Kress, Bob Hodge and Tony Trew.

Acknowledgements

I am grateful to the editors and publishers of the journals and books in which the essays first appeared for granting permission to reprint. The sources are as follows:

'Linguistic Criticism', Inaugural Lecture at the University of East Anglia, Norwich, November 20, 1979, and *UEA Papers in Linguistics*, 11 (January, 1980), 1-26.

'Literary Stylistics', review of Anne Cluysenaar, *Introduction to Literary Stylistics* London: Batsford, 1976, *Language and Style*, 12 (Winter, 1979), 50-51.

'Inclusive (Sociolinguistic) versus Exclusive (Formalist) Stylistics', review of William O.Hendricks, *Grammars of Style and Styles of Grammar* Amsterdam: North-Holland Publishing Co., 1976, *Style*, 11 (Spring, 1977), 199-204.

'Against Genteel Poetics', review of Andrew Welsh, *Roots of Lyric* Princeton, N.J.: Princeton University Press, 1978, *Journal of English and Germanic Philology*, 78 (April, 1979), 278-280.

'For Semiotics', review of Umberto Eco, *A Theory of Semiotics* Bloomington: Indiana University Press, and London: Macmillan, 1977, *Notes and Queries*, 124 (April, 1979), 163-165.

'Cohesive, Progressive and Localizing Aspects of Text Structure', in Teun A. van Dijk and János S. Petöfi, eds., *Grammars and Descriptions* Berlin: Walter de Gruyter, 1977, pp. 64-84.

'Literature as Discourse', Royal Institute of Philosophy Lectures, 1975-6 and Godfrey Vesey, ed., *Communication and Understanding* Hassocks: The Harvester Press, and Atlantic Highlands, N.J.: Humanities Press, Inc., 1977, pp. 174-194.

'The Referential Code and Narrative Authority', *Language and Style*, 10 (Summer, 1977), 129-161.

'The Reader: A Linguistic View', *Cahiers roumains d'études littéraires*, 4 (1977), 47-60.

'Anti-language in Fiction', *Style*, 13 (Summer, 1979), 259-278.

'Linguistics and, and versus, Poetics', *Journal of Literary Semantics*, 8 (1979), 3-21.

'Preliminaries to a Sociolinguistic Theory of Literary Discourse', *Poetics*, 8 (1979), 531-556.

Grateful acknowledgement is also made for permission to reprint the following copyright material: in Chapter Four, 'The Lover and his Lass' from James

Acknowledgements

Thurber, *Further Fables for our Time*, Hamish Hamilton Ltd, and Simon and Schuster Inc., copyright © 1962 by Helen W. Thurber. In Chapter Five, 'Missing dates' from William Empson, *Collected Poems*, by permission of Chatto and Windus Ltd and Harcourt, Brace, Jovanovich Inc; and extracts from 'Brothers, who when the sirens roar' (formerly known as 'A communist to others') from W.H. Auden, *The English Auden: Poems, Essays and Dramatic Writings 1927-1939*, Faber and Faber Ltd and *On This Island*, Random House Inc, by kind permission of Professor Edward Mendelson.

The texts of the essays are exactly as they appeared on first publication except for the correction of typographical errors; replacement of some references to articles 'forthcoming' by specific references to the dates of actual publication; conflation of separate bibliographical lists into one consolidated list of references; and provision of titles for the previously untitled book reviews reprinted as Chapter Three.

CHAPTER ONE

Introduction

The essays reprinted in this collection represent a second stage in my research in *literary stylistics*, or *linguistic stylistics*, an activity on which I have been engaged for some twenty years. Readers who are interested in how ideas develop and become transformed in a field such as stylistics may consult an earlier book of mine which reprints papers written in the 1960s, *The Languages of Literature*, published in 1971.[1]

Stylistics is 'literary' from the point of view of linguistics, or 'linguistic' from the perspective of literary studies. In either case, what is meant, in a nutshell, is the application of theoretical ideas and analytic techniques drawn from linguistics to the study of literary texts. The purpose of this Introduction is to locate the arguments of the present book within the context of previous and current stylistics. In the Introduction I am going to use the term 'stylistics' in a very inclusive sense, without theoretical precision, to refer to a diverse body of Anglo-American linguistic work on literature undertaken in the last twenty years. As a matter of fact, I do not like to refer to my own current research as 'stylistics', preferring *linguistic criticism*. Chapter Two, entitled 'Linguistic Criticism', is a fairly non-technical exposition of my present approach, while Chapters Three, Nine and Ten indicate — in rather polemical terms — both my sense of how linguistic criticism relates to alternative approaches, and also what I see as priorities for future research.

The intellectual context within which stylistics originated and developed was formed from three areas or schools of study: Anglo-American literary criticism using verbal analysis; modern American and contemporary European linguistics; and French structuralism.

Traditional literary scholarship, going back as far as the medieval and classical handbooks of rhetorical devices, had recognized the fundamental importance of linguistic structure in literature. Thanks to the tradition of rhetoric, the close verbal analysis of texts was a central activity in literary education, and so it continued into the twentieth century. In the 1920s and 1930s, verbal analysis received a new impulse from the theoretical and descriptive investigations of literary language pioneered by William Empson and I.A. Richards.[2] This approach too became firmly enshrined in literary education: in England with the teaching of 'practical criticism' at Cambridge University and elsewhere, and in America with the development of what came to be known as the 'New Criticism'. The New Criticism, strongly influenced by Empson and Richards, was the

11

product of a group of Southern writers and critics, notably Cleanth Brooks, John Crowe Ransom, Allen Tate and Robert Penn Warren. In 1938 Brooks and Warren published their textbook *Understanding Poetry* which provided models for the verbal analysis of poems at all levels of linguistic structure, and which exerted a massive influence on the way American students and teachers regarded and talked about poetry. After the Second World War came the theoretical articulation of the premisses which were assumed by the New Critics. Three books are particularly clear in their statements of the New Critical position on language in literature: René Wellek and Austin Warren's *Theory of Literature* (1942); W.K. Wimsatt's *The Verbal Icon* (1954); and Cleanth Brooks's *The Well Wrought Urn* (1947). For these writers, the literary text (of which the short lyric poem seems to be the paradigm) is a self-contained verbal artefact, a unique structure of language. Its mode of existence is linguistic, not historical; it is to be studied as a complex of integrated verbal patterns, not as the product of social forces or of the psychology of an author. Nor is the literary text a social force in its own right, according to these apologists for poetry: in their opinion, it is irrelevant and misleading to regard the text as in any way influencing the world around it. From my point of view, this anti-historicism, this insistent attempt to treat texts in isolation from their contexts, is unrealistic to say the least, and in effect prejudicial to a proper understanding of texts (see Chs nine and ten below). Nevertheless, the New Critics' concentrated focus on language did establish an encouraging context for the emerging discipline of linguistic stylistics in the 1950s: students of literature assumed that close analysis of language was the normal critical procedure, so there was an opportunity for linguists to offer methodological contributions to the verbal analysis of literary texts.[3]

Let us turn to the second influence on the development of stylistics, linguistics itself. I have outlined the linguistic background in *The Languages of Literature*, and there are a number of other accounts of the rise of modern linguistics, so I shall be very brief.[4] Three phases, or schools, of linguistic theory are relevant: relevant in very specific ways to growth and change in stylistics, and to the development and modification of my own aims and practices towards the formulation of an effective technique of linguistic criticism. The earliest phase, in the 1950s, was the closing decade of American structural or descriptive linguistics. American structuralism was a school of linguistic analysis which had been developed by one consistent and single-minded group of linguists on the basis of the ideas of Edward Sapir and Leonard Bloomfield in the 1920s and 1930s. By 1950 these linguists had devised a fairly complete and systematic set of procedures for analyzing the phonological and syntactic structure of sentences. The theoretical model implied by structural linguistics is much criticized today; but undeniably it provided an analytic terminology which could expound linguistic structure quite informatively and to a fair degree of detail, without dependence on the prejudicial theoretical terms of classical or school grammar. The earliest stylistic descriptions, in the 1950s, used the terminology of this model with confidence, and, particularly in the field of metrics, undoubtedly advanced our knowledge of literary structure.

The next stage in the history of linguistics was the overthrow of American structuralism by a new model, *transformational-generative grammar* ('TG'). In 1957, Noam Chomsky's revolutionary book *Syntactic Structures* was published. Chomsky argued that the linguistic theory of his predecessors was defective in several respects. He claimed that it misunderstood the purpose of linguistics, which he maintained was not the analysis of individual sentences but the formation of a theory of the linguistic abilities of speakers. Chomsky's arguments on this point were a valuable stimulus to research in the psychology of language. Of more interest to stylistics are his criticisms of the limitations of structural linguistics as an instrument of analysis. Insofar as linguistics concerns itself with sentence-structure, he argued, there are several properties of sentences with which structuralism cannot cope: notably, relationships between types of sentence such as active and passive; ambiguity ('Flying planes can be dangerous'); major structural differences concealed by superficial syntactic similarities ('John is easy/eager to please'); discontinuity ('He *held* the bank *up*'); degrees of grammaticalness; and several other properties. Chomsky's main remedy was to propose an additional level of 'transformational' structure, a set of rules of permutation, addition and deletion which would relate sentences to each other and to their underlying, abstract, forms. Now the concept of transformation was itself of great value to stylistics as an analytic tool, as will be amply evident from my own use of it below and from its use by others. But the Chomskyan revolution made an impact on many fronts. Chomsky demonstrated that language is very much more structurally complex than his predecessors had recognised; and the elaboration (and criticism) of Chomsky's theories in the 1960s and 1970s was motivated by a need to account for further and further layers and facets of linguistic structure. By radically questioning the structuralists' conception of language, Chomsky threw linguistics into sustained ferment and growth. Related disciplines such as stylistics received continuous stimulation from the development, the increasing power, of the parent linguistics. As new aspects of language came under the scrutiny of linguists, stylisticians followed each development and added a succession of new analytic tools to their technical equipment. Through this process of methodological enrichment, stylistics moved towards a capacity to discuss verbal structure in literature with something of the delicacy of the literary critic (impossible in the pre-transformational phase) but with a much more disciplined precision.

However, Chomskyan linguistics does not go far enough to provide a complete basis for stylistics. The transformational-generative model is limited in two related ways. First, it makes no claim to *explain* variations in linguistic structure. For example, TG argues plausibly that active and passive constructions are related to one another, that they are variant phrasings which are available to express the same idea. But if a passive has the same meaning as its active equivalent, one is bound to ask why the alternatives are provided by the structure of the language: what functions do the different constructions fulfil? TG does not concern itself with considerations of function, and this is a substantial limitation for literary study, which normally engages freely in functional explanations. Second, TG makes no offer to relate linguistic structure to social context — a rich source of functional explanations and a major obligation of linguistic criticism as I conceive of it. To make good these deficiencies in generative grammar, stylistics needs to draw concepts from some 'functional' and 'sociological' linguistic theory. Just such a linguistics is furnished by the British linguist M.A.K. Halliday, whose work has in fact already strongly influenced stylistics. Halliday's linguistic theory will receive extensive discussion below (Chapters four, eight and ten).

In addition to literary criticism and linguistics, the third school of thought which contributed to the development of stylistics was French structuralism. There are some excellent introductory textbooks on this movement,[5] so I shall say little about it here, reserving discussion of particular structuralist concepts until later chapters. What is generally known as 'French structuralism' is a diffuse set of intellectual movements including French linguistics, literary theory, anthropology, the semiotics of language and of culture. The theoretical basis is taken from the seminal *Course in General Linguistics* (1916) by the Swiss Ferdinand de Saussure.[6] Saussure sketched the design for a new science of signs within society, which he called 'semiology'. Semiology would cover the meanings and structures of all types of signifying systems, from language itself to gesture, fashion, architecture, eating habits, currency, etc., etc. Saussure concentrated on the linguistic system proper, which he regarded as structurally typical of the other systems; modern semiologists, such as Roland Barthes, have preferred to see language as the central semiological system *par excellence*, the others secondary systems modelled on the structure of language.[7] So Saussure's exposition of the general structural properties of language provided a theory and terminology which could be applied by extension to all the other language-like systems. The importance of Saussurean structuralism for literary studies is that it provides three linked perspectives on texts: the text may be seen as a sequence of sentences each to be analyzed linguistically; or as a single unified construction with its own particular internal structure in addition to the sentence-patterns it draws from the rules of the language; third, a literary text may be seen as a unit within a literary system, within the context of a set of relevant other works (e.g. English Shakespearean sonnets, or Miltonic verse narrative) related to the semiotic structure of the whole culture. These three structural perspectives on texts are thoroughly investigated in the work of Roman Jakobson — who has analyzed French and English short poems in minute detail — and in the writings on narrative structure of Roland Barthes and Tzvetan Todorov.

Literary structuralism in France in the 1960s and 1970s is really an independent school of literary theory developing in parallel with stylistics, and in some respects influencing it. Perhaps the chief importance of the movement is that, being based essentially in linguistics, French structuralism provides implicit support for other literary studies using linguistics, as well as suggesting specific concepts for incorporation in linguistic stylistics. These specific influences will be dealt with as they arise, below.

It is unnecessary to give a chronological survey of the development of stylistics;

rather, I want to indicate what facilities the discipline offers today, and the ways in which these resources were formed, with reference to some major innovations during the earlier stages of the discipline. I will also suggest some directions in which stylistics could profitably move in the future, and place my current work within that developmental context. This exposition will lead naturally to Chapter Two, which, written later than the other papers in this collection, articulates as simply as possible the major theoretical assumptions which have been emerging and being subjected to progressive reformulation over the last ten years. Chapter Five is a simple statement and illustration of another strand of my argument for a new orientation in stylistics, while Chapters Nine and Ten (which presuppose a more technically informed kind of reader) take a tough line in condemning attitudes which I regard as complacent and non-progressive in established stylistics and poetics (not exempting some of my own earlier and more modest claims for stylistics!).

The achievements of stylistics seem to me to fall into two categories, descriptive and theoretical, and I will discuss them in that order. As we have seen, literary criticism and literary education in recent years generally accept that literature is basically constituted in language; cumulatively, by advances in a large number of specific areas of language structure, stylistics has consolidated a descriptive apparatus which now embraces all levels of linguistic structure, which ventures into most traditional categories of literary from (metre, metaphor, point of view, etc.), and which has now been applied to all the major literary genres of poetry, prose fiction, and drama. Understandably, progress in descriptive stylistics has been from the most palpable, observable levels of structure to the more abstract: from phonology through syntax to semantics and pragmatics. Studies of metre, and of sound-texture in lyric poems, were among the first applications of linguistic analysis to literary works. In the late 1950s and early 1960s a number of studies of English verse were published using the four-stress-level system devised by the American structuralists Trager and Smith. The analysis was debated in a special issue of the literary magazine *The Kenyon Review* in 1956; Epstein and Hawkes published a detailed monograph in 1959; and in 1965 Seymour Chatman produced a full, considered study of the linguistic basis of English metre, reviewing earlier linguistic studies of prosody and devising his own exhaustive method of analysis based on an adaptation of the Trager-Smith system.[8] By this stage we had a working technique for metrical description which was capable of accounting for the subtle differences between English verse lines, and the individualities of different poets' metrical styles, with greater precision than the crude and misleading analysis based on the 'long' and 'short' syllables of classical prosody. The analysis could readily be used by literary critics who were not fully qualified in linguistic theory, as can be seen from an excellent book on sixteenth century English versification, John Thompson's *The Founding of English Metre*. Then something happened which is very typical of the evolution of stylistics. The Trager-Smith theory of stress and pitch came under strong attack from the new generative grammarians, who replaced it by an alternative account of English stress closely integrated with the syntactic and morphological construction of sentences. The ensuing debate about theories of stress within linguistics quickly sent waves of energy into stylistics: Halle and Keyser, Freeman, Beaver and others began to reanalyze English iambic pentameter verse in terms of the new generative model, disputing and refining the techniques. The product of this activity, by the early 1970s, was a reinvigoration of the study of prosody which, in English, had remained dormant and, when active, erroneous, for centuries. And for the descriptive critic, a choice of well-considered models of analysis was available, offering firm bases for prosodic description. The fact that by this time metrics was well re-established is reflected in the appearance in 1972 of *Versification*, edited by W.K. Wimsatt, a basic and informative linguistic account of metrical structures in a number of the world's major languages.

Traditional and modern syntactic categories (i.e. pretransformational syntax) provided a reliable basis for stylistic description; after all, a great deal was known about the syntax of English by the early years of this century, and major grammars such as Jespersen's multi-volume one were written decades before TG. Stylisticians such as Leo Spitzer and Roman Jakobson employed an essentially traditional terminology when they commented upon syntactic structure; literary critics in the Empson-Richards stream of practical criticism — Donald Davie, Winifred Nowottny, Christopher Ricks, for instance — make do with the familiar syntax that is so firmly established in our educational system, sharpened somewhat by the modern age's closer scientific scrutiny of language. From the point of view of contemporary linguistics (with hindsight), the syntactic analysis provided by American structural linguistics was no great improvement over traditional grammar; the two together gave a solid but uninspiring foundation for description of the surface structure of sentences. A major stimulus to the study of syntax within stylistics — and a boost to stylistics in general — was the introduction of transformational grammar in 1957. As we have seen, this new linguistic model not only added an extra dimension to syntactic description, it also provoked discussion of a range of supplementary issues, and, in response to problems which arose with the model, the development of new techniques and concepts. I will illustrate how two aspects of the development of TG inspired new enquiries into the workings of syntax in literary texts.

Transformations are structural relationships between syntactic entities. Just what kinds of syntactic structures they relate had been a matter for considerable debate among linguists; in my opinion 'transformation' may be used to cover different kinds of relationship so long as one is careful not to confuse usages. In the work of Chomsky's teacher Zellig Harris, transformations are relationships between sentences within one text — a notion which has very clear applications for stylistics as a way of showing links between different parts of a text, helping to map the internal structure of a text. Alternatively, transformations can be seen as relating sentences in paradigms existing as potential sets of options independent of any particular text: providing stylistic choices between transformationally related alternatives such as 'We can make an omelette' and 'What we can make is an omelette'. In Chomsky's own writings between 1957 and 1965, the transformational relationship is between a sentence and the underlying, more abstract, form from which it is derived: the *surface structure* and the *deep structure* of the sentence. The syntactic surface structure (the actual orderings of words, phrases and clauses) is a transformational rendering of an abstract deep structure or semantic structure. An important feature of the theory of deep structure and surface structure is that it includes a theory of paraphrase or synonymy, in the sense that the same deep structure may have two or more different surface structures, without change of meaning: the two sentences about omelettes just cited have the same meaning, in some reasonable sense of 'meaning', but the transformational routes from deep to surface structure are different. The stylistician Richard Ohmann seized upon this linguistic distinction as a possible illumination of one of the fundamental assumptions of stylistics: the form/content or expression/content distinction. The claim is that it is possible to say the same thing (content) in different ways (expressions), and that the sum of a writer's preferred forms of expression constitutes his style. In the new theory, expression is surface structure, content is deep structure, and the writer's preferred style consists of the characteristic transformations he uses. Whether or not this is the correct account of the form/content distinction (it now seems to me to be invalid), at least the surface structure/deep structure dichotomy offered a conceptual apparatus for thinking about this part of the theory of style, and a terminology for describing stylistic preferences. A number of writers followed Ohmann's lead in producing transformational analyses of authors' styles, often attempting to explicate characteristic literary-critical responses in terms of transformational structure. Examples are Chatman on Henry James, and Freeman on Dylan Thomas and on Keats.

A second example of cross-fertilization of TG and studies of poetic syntax is the research into *ungrammaticalness* which was stimulated by Chomsky's enquiries in the early 1960s into the status of sentences such as 'Colourless green ideas sleep furiously' and 'Sincerity admires the boy'. The technical problem in transformational-generative grammar is to ensure that such sequences are not generated as fully grammatical sentences of English; however, they are partly congruent with the syntactic rules of English, and they can often be assigned some kind of interpretation, so they must not be rejected absolutely. Now, although these sentences are ungrammatical or partly grammatical — so that one would not wish to, for instance, teach a foreign learner rules which would allow him to produce them — they do occur frequently in literature, and with particular regularity in modernist and post-modernist poetry. So while linguists worked on 'fixing' the grammar to account for the intuitively semi-grammatical status of such sentences, stylisticians eagerly joined in the discussion, gleaning whatever terminology emerged and proving it by application to standard modern poets of syntactic deviance such as e.e. cummings and Dylan Thomas. A series of articles by Levin, Thorne, Fowler, Hendricks and others explores this problem, I think adding substantially to our knowledge of the language of syntactic deviance; and probably contributing to general linguistic theory too, by bringing genuine (ungrammatical) texts to the discussion of a theoretical issue.

Stylistic studies utilizing linguistic theories of semantics (meaning) and pragmatics (use of language in personal interaction) have lagged behind. There is one obvious reason for this: the semantic level of language is abstract and difficult, so progress in linguistic semantics was very slow until recent years.[9] Another reason for the neglect of semantics in stylistics will emerge below in my critique of mainstream stylistics. But there has been a certain amount of research in semantic dimensions of literature. In the mid-1960s, a semantic theory was developed called *componential analysis:* the analysis of word-meanings into sets of semantic features or semantic components such as 'animate', 'non-human', 'quadruped', 'female' and the like. This theory provided a way of investigating metaphoric language, particularly usages where clashes of features are involved: in *the stream danced*, for instance, a verb which normally takes a human or at least animate subject is given a non-animate subject. Samuel Levin's *The Semantics of Metaphor* explores this approach in some detail, and though his own conclusions are somewhat suspect, the book is a good guide to the ways other stylisticians have used componential analysis in the study of metaphor. Another excellent stylistic study in which the findings of modern semantics have been fruitfully absorbed is Michael Riffaterre's *Semiotics of Poetry*.

As for pragmatics, two sets of ideas have recently been explored by stylisticians: the theory of *speech acts* and the theory of *implicature*. Both originate with linguistic philosophers rather than linguists: speech act theory was first developed by J.L. Austin and subsequently by J.R. Searle, while the notion of implicature was devised by H.P. Grice. The basic principle of speech acts, or illocutionary acts, is that a speaker in uttering a sentence not only communicates a proposition about some state of affairs in the world, but also, by the same utterance, performs an action. Some of the speech acts are formal and conventional: 'I hereby name this ship *The Skylark*', or 'I declare you man and wife', if spoken in appropriate circumstances, accomplish the social actions of ship-naming and marrying. There are also, besides those kinds of ceremonies, everyday speech acts such as requesting, denying, stating, commanding, informing, and so on. Every utterance performs a speech act of some kind, although this may not be obvious from the surface structure of the sentences concerned. This means that continuous utterance or writing by one person, or dialogue, is a continuous sequence of changing speech acts. In fictional discourse, the status of speech acts is, admittedly, problematic because they do not occur in real contexts of situation, the temporal location of the language is unclear, and so on. Perhaps literature works with pretend speech acts, or imaginary speech acts, or representations of speech acts. The problem has been explored in a series of articles by Richard Ohmann, a book by Mary Louise Pratt, and several other writings. Despite the uncertain status of speech acts in literature, the inclusion of this dimension of language in stylistic studies meets with my approval because it increases attention to interpersonal and discursive, rather than merely formal, aspects of literature: see below, Chapter five.

Implicatures fall in the same area of pragmatics as speech acts. They are unstated propositions which a reader or hearer conventionally deduces from what is actually said. The best introduction to this notion is still Grice's article 'Logic and Conversation'; for the application to literature, see Pratt's book and the chapter on dialogue in Leech and Short's *Style in Prose Fiction*.

In the foregoing pages, I have not tried to give a complete history of stylistics in the last twenty years, but only to pick out studies in each area of linguistic structure which have progressed the discipline. It seems to me that the net product of this work has been a vast improvement in the level of reliability and detailed delicacy at which critics can describe the verbal structure of literary texts. This gain is evident from the specialist studies cited above, for instance Chatman's account of transformational syntax in Henry James, or Riffaterre's *Semiotics of Poetry* in which we find a number of superbly sensitive and disciplined semantic readings of French poems. Such work is rather advanced, but the research studies have given their practitioners the expertise to teach and write at a lower level of technicality. There are now several good introductory textbooks such as Leech's *Linguistic Guide to English Poetry*, or Cluysenaar's *Introduction to Literary Stylistics*.[10] Stylistics is readily accessible to undergraduate students, and in my experience literature students in those departments which teach stylistics courses perform noticeably better in their ordinary (literary) practical criticism than do those students who do not have a basis in linguistic stylistics.

One further comment on the use of linguistics in textual description. I would like to emphasize that not only do I regard stylistics as having matured to offer a precise instrument of textual description, I also consider that description of the specific actual constructions in texts is the most desirable way of using linguistics in literary studies. Most of the papers in this book contain close scrutinies of the language of texts or of some specific linguistic construction (e.g. the generic sentences studied in Chapter six); and where the papers are general and programmatic, they call for textual studies with close analysis of language using the techniques of linguistics. It is necessary to stress the priority of linguistic *description* because description *per se* is not the only way in which linguistics has been recommended and employed in literary studies. In structuralism/semiotics particularly, linguistic concepts have often been used loosely and metaphorically to provide *models* of textual structure rather than *accounts* of the specific structures of sentences and texts.[11]

Granting the primacy of a descriptive application of linguistics, we still ought to ask to what extent stylistics has advanced the *theory* of literature. In many places in this book, I argue that the theory of literature announced or implied by practitioners of stylistics is inadequate or unadventurous. Stylistics in Britain and America has on the whole tried to be compatible with the principles and practices of modern literary criticism, or at least accepted them as natural; this acceptance has facilitated practical criticism at the cost of a complacent and unprogressive ideology of 'literature' (see my review of Cluysenaar's book, pp.46-48 below). Although the schools of Anglo-American criticism described above provided useful working hypotheses and a hospitable environment for stylistics, their principles (as for example voiced in Wellek and Warren's *Theory of Literature*) were by no means 'natural' but extremely tendentious. The same must be said of two continental theories which have had much influence on stylistics: the theory of *defamiliarization* or *dehabitualization* of the Russian Formalist Viktor Shklovsky, and the Czech structuralist Jan Mukařovský's theory of *foregrounding* (derived from Shklovsky's ideas).[12] The limitations of all of these theorists are in two related areas. First, they argue that all literature is a special kind of entity distinct from ordinary communication; linguistic structuralists such as Roman Jakobson and Tzvetan Todorov then go in pursuit of some quality of 'literariness' which is presumed to characterize this entity and which is supposed to find its expression in a distinctive 'literary language' opposed to 'ordinary language'. These hypotheses seem to me to be quite false, and what is worse, socially detrimental in striving to reserve a culturally privileged area of linguistic practice for a trained elite of producers and consumers of texts. Second, our apologists for literature, including conventional stylisticians, are preoccupied with the *formal* structures of texts to the neglect of semantic interpretation and of historical context and social function. These omissions are partly the product of the doctrine that literary works have no real context or function. They also have methodological causes within stylistics. As we have seen, semantics and pragmatics have lagged behind syntax and phonology in the linguistics available to stylisticians, so the emphasis on formal structures of sound and of syntax is understandable in view of the technical potentialities of stylistics. However competent formal description is, the neglect of interpretation and of functional explanation is highly regrettable. Making up these particular deficiencies seems to me the next goal of stylistics (or linguistic criticism): and achieving this objective would not only be a methodological gain, it would also contribute to developing a theory of literature which would be a radical alternative to the formalist premises of which I have complained.

The critique of formalism in stylistics is argued at length in several chapters below, especially Part 2 of Chapter Three, and Chapters Five, Nine and Ten. Chapter Nine argues specifically against the theoretical implications of 'Jakobsonian' poetics; Chapter Ten extends this critique of formalism and of the notion of a unitary, special, 'poetic language'. Chapter Ten also sketches the basis of a positive replacement theory, a descriptive sociolinguistic stylistics; Chapter Ten should be read in conjunction with Chapter Two (which was written just after Chapter Ten) in which I outline the idea of a linguistic criticism founded on the sociolinguistics of styles. Chapter Two, written as a lecture for a general audience, is a straightforward introduction to linguistic criticism — in the context of the present book, 'linguistic criticism' constitutes the new direction in stylistics for which I have been calling in the last few pages — so I will merely summarize its basic assumptions very briefly at the present point. They are:

1. PLURALITY OF LINGUISTIC VARIETIES
A language (English, or French, etc.) is not a single unified entity, as the grammar-books suggest, but a large set of varieties or registers in the sociolinguistic sense.[13] These varieties are distinguished one from another by the occurrence of characteristic linguistic patterns which might be phonological, syntactic, lexical, or semantic, or some combination of patterns at more than one

linguistic level. A written text, or a spoken discourse, is (among other relevant ways of looking at it) the mediation of a set of ideas using forms of expression drawn from one, or more usually, more than one, variety/ies. 'Literature' is *not* a distinct variety; any of the texts which are regarded as 'literary' can be analyzed as being built out of one or more varieties just as other texts are. Some of the varieties used in the constitution of a specific 'literary' text may tend to occur regularly in some, but not all, other 'literary' texts, but they are not restricted to 'literary' texts (rhyme and alliteration are found in advertisements); and 'literary' texts also draw upon patterns which tend to occur in 'non-literary' texts (conversation, news report). This stylistic overlapping, and the absence of any necessary and sufficient linguistic criterion for the 'literary' text, is well known though often ignored. My suggestion is that stylistics, and literary studies, must take sociolinguistic variety theory and methodology seriously as a way of accounting for the specific linguistic properties of the texts concerned.

2. LANGUAGE AS SOCIAL PRODUCT AND SOCIAL PRACTICE

Sociolinguists have in the last twenty years demonstrated that variation within a language correlates regularly and intricately with factors in the social circumstances within which discourse occurs (see note 13). There is no reason to believe that 'literary' texts are exempted from these correlations, nor from the stronger, causal, explanations that have been offered for such correlations. There is a dialectical interrelationship between language and social structure: the varieties of linguistic usage are both *products* of socioeconomic forces and institutions — reflexes of such factors as power relations, occupational roles, social stratification, etc. — and *practices* which are instrumental in forming and legitimating these same social forces and institutions.[14] The New Critics and the Formalists vehemently denied that 'literature' had social determinants and social consequences, but a sociolinguistic theory of the kind which these papers presuppose will show that *all* discourse is part of social structure and enters into the effected and effecting relationships which I have just described.

3. LANGUAGE AS SOCIAL SEMIOTIC

This is the title of a recent book by M.A.K. Halliday (London: Edward Arnold, 1978) which argues for a theory of the social origin of meanings which is extremely valuable for the purposes of linguistic criticism. Details are given, and the theory interpreted and extended, at several places in this book.[15] Briefly, following Halliday, I propose that beyond a few natural meanings which are encoded in most languages (e.g. basic colour terms), the majority of meanings in languages, and in different varieties of a language, are crystallized in response to the social, economic, technological and theoretical needs of the cultures concerned. Bearing in mind the fact that language is practice as well as product, note that language use is effective in the formation and reproduction of ideas, rather than simply reflecting a stock of preexisting ideas independently formed within the culture. Halliday insists that linguistic varieties (cf. 1 above) or 'registers' are not merely formally differentiated versions of a language, but 'ranges of semantic potential':

speakers can mean different things in different varieties; and on the dialectical principle (2), they constitute as well as express meanings in speaking. This theory opens the way for an analysis of the formal structure of any text as encoding and constituting a version of reality: for full details, see Chapter Two.

4. CRITICISM, DECONSTRUCTION AND DEFAMILIARIZATION

Again, this last stage of the argument, which moves stylistics towards linguistic criticism, is detailed in my next chapter. It is proposed (cf. 3 above) that any text embodies a version or theory of reality — socially based and accessible linguistically in the culture's repertoire of varieties. The activity of linguistic criticism is deconstructing a text, using linguistic analysis and with the social contexts of the discourse very much in mind, in order to understand how the text constitutes its own theory of reality, and under what social constraints: unpacking the ideology from the linguistic patterns in which it is encoded. (At a practical level, an informal list of constructions which I have found promising areas to probe is given on pp.40-44 below.) The ideologies which are embedded in language, and thus implicitly spoken in the practical use of language, are often hidden from the consciousness of readers and hearers, so linguistic criticism, especially applied to public discourse such as newspapers, reports, etc., is a practice of demystification (see the two books cited in note 14). Now according to Shklovsky's aesthetic theory (note 12), literature differs from ordinary language in being so structured as to make obvious the artificiality of its version of its presented world, and thereby to suggest to us that our own habitual, accepted, assumptions about 'reality' are equally artificial and in need of critical scrutiny. I do not accept that 'literature' always and exclusively has this property; but much literature is nowadays written, and read, with this expectation of dehabitualization. But language and society change, while 'literary' texts are preserved over centuries: so it is not surprising that defamiliarizing texts lose their force and perspicacity, so that their original analysis of ideology may become just as fixed and invisible as the unexamined ideologies of contemporary 'ordinary' discourse. In that historical context of the reception of older literature, linguistic criticism serves as a practice of appreciative resuscitation. Criticism is not necessarily negative. And linguistic criticism, unlike earlier formalist stylistics, is very much like traditional literary criticism (but methodologically and theoretically superior!) in interpreting texts for whose language and ideas it has great respect.[16]

Notes

1. Roger Fowler, *The Languages of Literature* (London: Routledge and Kegan Paul, 1971).

2. I.A. Richards, *Practical Criticism* (London: Routledge and Kegan Paul, 1929); *The Philosophy of Rhetoric* (New York and London: Oxford University Press, 1936); William Empson, *Seven Types of Ambiguity* (London: Chatto and Windus, 1930).

3. Curiously, some literary critics were less than welcoming to linguistic stylistics: for debate, see Chs. 3-6 of the *Languages of Literature*; also Barbara Herrnstein Smith, *On the Margins of Discourse* (Chicago: University of Chicago Press, 1978), Ch. 7; my review of that book in the *Journal of English and Germanic Philology*, forthcoming; Donald C. Freeman, 'Literature as Property' forthcoming in *Language and Style*.

4. *The Languages of Literature*, pp. 3-9; see also R. Fowler, *Understanding Language* (London: Routledge and Kegan Paul, 1974), pp. 20-33; John Lyons, *Chomsky* (London: Fontana, second edition, 1977); J.T. Waterman, *Perspectives in Linguistics* (Chicago: University of Chicago Press, 1963).

5. See Terence Hawkes, *Structuralism and Semiotics* (London: Methuen, 1977); Jonathan Culler, *Structuralist Poetics* (London: Routledge and Kegan Paul, 1975). It is an unfortunate coincidence that the school of linguistics derived from Bloomfield, and also the school of poetic, anthropological and semiotic theory derived from Saussure are both known as 'structuralism': they are quite independent of one another.

6. Ferdinand de Saussure, trans. Wade Baskin, *Course in General Linguistics* (London: Fontana, 1974).

7. Roland Barthes, trans. Annette Lavers and Colin Smith, *Elements of Semiology* (London: Cape, 1967).

8. For brevity and convenience, all the major works in stylistics mentioned in this section are listed among the Further Reading on pp.207-9, with full bibliographical information.

9. Good accounts and critiques of modern linguistic semantics are R. Kempson, *Semantic Theory* (London: Cambridge University Press, 1977) and J. Lyons, *Semantics* (2 Vols; London: Cambridge University Press, 1977).

10. More recently, E.C. Trangott and M.L. Pratt's excellent *Linguistics for Students of Literature* (New York: Harcourt, Brace, Jovanovich 1980).

11. For the various non-descriptive uses of linguistics, see Culler's *Structuralist Poetics* (note 5 above).

12. Viktor Shklovsky, 'Art as Technique,' (1917) in L.T. Lemon and M.J. Reis (eds.), *Russian Formalist Criticism* (Lincoln, Nebraska: University of Nebraska Press, 1965), pp. 5-24; Jan Mukařovský, 'Standard Language and Poetic Language,' (1932) in P.L. Garvin (ed.), A Prague School Reader on *Esthetics, Literary Structure and Style* (Washington: Georgetown University Press, 1964), pp.17-30.

13. See P. Trudgill, *Sociolinguistics* (Harmondsworth: Penguin, 1974); P.P. Giglioli (ed.), *Language in Social Context* (Harmondsworth: Penguin, 1972) for basic introductions to sociolinguistics and references to research studies of sociolinguistic variation.

14. See R. Fowler, R. Hodge, G. Kress and T. Trew, *Language and Control* (London: Routledge and Kegan Paul, 1979); F. Burton and P. Carlen, *Official Discourse* (London: Routledge and Kegan Paul, 1980).

15. See also my review-article on three books by Halliday explaining the relevance of his theory to linguistic criticism, in *Comparative Criticism Yearbook* (Cambridge: Cambridge University Press, 1981).

16. For this emphasis, see my book *Linguistic Criticism* (Oxford: Oxford University Press, forthcoming).

CHAPTER TWO

*Linguistic Criticism**

The heading 'Linguistic Criticism' is meant to abbreviate a range of meanings. It means, first of all, criticism of language. To spell it out, critical analysis of the social practices that are managed through the use of language. Next, my title means criticism which employs the concepts and methodology of linguistics: it is possible, but undesirable, to talk about language non-linguistically, a procedure which is guaranteed to get you into trouble. Third, the phrase 'linguistic criticism' is intended to recall the phrase 'literary criticism'. One of my most enduring academic interests has been the linguistic analysis of literary texts. Since it is well known that I have a strong dislike of the motives and practices of literary criticism as carried out by literary critics, you will realise that I'm offering linguistic criticism as an alternative to and improvement on literary criticism. I will be discussing the linguistic criticism of 'literary' texts in the latter part of this talk, after illustrating the analysis and expounding the theory in relation to a variety of texts that would not normally be called 'literary'. Let me make it clear, however, that I don't believe any special assumptions have to be made about 'literature'. There isn't any special 'literary language' qualitatively distinct from 'ordinary language', so the methods of linguistic criticism can be applied to literary texts without any special adjustment. There are of course some peculiar conventions concerning the ways readers are supposed to respond to 'literary works', and these need to be kept in mind. However, they are conventions in the social psychology of literary communication, and don't affect the nature of the texts as language. The techniques of linguistic criticism apply universally, whatever the genre of the text under consideration.

To appreciate the necessity of criticism, and the importance of linguistic criticism, we need to consider some basic principles in the sociology of knowledge. The world of perception and cognition — the world as we know it — is an artifice, a social construct. We have a variety of names for this world: commonsense, everyday life, the natural attitude, ideology. All of these designations refer to the world as we take it for granted, the habitualized world. Cultural anthropologists have observed the extreme variability of everyday life in different civilizations, and it is from these observations that the principle of a socially constructed commonsense has arisen. A popular account of the processes involved is Berger

*This chapter is a slightly revised version, with full references added, of the author's inaugural lecture as Professor of English and Linguistics at the University of East Anglia.

24

and Luckmann's book *The Social Construction of Reality*.[1] Berger and Luckmann give a picture of each human society transforming and structuring its environment by a process which they call 'objectification'. Typical and repeated patterns of interaction, technological procedures and the development of roles and institutions cause the members of a society to represent the world as a system of recognisable objects: habituated categories of perception and action which simplify the society's management of itself and of its habitat. These categories are not the deliberately contrived instruments of scientific analysis (though some may have started life as such) but automatically assimilated ways of dividing up the world. Together, the complete set of objectivations in a culture constitutes the representation of reality, or world-view, enjoyed by the community and its members. In a nutshell, we see the world in terms of the categories through which we and our society have constituted it.

Berger and Luckmann acknowledge the power of symbolic systems, and especially language, in the social construction of reality. Language provides labels for the objects which a culture has determined are relevant to its functioning: the existence of linguistic signs ensures the identity of the objects we call 'trees', 'government', 'riots', 'imagination', 'literature', 'girls', 'inaugural lectures', etc.: vocabulary *segments* the world into culture-relevant categories. Language also *classifies* these objectivations by groupings into lexical sets, e.g. kinship terminologies or the jargons of specific occupations or fields of knowledge such as medicine. As Berger and Luckmann observe, occupational jargons are of paramount importance in maintaining the identity of specialized groups and their members: swearing like a trouper or talking like a book maintains the position of the individual as a soldier or an intellectual, and preserves the role of his group within society. Furthermore, because language is a systematic code and not just a random list of labels, it facilitates the storage and the transmission of concepts. Finally, since language is used in interaction between people as well as being a form of knowledge possessed by people, concepts can be negotiated in communication between people. For instance, two persons can discuss whether a third is a 'girl', or a 'woman', or a 'lady', and in so doing they are necessarily exchanging and formulating the social concepts encoded in the words.

How does criticism apply to these processes? By 'criticism' I don't mean the appreciative, supportive role played by the flood of writings about texts and authors which calls itself literary criticism. Nor do I intend the sense of intolerant unreasoned fault-finding, as when someone tells me that I am being very critical today. I mean a careful analytic interrogation of the ideological categories, and the roles and institutions and so on, through which a society constitutes and maintains itself and the consciousness of its members. As we have seen, all knowledge, all objects, are constructs: criticism analyzes the processes of construction and, acknowledging the artificial quality of the categories concerned, offers the possibility that we might profitably conceive of the world in some alternative way.

In his introduction to the Penguin Frankfurt School anthology *Critical Sociology*,[2] Paul Connerton offers a useful discussion of criticism or critique in this sense:

> Critique denotes reflection on a system of *constraints* which are humanly
> produced: distorting pressures to which individuals, or a group of individuals,
> or the human race as a whole, succumb in their process of
> self-formation. (p.18)

> Criticism . . . is brought to bear on objects of experience whose 'objectivity' is
> called into question; criticism supposes that there is a degree of inbuilt
> deformity which masquerades as reality. It seeks to remove this distortion and
> thereby to make possible the liberation of what has been distorted. Hence it
> entails a conception of emancipation. (p.20)

I would just query in this an excessive optimism: a hint that criticism could
somehow remove the veil entirely to reveal an undistorted reality. It is not the case
that there are some representations of reality which allow it to be experienced
in its true nature, and on the other hand other representations which impede and
falsify. *All* knowledge and communication is, precisely, representation. What
criticism cannot do is disperse illusion and reveal truth. What it can do is
demonstrate the representedness of knowledge, the ordering of the symbolic
structures through which this is achieved, and postulate the causes and
consequences of these processes: and it can offer the possibility of alternative
representations.

Connerton offers as a main function of criticism the removal of 'a false or
distorted consciousness'. Now 'false or distorted consciousness' is one of the
popular meanings of the word *ideology*. Please note that, although ideology is a
central concept in my argument, I do not use the word in that pejorative sense.
An ideology is just a theory, a system of beliefs which has come to be constructed
as a way of comprehending the world. No person can engage with the world
without the cognitive support of ideology in this sense. Ideology cannot be
removed. It can be replaced — by alternative ideology. Criticism demonstrates
that there are ideologies; compares their structural characteristics, their geneses,
their consequences; cannot disperse them.

Alternative ideologies, and the variant linguistic structures which encode them,
are strikingly visible in comparable variant phrasings. Good examples are rare, to
be spotted only by assiduous scanning of news reports or translations. Presumably
the world of language usage is regulated so that the consumers of language do not
routinely find comparable phrasings, for they are a give-away: being able to see
that some thought could have been worded in an alternative fashion, a reader can
imagine that thought replaced by an alternative thought. Comparison reveals the
relativity of representations.

I've included some choice examples from newspapers as examples 1 and 2 in
Appendix A. I'm not going to analyze these fragments, but allow you to figure out
for yourselves which newspapers they appeared in. You should also consider
whether they are interchangeable; I don't think so: the paper which headlined the
confrontation of Keith Joseph and the NUS as 1(a) could never print 1(c), and
vice-versa.[3]

Our intuitions about these newspaper headlines tell us that each is located in a specific recognisable system of beliefs. 2(a), for instance — LEYLAND PLANS FOR SURVIVAL REJECTED — can only be uttered by someone who believes that any commercial concern, even a company as unsuccessful as British Leyland, is to be credited with taking a laudable initiative if it proposes to sack large numbers of its workers. 2(b), by contrast, is prepared to grant union officials the right to resist management's plans on the grounds that they involve sackings, regardless of the prediction that such redundancies might be the condition of successful commercial continuation. Our knowledge of economic practices and institutions in British society leads us to associate the beliefs implied by these sentences with certain positions in socio-economic structure. The readership of the newspaper which supplied 2(a) is committed to industry and commerce financially as well as ideologically, and is actively hostile to trades unions.

It comes as no surprise that there is a manifest relationship between socio-economic structure and ideology. More important in this context of linguistic criticism is the role of language in mediating the relationship. From the point of view of the sociologist, linguistic analysis provides a novel point of entry for investigating the relationships between belief systems and social structures. Despite the acknowledgement of the importance of language by theorists like Berger and Luckmann, there has so far been little detailed linguistic research into sociologically and ideologically interesting language. Language has been mined for *content*, or used to elicit content, with insufficient recognition of the power of structural arrangements in the shaping and slanting of propositions. As for sociolinguistics, linguistic variation has been studied largely as an index of such sociological variables as stratification, role and status. Semantically empty variables such as single phonemes have been observed by linguists such as William Labov, with little attention to the mediation of social *meanings* by varying linguistic structures.[4]

So there is an analytic methodology to be developed. Examples 1 and 2 suggest that, although the belief-system embodied by a piece of text may be easily read off by anyone who is attuned to the relevant vibrations, the structural mechanisms involved in shaping the ideas are extremely delicate. Examples 1(a)-(c), though very evidently different in tone when they are set alongside one another, don't differ grossly in structure. There are profound but not easily visible differences such as, for instance, the different case-relationships implied by the nominalized predicates *fury*, *insult* and *attack*, or the reflexivity of *regret* versus the transitivity of *condemn*. Such structural minutiae must be established within the methodological scope of linguistic criticism.

Against this background of objectives, I'd like to refer to some work in linguistic criticism on which a number of my colleagues and I have been engaged. The people I have been working with most closely are Bob Hodge and Gunther Kress, now alas returned to Australia, and Tony Trew and Gareth Jones from the School of Economic and Social Studies. Other colleagues are also working in this area, and it has some claim to being UEA's distinctive contribution to linguistic theory and the sociology of language. From about 1975, we have been working on various genres of what I would call 'public discourse'. By this I mean partly language published on the open market, like newspapers and broadcasts, and partly the language of individuals in communicative situations formalized by public roles and statuses: for instance, interviews, school lessons, committees. We were initially interested in such materials for a variety of individual purposes, but as we discussed our separate research and our teaching, a number of common concerns emerged. We have now come to regard language as not just a tool in the social construction of everyday life; not just a subservient instrument or medium adapting to the necessities of a preexisting social structure, economic base or whatever. Rather, we regard language use as a continuously active social practice, and the production of ideology or theory as an inevitable and ongoing function of the use of language. Every time people speak or write, the form of their sentences necessarily articulates and so reproduces elements of ideology. Just how, we have asked ourselves, is this done?

Our interest in this question has been partly theoretical and methodological — as linguists and sociologists — and partly practical — as socialists. Trying to describe and interpret the linguistic constructions through which people and institutions articulate their views of the world, we became impressed with the inadequacy of existing linguistic theories for handling the questions we were asking. So with the help of our students, doing textual analysis on a large scale and across a great variety of texts, we developed a suitable technique of analysis. Our starting-point was the *functional* linguistic model of M.A.K. Halliday. In Halliday's own words,

> The particular form taken by the grammatical system of language is closely related to the social and personal needs that language is required to serve.[5]

Linguistic structure is not arbitrary, but is determined by, or motivated by, the functions it performs. Furthermore, *all* parts of language are functional in this sense, not just the structures that explicitly serve social and interpersonal ends like personal pronouns, address forms, speech acts and so on. It follows for the interpretation of discourse that any choice of words and syntactic constructions can have some significance assigned to it. But not randomly: within a given community, particular ranges of significances tend to be conventionally attached to specific types of construction. Not in a one-to-one relationship: each construction we have studied has offered different meanings depending on the contexts in which it is used. There is, necessarily, a degree of unpredictability, so that we can't supply a dictionary of ideological significances. We have, however, identified a good many constructions which regularly respond to critical interpretation, and I have listed and illustrated the main ones in Appendix B. This is a checklist of the important structures which we find ourselves constantly studying; in a metaphor once applied by Professor Broadbent to this work, a 'box of knives' for performing investigative surgery on texts. You will see that the categories are quite eclectic: we have cannabalized several linguistic theories and still have to do a lot of work to raise our model to a coherent whole.

Formalizing the linguistic apparatus is an urgent priority for our future work. A major attraction of linguistic criticism is that it offers precise, potentially formal, descriptions of patterns of language: it differs in this respect from various less plausible existing alternatives, including content analysis and impressionistic practical criticism.

Returning to our practical motives, we have been studying the meanings and functions of public discourse in a divided society, a society based on inequalities of power and opportunity: contemporary British society. The title of our recent book, *Language and Control*,[6] indicates the topic to which we have directed our version of the language-and-ideology thesis. Given the nature of the society we live in, much communication is concerned with establishing and maintaining unequal power relationships between individuals, and between institutions and individuals. Our studies of various genres of discourse argue that this practice is carried out through a much wider variety of language usages and speech acts than just the rules and directives by which interpersonal control is obviously managed. Because language *must* continuously articulate ideology, and because ideology is simultaneously social product and social practice, all our language and that of others expresses theories of the way the world is organised, and the expression of these theories contributes to the legitimation of this theorized organization. Tony Trew's studies of mediation in the press, for instance, show that the preferred phrasings and wordings of newspapers insist on events and people being classified in some consistent way. That classification is likely to be of service to the position in power structure represented or favoured by the newspaper. Similarly, the interviews analyzed by Gareth Jones, and by Gunther Kress and myself, show the participants hard at work (partly unconsciously, no doubt) defining their identities, statuses and rights through language. Since interviews are profoundly asymmetrical in their distribution of power, the act of self-definition is likely to be prejudicial to the chances of the interviewee as job candidate or whatever role she is performing. In the Liz and Mary interview studied in the book the unemployed Mary unwittingly but cooperatively defines herself as inferior and unemployable.

I'd like now to give you an example, adapted from *Language and Control*, of how linguistic style simultaneously expresses and constructs an ideology. Since criticism is supposed to be reflexive, that is, to engage in critique of the critic's own location within the language-thought-society nexus, the most appropriate example for this university occasion is the examination I did of UEA's General Regulations for Students; example 3 of Appendix A is an extract.

Although this text is lacking in directive speech acts, it is clearly intended to be an instrument in controlling behaviour. This control is to be achieved not by regulating specific actions, but by enforcing a set of attitudes. By adopting a familiar bureaucratic style of 'impersonality' (ready-made and available generally for institutions, not invented by UEA) the people responsible for publishing the text have obscured the fact that they intend to control the behaviour of the people to whom the text is addressed. But there is a degree of over-kill; the writer is absolutely unidentifiable, and the addressees are absolutely depersonalized. In these respects, the language is so unlike any discourse which might be spoken by one person to another person that the text is alienating, symbolic of an utter separation of the interests of the source and the addressees (while both parties are, after all, members of the same university community).

Not only is the nature of the power relationship obscured or mystified by the language, so also is the content which is being communicated. The addressee is given very little specific guidance about what activities are approved and what proscribed, and yet the structure of the language expresses an implicit and demanding orthodoxy, a special system of attitudes required of members of the community.

The text is impersonal in the way that rate demands, government circulars, official notices are, and this impersonality has the same linguistic origins, and the same causes in the needs of institutions to interact with individuals in a formal manner. But the subject-matter, and the act of speech, are in fact far from impersonal. The Regulations have for their topic a set of relationships between institution and addressee — rights and obligations, permitted and proscribed behaviour. In these circumstances the impersonality of the language is exceedingly conspicuous. There are no 'you's', and the only first-person pronouns which occur are the 'I' and 'me' in the quoted 'Declaration of Obedience'. The 'you' addressed by this text is consistently transformed into third person: 'a student', 'students', 'persons', 'those', 'they', etc. The effect is to turn the person who is being addressed into someone who is being talked about; like a child whose parents talk about her to other people in her own presence. There is no 'I' in this text; only 'the Authorities of the University' and 'the University', with 'the General Regulations' serving as an intermediary between source and addressee. Notice how both the source and the addressee are expressed in plural form: 'the Authorities', 'students'. Pluralization aggrandizes and obscures the source, as with the royal plural. Pluralization of the addressee, on the other hand, confirms the source's refusal to treat the individual addressee as an individual person.

Impersonality also arises from the avoidance of any explicit command structure: there are no requests or imperatives. However, a weighty burden of authority is carried by the modal verbs 'shall', 'must' and 'may'. 'Shall' suggests an inexorable obligation, usually imposed on the student but, occasionally, in later paragraphs, the obligation of the university: 'The days on which students register shall be announced annually by the University . . .' 'Must' means an absolute condition. One revealing modal attached to 'the University' is 'may', which ascribes a right, not an obligation: the University may if it chooses dispense with some condition, or has the right, if it chooses, to punish the breach of a regulation.

In most styles that people find 'formal' and 'impersonal', two syntactic constructions are prevalent: *nominalization* and *passivization*. Both abound in this passage. Passives include 'engaged in their duties', 'bound by the following Regulations', 'not normally admitted', 'allowed to matriculate', etc. Nominalization is a transformation which reduces a whole clause to its verb, and turns that into a noun. For example, the noun 'freedom' is derived from 'someone is free', 'study' from 'someone studies something', 'thought' from 'someone thinks', 'Regulations' from 'someone regulates somebody else', and so on. Many derived nominals can be spotted by their ending in *-ion*, *-ience*, *-ness*, etc., and many are learned words of classical origin: 'expression', 'protection', 'regulation', 'matriculation', 'declaration'. The impression of formality derives partly from their etymological pedigree, partly from the fact that large numbers of scientific and technical terms have this form.

Nominalization facilitates *relexicalization*[7], the coding of new, specialized, sets of concepts in new sets of lexical terms. The student can conform to the Regulations only by learning a new technical vocabulary which expresses the relationships of which the regulations speak. The word 'matriculation' illustrates the essence of this process. This arcane term, meaning admission to the register of students when entering the university for the first time, or the ceremony associated therewith, refers to one sole experience in the life of a person who goes to college. By its intense specialization of reference, the word becomes talismanic in the relationship of student and university. Apparently the student must acquire the meaning of this word as a precondition for a well-formed relationship between the parties: a patently ritual function of language.

Another example, which illustrates how relexicalization generates *systems* of new terms, is the series 'examination requirements', 'course requirements', 'general entrance requirements'. Since the series is productive, the student may feel some unease lest it spawns other terms, unexpressed here and perhaps to be unleashed elsewhere — 'residence requirements', 'political affiliation require-ments', 'dietary requirements' are all too plausible offspring of the system.

Nominalization has syntactic as well as lexical repercussions. The personal participants, the 'someones' whoever they may be, are deleted as a clause turns into a noun; so is modality (thus many potential 'may's' and 'shall's' disappear.). The deletion of references to persons is entirely compatible with the strategy of suppressing 'I' and 'you': the single word 'Regulation', and all other words like it ('requirement', 'obedience', etc.) is effectively a euphemism, the nominalization allowing the university to avoid telling the truth in its full syntactic form: 'I, the university, require you, the student, to do such-and-such'; 'you, the student, obey me, the university'. Similarly with passives: 'not normally admitted' really means 'the University does not normally amit' — the passive structure, allowing agent-deletion, permits a discreet silence about *who* might refuse to admit the applicant. Usually the agents and patients can be retrieved in an analytic reading, though of course the style discourages such analysis. Sometimes nominalization or passivization makes it extremely difficult to infer the persons associated with the underlying verb: 'matriculation' is a case in point: it is not clear, even if you read the sentences concerned carefully, who does what to whom, in this ritual. 'The act of placing a student's name . . .' suggests that matriculation is something done *to* the student, but the next sentence, 'Before being allowed to matriculate . . .', implies that matriculation is reflexive, something a student does to himself. As the whole text is about the responsibilities and obligations of the two parties, this is a crucial ambivalence.

Syntax may do something even more treacherous. Rather than just clouding the relational responsibilities of the deep structure (who does what to whom), it may

31

actually *reverse* the distribution of rights and duties. Thus someone who has something done to him by another can be made to seem responsible for what happens to him. Consider, for example, the sentence

> All students matriculating in the University shall, so long as they remain in attendance, be bound by the following Regulations and by such other Regulations as the University may from time to time determine.

The deep structure is actually something like 'The University binds all students by Regulations'. But in the passive surface structure, the nominal designating the object ('all students') has been placed in the position of theme, i.e. the left-most noun phrase in the sentence, a position normally associated with the agent. The syntax strongly encourages one to read the first part of this sentence with the expectation that it is going to mention some action carried out by 'all students'; this illusion is heightened by the presence of an active verb of a subordinate clause ('matriculating') immediately following 'all students'; and by the extreme distance between the subject 'all students' and the main verb 'be bound', a distance which forces the reader to cling on to a hypothesis about the way the sentence is going to turn out. The easiest hypothesis is that we are waiting for a main verb which will tell us what action 'all students' perform; but this hypothesis will prove incorrect, since it is actually the university which is doing something.

A linguistic style is 'constitutive': an important function of rules-style is to systematize the special concepts of the society they regulate. Now there is something very odd about the way this text's language analyses the community it refers to. The General Regulations apply to individuals living and working in a large, complex community which encourages and stages a great variety of academic, social and domestic work and interaction. A university, particularly a residential one, is a hive of activity. But this language is used to neutralize the activity, and gives no sense of transaction or productivity. The avoidance of transitive verbs, the use of abstractions as subjects, and pervasive nominalization, account for a large part of the effect. Nominalization permits deletion of reference to the persons responsible for and affected by the processes described by the verbs; nominalization can depersonalize, depopulate. It can also drain the language of actional vitality — an effect recognised in style handbooks which teach aspiring writers to prefer verbs to nouns. The processes and work which go on within the university are presented as nouns (study, assembly, academic pursuits); thinking, talking, writing, etc. become, grotesquely, static 'things' located in a peaceful, stable landscape. Nominalization transforms the processes of studying and working into objects possessed by the institution, capital items to be accumulated, counted, deployed. The alternative view, that intellectual progress springs from work, dialogue, even conflict, is tacitly discouraged by this style.

My lettrist colleagues may by this point be starting to get a little bothered. This 'linguistic criticism' is labelled as if it were a form of literary criticism, but it seems rather to be a branch of sociolinguistics or discourse analysis. My examples, taken from regulations and from newspapers, may confirm your belief that linguistic criticism is a secular or even profane trade which doesn't apply to literature. If you believe that — and I know that many people do — then you need reminding that literature is indeed a secular institution: a social and economic practice through which cultural values are transmitted, a body of texts which encode and transform belief-systems, a whole set of industries for regulating the conditions of production and consumption of the texts, with a profession of ideologues — yourselves — employed to administer the practice of literature within the educational system.

What I have just said was meant merely as the starting-point for an analysis of the institution of literature which I don't actually intend to pursue this evening. If it sounds antagonistic to you, my antagonism is directed to the institution and not to the texts which the institution administers. On the other hand, my interest in literature, and my implicit respect for the texts, doesn't mean that I believe, as linguistic poeticians such as Jakobson and Culler do, that there is some essential property of literariness which makes literary works 'special'[8]. I have argued against these claims in a number of recent papers and there is no need for me to rehearse the arguments here.[9]

Jakobson's claim of a special, distinctive poetic language forced him and his followers into a very narrow concept of significant literary patterning and consequently they paid attention to a quite restricted range of linguistic features presumed to be the exponents of these patterns. I have found no good reason to separate off literature from other kinds of discourse, and so can open up linguistic investigation to the study of any parts of textual structure.

There is some redressing of balance to be done. The extreme formalism of Jakobson's syntactic and phonetic descriptions meant an equally extreme neglect of interpersonal, expressive and referential dimensions of literary works. Jakobson never offers interpretations of a degree of richness which would satisfy literary critics or literary historians; he exercises such caution in his statements about the relationships of texts to the world around them that one would hardly think there is a world around them. Interestingly, Jakobson's calvinistic formalism is in accord with the prevailing anti-historical, anti-kinetic dogmas of modern literary criticism as expressed by the 'New Critics' and their successors.[10]

The present model of linguistic criticism attacks these limitations on two fronts. To take the simpler part of my proposal first. In formalist poetics, and in traditional and even transformational linguistics, there is very little recognition of *interpersonal* aspects of language. But as even the sketchy description in section 3 of Appendix B shows, several different theoretical categories need to be distinguished in this area: modality, speech acts, implicatures, categories of address, naming, and so-on. And these abstract categories are provided with several complicated systems of surface structure forms. The Fowler-Hodge-Kress-Trew model would relate all of these categories to dimensions of social structure, after the fashion of Brown and Gilman's treatment of 'The Pronouns of Power and Solidarity' (*vous* and *tu* in French, etc.)[11], so on our theory they are of massive significance for interpretation. But a more elementary step in this study is simply to get interpersonal features noticed in practical criticism. In my undergraduate teaching, therefore, it is a particular emphasis: poems like 'My Last Duchess', the more argumentative and exclamatory lyrics of Donne, and almost anything by Blake or by Yeats, are a revelation to students, who generally have little conception of the complexity of the structures which are needed to constitute a written text as a representation of a speech act. Another area ripe for research is the study of dialogue. Dialogic structures are becoming of interest to literary critics through the attraction of the newly available ideas of Bakhtin and Vološinov, but a lot of spadework still has to be done.[12] Conversation as interaction is vitually unstudied: there is the recent book *Therapeutic Discourse* by Labov and Fanshel[13], and the discourse analysis research at Birmingham.[14] At UEA, we reported analyses of interviews in *Language and Control*; and Bill Downes has some important research in progress on implicatures, belief-systems and speech acts in dialogue, including some fictional materials.[15]

I'd like to mention briefly a third literary topic involving interpersonal structures which particularly interests me and on which I have done some work: the characterization of narrators, implied authors and implied readers in prose fiction texts. So far, I have studied only very overtly characterised narrators, in Fielding, Sterne and George Eliot, narrators, or authors' personae, who draw attention to themselves and to their relationships with their implied readers.[16] Pronouns, address forms, modality, speech acts (or pretend ones) and many other interpersonal structures are involved in the characterization of narrators and readers. Description of the languages of narration and reader-creation connects with Wolfgang Iser's stimulating but pre-linguistic work.[17] I think that theories of reception and of the rhetoric of fiction are crying out for the solidity and precision of linguistic description. Iser's recent work is much concerned with ideology: with the ways in which the semantic repertoire of a text interacts with the systems of ideas of a community. This is a central preoccupation of linguistic criticism in my sense, and, to conclude my lecture, I'd like to sketch an example, taken from work in progress, of the study of language and ideology in fictional texts (specifically, novels).

At the beginning of my talk, I spoke about the ways in which language is implicated in the construction of theories of reality within the arena of social practice. Let us think about fiction in this light: and I'd like to suggest that the most natural definition of a fiction is a theory of reality constructed through a particular use of language. The novelist creates a world, an analysis or representation of a world, in the normal way in which a journalist, historian, or regulations-writer does. Whether any of these linguistic practitioners refers to real entities is beside the point, which has to do with representation, not existence.

The fictionality of fiction should be acceptable to you! I started out this talk with a theory of the fictionality (constructedness) of reality, then explained the role of language in constructing this fictional commonsense, and then offered an analytic methodology from linguistics for unpacking the relationship of ideas and the language that constructs them. I am now suggesting that these analytic procedures apply unproblematically to fictions produced within the institution of literature.

I do not take the vulgar Marxist position that the language of a novel reproduces the ideology of the society that, through the author, produced the novel-text. Rather, I want to say that a novel is a linguistically constructed system of beliefs which bears some interesting, usually critical and defamiliarizing, relationship to the numerous ideologies current at its time, in our time, and encoded in the earlier texts in the genre. If this sounds bland, well, I'm sorry, but you have to interpret the claim in the light of the theoretical and methodological innovations I have suggested in the earlier part of this lecture. The linguistic critic must suspect that each and every stylistic choice carries a socially interpretable meaning, and his analytic method dictates a searching, minute and systematic empirical study of the texture of, in this case, very long texts. What is more, linguistic analysis by itself will not give the answers that are required: this analysis must be accompanied by historical research to validate the interpretations which the critic offers.

So far, my own research has concentrated upon easily manageable fragments of novel-texts, and upon grossly distinguished sociolinguistic styles through which a novelist is clearly encoding contrasting ideological positions. I can illustrate what I have done with fragments only by citing a recent article: 'The Referential Code and Narrative Authority'. (chapter six) In this paper I re-analyzed the so-called 'referential code' which Roland Barthes identified in Balzac's short novel *Sarrasine*. According to Barthes, this code is a set of cultural references or footnotes: sentences or phrases which articulate the conventional wisdom of Parisian society at the time in which the story is set: assumptions about women, the rich, Germans, Italians, and so on. These prejudices are continuously invoked by the internal narrator in Balzac's story. I looked for structural consistency in the segments of Balzac's text which Barthes labelled REF, and in fact some consistency emerged. Many of the cultural aphorisms were cast in generic or nomic syntax — i.e. proverbial form; there was also an insistent presence of generic noun-phrases such as *gens, espèce, type* followed by qualifying relative clauses; and a number of other transformations away from the canonic form of the generic. Since I am not an expert on Balzac or his society, I leave to my colleagues the question of why Balzac puts these nuggets of ideology in the mouth of an ironically treated internal narrator. For myself, the direction out of this study has been the beginnings of research into the ideological functions of generics and other transformations in English nineteenth century novelists, and I have made a start on this aspect of the language of George Eliot, whose wit and wisdom have been copiously and misleadingly anthologised. There is a relevant passage in section 3 of Appendix B, but I have not time to analyze it. Generics cast in the syntax of rhetorical questions with first person plural subjects — 'Do we not . . .?' — are particularly interesting in this author.

Finally, I have started a project on the significance in novels of representations of class languages and sub-culture languages. I've been looking particularly at texts which present sociolects expressing dialectical resistance to the linguistic norms of the bourgeois novel institution: the fictional analogues of what Michael Halliday calls 'anti-languages', the linguistic expression of the world-views of deviant societies or anti-societies. I have a pilot study of anti-languages in William Burroughs' *Naked Lunch* and Anthony Burgess' *A Clockwork Orange* forthcoming in the journal *Style*. Work in progress includes more detailed analysis of some 'social novels' of the 1840s and 1850s: Mrs. Gaskell's *Mary Barton* and *North and South*, and Dickens's *Hard Times*. A central compositional technique of all three novels is the juxtaposition of linguistic styles associated with representatives of diverse social groups. I maintain that each such representation is an encoding of an ideological analysis from some perspective which is central to the novel's own ideology. Mrs. Gaskell is more straightforward than Dickens but no less interesting. The dialect speech of the Bartons, the Wilsons and the Davenports in *Mary Barton* is startingly differentiated from the style of the authorial voice and from the speech of the upper classes, by Mrs. Gaskell's use of a small but highly visible set of special spellings and dialect words. But it is accompanied by some very self-conscious explanatory footnotes whose function seems to be to mediate between this estranged speech and the language of the middle classes (eg. dialect words and morphological forms are dignified by being given a literary pedigree with Chaucer, Wyclif and Spenser as ancestors). What is interesting in *Mary Barton* is the way in which Mrs. Gaskell draws attention to this act of mediation or bridging between the speech styles of the classes. In *North and South* the dialect representation is still there, but the footnotes have gone. Instead we are given as set pieces a number of lengthy conversations between the Hales, representatives of the southern middle classes, and the Higginses, the worker and his sick daughter whom the Hales have taken under their wing. What is impressive about these conversations is their immense cooperativeness: I have started analyzing these interactions in terms of the linguistics of speech acts and of conversational implicatures. I'm going to suggest that the conversations between the Hales and the Higginses embody, in the details of their language, the ideology of class reconciliation, and common interest to which Mrs. Gaskell had become firmly committed by *North and South*.

The final text in this group which I want to mention is Dickens's *Hard Times*, which was of course influenced by Dickens's reading *Mary Barton*. I've put four extracts from this novel in the Appendices (B, section 2, and A, section 4), and these begin to illustrate one of its salient compositional devices: an extreme variety of speech styles attributed to the characters. The opposition is not simply a dichotomy between one style for the masters and one style for the men, as in Mrs Gaskell, but within the warring classes there are distinctions. Gradgrind and Bounderby employ different syntaxes, and Harthouse different again. Stephen Blackpool has his own idiolect, the circus people speak in — in Dickens' own words — 'a variety of voices', Slackbridge the orator a distinct mode of speech again; and so on. Within the speech of individuals, too, there are shifts of tone and register. In the case of Stephen Blackpool, for instance, there are noticeable and consistent differences of syntax, intonation and vocabulary between his conversations with Rachel or his dying words, for instance, and on the other hand the language of his responses to the orator and to Bounderby. Finally, there are shifts in the narrative voice itself, which constantly adapts itself by ironic parody, sympathetic reflection, or elaborating contrast to the modes of speech within different scenes. Now I can assure you that all of these styles are linguistically characterizable in the terms which my lecture, and the analytic categories on the handout, offer. The question is what one makes of this variety: is it to be put down to Dickensian caricature, rhetoric and inconsistency, or are each of the styles, and the mixture and the oppositions, functional? I think the latter is the answer. In each case that one cares to take — Blackpool or Bounderby, for example — the linguistic construction of the character is an analysis of an ideology, and this can be demonstrated. But taking the novel as a whole, the analysis is unresolved, incomplete, lacking the kind of decisive judgement that Mrs Gaskell arrives at in *North and South* through her own words and the symmetrical juxtapositions of the characters' speech-styles. By general consent, *Hard Times* is a more satisfying novel, compositionally, than *North and South*; it is certainly much more interesting for the student of ideology, linguistic or other. It shows Dickens experiencing class conflicts and solidarities, affiliations and transitions, as a much richer problematic than Mrs Gaskell did.

The foregoing position statement and fragmentary notes on my work in progress are a preamble to the real substance, the box of knives given in Appendix B. These knives should be used to carve up your own linguistic puddings: to dissect your own language, and the language which is offered you in such gargantuan portions for daily consumption.

Appendix A

1. (a) NUS REGRETS FURY OVER JOSEPH

   (b) STUDENT LEADERS CONDEMN INSULT TO KEITH JOSEPH

   (c) STUDENT CHIEFS 'REGRET' ATTACK ON SIR KEITH

2. (a) LEYLAND PLANS FOR SURVIVAL REJECTED

   British Leyland's plan for survival was rejected yesterday by senior shop stewards representing 165,000 workers.

   (b) STEWARDS DEFY BL CLOSURE THREAT

   Shop stewards from all BL's plants yesterday rejected overwhelmingly the redundancy programme drawn up by chairman Sir Michael Edwardes.

3. **General Regulations for Students**

PREAMBLE
The University can function effectively only if all its members can work peaceably in conditions which permit freedom of study, thought and expression within a framework of respect for other persons. The General Regulations exist to maintain these conditions:

(1) by the protection of free speech and lawful assembly within the University.

(2) by the protection of the right of all members or officers or employees of the University to discharge their duties.

(3) by the protection of the safety and property of all members or officers or employees of the University while engaged in their duties or academic pursuits.

(4) by the protection of the property of the University.

All students matriculating in the University shall, so long as they remain in attendance, be bound by the following Regulations and by such other Regulations as the University may from time to time determine.

1 AGE OF ADMISSION

Those who intend to follow courses for University degrees and diplomas are not normally admitted if they are under the age of seventeen years on 1 October of the year of admission.

2 MATRICULATION

Matriculation is the act of placing a student's name upon the *matricula* or roll of members of the University. Before being allowed to matriculate a student must have fulfilled the examination requirements laid down by the University in respect of general entrance requirements and in respect of course requirements for the programme of study which the student wishes to pursue.

All persons entering the University as students in residence shall sign a Declaration of Obedience to the Authorities of the University, in the following terms: 'I hereby promise to conform to the discipline of the University, and to all Statutes, Regulations and rules in force for the time being, in so far as they concern me'.

4. Extracts from Charles Dickens, Hard Times

(a) 'By your leaves, gentlemen,' said Mr. E.W.B. Childers, glancing round the room, 'It was you, I believe, that were wishing to see Jupe?'

'It was,' said Mr. Gradgrind, 'His daughter has gone to fetch him, but I can't wait; therefore, if you please, I will leave a message for him with you.'

'You see, my friend,' Mr. Bounderby put in, 'we are the kind of people who know the value of time, and you are the kind of people who don't know the value of time.'

'I have not,' retorted Mr Childers, after surveying him from head to foot, 'the honour of knowing *you*; — but if you mean that you can make more money of your time than I can of mine, I should judge from your appearance, that you are about right.'

'And when you have made it, you can keep it too. I should think,' said Cupid.

'Kidderminster, stow that!' said Mr. Childers. (Master Kidderminster was Cupid's mortal name.)

'What does he come here cheeking us for, then?' cried Master Kidderminster, showing a very irascible temperament. 'If you want to cheek us, pay your ochre at the doors and take it out.'

'Kidderminster,' said Mr Childers, raising his voice, 'stow that! — Sir,' to Mr. Gradgrind, 'I was addressing myself to you. You may or you may not be aware (for perhaps you have not been much in the audience), that Jupe has missed his tip very often, lately.'

'Has — what has he missed?' asked Mr Gradgrind, glancing at the potent Bounderby for assistance.

'Missed his tip.'

'Offered at the Garters four times last night, and never done 'em once,' said Master Kidderminster. 'Missed his tip at the banners, too, and was loose in his ponging.'

'Didn't do what he ought to do. Was short in his leaps and bad in his tumbling,' Mr. Childers interpreted.

'Oh!' said Mr Gradgrind, 'that is tip, is it?'

'In a general way that's missing his tip,' Mr E.W.B. Childers answered.

'Nine-oils, Merrylegs, missing tips, garters, banners, and Ponging, eh!' ejaculated Bounderby, with his laugh of laughs. 'Queer sort of company, too, for a man who has raised himself.'

(b) 'I was to pull through it I suppose, Mrs Gradgrind. Whether I was to do it or not, ma'am, I did it. I pulled through it, though nobody threw me out a rope. Vagabond, errand-boy, vagabond, labourer, porter, clerk, chief manager, small partner, Josiah Bounderby of Coketown. Those are the antecedents, and the culmination. Josiah Bounderby of Coketown learnt his letters from the outsides of shops, Mrs. Gradgrind, and was first able to tell the time upon a dial-plate, from studying the steeple clock of St. Giles's Church, London, under the direction of a drunken cripple, who was a convicted thief and an incorrigible vagrant. Tell Josiah Bounderby of Coketown, of your district schools and your model schools, and your training schools, and your whole kettle-of-fish of schools; and Josiah Bounderby of Coketown, tells you plainly, all right, all correct — he hadn't such advantages — but let us have hard-headed, solid-fisted people — the education that made him won't do for everybody — such and such his education was, however, and you may force him to swallow boiling fat, but you shall never force him to suppress the facts of life.'

Appendix B

Check-list of critically/ideologically interesting linguistic structures.

1. VOCABULARY
Lexicalization, e.g. specialist vocabulary: track, album, spin, disc, release, group, single; transformation, phoneme, nominalization.

Relexicalization: upright man, prigger of prancers, counterfeit crank, doxy, snappings, lifting law, wresters (Elizabethan underworld)

Overlexicalization: vandals, hooligans, thugs, punks, louts, kids, yobboes, youths, teenagers, misfits, layabouts (Various newspapers)

Underlexicalization: curly iron fences, raw fish and sort of meat fritter, huge pink fish (Jenny Bunn in Amis, *Take a Girl like You*); curling flower spaces, the flower tree (Benjy in Faulkner, *The Sound and the Fury*)

Complex categories: juvenile criminal justice system, supervision order, secure care order, residential care order, care order, custodial care order, ordinary care order, community homes, foster homes, detention centre, juvenile system, young adult offender (*Guardian*)

Prenominal adjectives: a mythic quest, a passionately detailed and evocative work, a brilliantly managed scene, a riveting novel, punchy dialogue, action-packed war-time scenes, a more light-hearted but equally exciting satire, stylish ingenuity, a delicate elusive manner, broad comedy, an intriguing and stylish attempt (*Observer* review)

verdant hillock, friendly shade, industrious bee, balmy dews, silken robe, fragrant breath, rude storm, hospitable scene, gladsome toils, ambrosial spoils, sylvan scenes, etc. (Akenside)

2. SYNTAX
Clause structure of sentences

Hypotaxis: If I might venture to remark that it is the least in the world deficient in that delicacy to which a youth mistaken, a character misconceived, and abilities misdirected, would turn for relief and guidance, I should express what it presents to my own view. (James Harthouse in Dickens, *Hard Times*)

Parataxis: Miss Gage brought a pitcher of water and a glass. I drank three glasses and then they left me and I looked out of the window a while and went back to sleep. I ate some lunch and in the afternoon Miss Van Campen, the super-intendant, came up to see me. She did not like me and I did not like her. She was small and neatly suspicious and too good for her position. (Hemingway, *A Farewell to Arms*)

Speech style: I've tried a long time, and 'ta'nt got better. But thou'rt right; 'tmight mak for talk, even of thee. Thou hast been that to me, Rachel, through so many year: thou hast done me so much good, and heartened of me in that cheering way, that thy word is a law to me. Ah lass, and a bright good law! Better than some real ones. (Stephen Blackpool in Dickens, *Hard Times*)

Transformations

Transformations are functional and significant, despite the denial of this by transformational grammarians. Any transformations may be important, but the ones illustrated — passive, nominalization, thematization — regularly call for interpretation.

Passive:
RIOTING BLACKS SHOT DEAD BY POLICE AS ANC LEADERS MEET (*The Times*)
All students matriculating in the University shall, so long as they remain in attendance, be bound by the following Regulations. (*UEA Regs.*)

Salt has long been associated with high blood pressure. (*Observer*)
The observations were carried out in the course of a therapeutic procedure. . . . The cortical surface electrodes were equally spaced at 1-centimeter intervals. (F. Morrell, 'Electrical Signs of Sensory Coding'.)

Note transition from active to passives in the following: The QUEEN has directed that the appointment of Professor Sir Anthony Frederick Blunt to be a Knight Commander of the Royal Victorian Order dated 31st May 1956 shall be cancelled and annulled and that his name shall be erased from the Register of the said Order. (*London Gazette*)

Nominalization:
freedom, study, thought, expression, respect, Regulations, protection, speech, assembly, etc, (*UEA Regs.*)

Being absent for more than three consecutive sessions without explanation to the membership secretary means automatic expulsion. (Swimming Club Rules)

In the majority of cases there is little wait if the matter is urgent. That should be recognised. Most of those who are having to wait are non-urgent cases. When a case becomes urgent, it goes to the top of the list. (David Ennals)

Thematization:
President Carter, for his part, has appealed for calm and patience. (BBC News)

She waited, Kate Croy, for her father to come in. (James, *The Wings of the Dove*)
Orange juice I drink every morning.

Of Man's First Disobedience, and the Fruit
Of that Forbidden Tree . . .
Sing Heav'nly Muse . . . (Milton, *Paradise Lost*)

3. INTERPERSONAL FEATURES
Speech acts:
Fill in the coupon right now. (Newspaper advertisement)
Please respect the facilities and equipment, and take particular care with

41

untrained children. (Swimming Club Rules)

I promise it won't hurt you.

Indirect speech acts:

Will't please you sit and look at her? (Browning, 'My Last Duchess')

Well you know, wdy'mind takin' the dustrag an' justdustaround? (Rhoda)

Can you pass the salt?

I promise you you'll regret it.

No outside shoes will be worn when in the pool area. (Swimming Club Rules)

Implicatures:

Patient: I'm a nurse, but my husband won't let me work.

Therapist: How old are you? (Therapeutic Interview)

(Implicature: Adults decide for themselves whether they work.)

There's good food in Ireland. You like plain meals? (Irish Tourist Board advertisment. Implicature: English tourists going abroad object to fancy foreign cooking.)

Deixis: That is no country for old men (Yeats)

Banish those washday blues (advertisment)

Presuppositions:

Why is your memory so poor? (advertisement)

How can we combat this Communist conspiracy?

Modality

Modal verbs: may, shall, will, can, should, etc.

Sentence-adverbs:

But he has perhaps some of the qualities needed . . . (*Guardian*)

It was this, precisely, that had set the Prince to think. (James, *The Golden Bowl*)

Generics:

Professors tend not to be much fun. As research students, lecturers, and even readers they may have been gay sprigs, but give them a chair and they become solemn. (*Sunday Telegraph*)

We learn to restrain ourselves as we get older. We keep apart when we have quarrelled, express ourselves in well-bred phrases, and in this way preserve a dignified alienation, showing much firmness on one side, and swallowing much grief on the other. (George Eliot, *The Mill on the Floss*)

Tense as modality:

I was wondering if you had marked my essay?

Hedging:

Er, um, I quite like it really, it's er, part of it I find, er sort of, a bit contrived, but I suppose that's er, that's sort of Byron's style that er, um . . . (Candidate for university admission)

An-nd — uh — mayb-y'know — maybe some of this has to be discussed together. Actually it — uh — usually . . . (Rhoda's therapist)

Personal pronouns:
We must keep up all our defences, whether nuclear or conventional. (Mrs. Thatcher)

You can't cut tax unless you curb public spending. (Mrs. Thatcher)

Sexually the naked ape finds himself in a somewhat confused situation. As a primate he is pulled one way ... (Desmond Morris, *The Naked Ape*)

                              ... be Kent unmannerly
When Lear is mad. What would'st thou do, old man?
Think'st thou that duty shall have dread to speak ... (*King Lear*)

Titles and names:
Mrs. Thatcher (*Observer*); Maggie (*Eastern Evening News, Sun*), The Prime Minister (*Telegraph*)
Sonia, Paul, Keith (children and wives, *Observer*)
Brady, Hudson, Cunningham (footballers, *Observer*)
The Bishop (Lord Carrington referring to Bishop Abel Muzorewa)
Professor R.G. Fowler, Mrs. R.G.Fowler, Miss Rosemary Jackson, Mrs. Lorna Sage, Dr. V.R.L. Sage, Smith, A.R. (EAS I), Smith, Joanne (EAS I) (from various UEA lists, envelopes, etc.)

4. COHESION
Call me Jonah. My parents did, or nearly did. They called me John. (Kurt Vonnegut, Jr., *Cat's Cradle*)

Madame Merle looked a moment at Isabel and at the master of the house. He was leaning against the parapet, facing her, his arms folded; and she at present was evidently not lost in the mere impersonal view, persistently as she gazed at it. As Madame Merle watched her she lowered her eyes; she was listening, possibly with a certain embarrassment, while she pressed the point of her parasol into the path. Madame Merle rose from her chair.
'Yes, I think so!' she pronounced. (James, *The Portrait of a Lady*)

(On cohesion see M.A.K. Halliday & R. Hasan, *Cohesion in English*, London: Longman, 1976); W. Gutwinski, *Cohesion in Literary Texts* (The Hague: Mouton, 1976).

5. TRANSITIVITY
Arguably the most fundamental category but difficult to illustrate because basically semantic (thus strictly unobservable) and expressed in a variety of often deceptive syntactic constructions. The semantics of actions, states and processes, and of the participants of which these are predicated. A Subject-Verb-Object sequence often indicates full transitivity:

1. I burned the letter.
2. Mary opened the door.

In 1 and 2 an agent intentionally performs a definite action which results in a change of state in some object. These structures seem so 'natural' that they go unnoticed, but are ideologically significant since they are options in a system. We have found pseudo-transitives also highly important:

3. We make a rapid reconnaissance. (*Observer*)
4. I take the trans-Europe to Paris. (*Observer*)
5. Egypt will continue its peaceful efforts. (*Observer*)

And intrinsically transitive predicates expressed intransitively:

6. I could see them hitting . . . . they were hitting . . . and he hit and the other hit. (Benjy in *The Sound and the Fury*)

Not to mention ordinary intransitives, which, foregrounded, contrast with transitives:

7. She laughed.

States (8) contrast with actions (7), but may look like them:

8. She sat (still).

Reflexives (actions performed on oneself) sometimes look transitive (9) and sometimes intransitive (10); in either case, a less 'active', 'controlled' world is communicated by the style if the constructions are used frequently:

9. The British understand themselves better when they see themselves through French eyes.(*Observer*)
10. Simon meditated.

Finally, it is always worth looking at what sorts of participants are associated with what kinds of actions and processes. Particularly important — the basis of some central metaphors and of the styles of gothic novels, depictions of limited and defective consciousnesses, etc. — is the combination of an inanimate subject with a verb or adjective which normally takes an animate subject:

11. The house creaked and groaned.
12. . . . dwarfish, doddered, leafless trees . . . and weeds rearing their unlovely heads . . . all waving and bending in capricious and unsightly forms . . . (Maturin, *Melmoth the Wanderer*)
13. Yea plants, yea stones detest, / And love (Donne)
14. Mushrooms and their hallucinogenic properties are creating a legal tangle in magistrates' courts. (*Observer*)

Other clashes of semantic feature between the elements of a clause are striking:

15. I am every dead thing. (Donne)

The permutations of semantic features, and of semantic structures with syntactic expressions, are considerable. For some analyses of these topics in 'literary' texts, see M.A.K. Halliday, 'Linguistic Function and Literary Style: An Enquiry into the Language of William Golding's *The Inheritors*', in *Explorations in the Functions of Language* (London: Edward Arnold, 1973), pp. 103-143; G.R. Kress, 'Poetry as Anti-Language: A Reconsideration of Donne's "Nocturnall upon S. Lucie's Day"', *Poetics and the Theory of Literature*, 3 (1978). 327-344.

Notes

1. Peter L. Berger and Thomas Luckmann, *The Social Construction of Reality*, (1966: repr. Harmondsworth: Penguin Books, 1976).

2. Paul Connerton, ed., *Critical Sociology* (Harmondsworth: Penguin, 1976).

3. For the solution to the puzzle, see my detailed linguistic analysis of these sentences in *UEA Papers in Linguistics*, (January 1977), 36-48.

4. For typical examples of indexical or correlational sociolinguistics, see W. Labov, *Sociolinguistic Patterns* (Philadelphia: University of Pennsylvania Press, 1972); P. Trudgill, *Sociolinguistics: An Introduction* (Harmondsworth: Penguin Books, 1974).

5. M.A.K. Halliday, 'Language Structure and Language Function', in J. Lyons, ed., *New Horizons in Linguistics* (Harmondsworth: Penguin, 1970), pp. 140-165; see also his *Language as Social Semiotic* (London: Edward Arnold, 1978).

6. R. Fowler, R. Hodge, G. Kress and T. Trew, *Language and Control*, (London: Routledge and Kegan Paul, 1979).

7. See M.A.K. Halliday, 'Antilanguages', *Language as Social Semiotic*, pp. 165 ff.

8. Jonathan Culler, *Structuralist Poetics* (London: Routledge and Kegan Paul, 1975), Ch. 6

9. 'Linguistics and, and versus, Poetics, *'Journal of Literary Semantics*', 8(1979), 3-21.

10. R. Jakobson, 'Closing Statement: Linguistics and Poetics', in T.A. Sebeok, ed., *Style in Language* (Cambridge, Mass.: MIT Press); cf M.H. Abrams, 'Orientation of Critical Theories', in *The Mirror and The Lamp* (New York: Oxford University Press, 1953).

11. R. Brown and A. Gilman, 'The Pronouns of Power and Solidarity', in *Style in Language*, pp. 253-76.

12. M. Bakhtin, trans. R.W. Rotsel, *Problems of Dostoevsky's Poetics* (Ann Arbor: Ardis, 1973); V.N. Vološinov, trans. L. Matejka and I.R. Titunik, *Marxism and the Philosophy of Language* (New York: Seminar Press, 1973).

13. W. Labov and D. Fanshel, *Therapeutic Discourse* (New York: Academic Press, 1977).

14. M. Coulthard, *An Introduction to Discourse Analysis* (London: Longman, 1977).

15. W.J. Downes, 'Language, belief and verbal action in an historical process', *UEA Papers in Linguistics*, 8(1978), 1-43.

16. See R. Fowler, *Linguistics and the Novel* (London: Methuen, 1977): 'The Referential code and Narrative Authority', *Language and Style*, 10 (1977), 129-161.

17. W. Iser, *The Implied Reader* (Baltimore: Johns Hopkins University Press, 1974); *The Act of Reading* (Baltimore: The Johns Hopkins University Press, 1978).

CHAPTER THREE

Orientation: Four Reviews

(i) Literary stylistics

Linguistic stylistics has for over ten years been a controversial proposal, perhaps, particularly in Great Britain where the literary establishment is very entrenched and conservative. Stylisticians tend to be defensive, and Anne Cluysenaar's book* is written 'in response to certain questions repeatedly posed by those who doubt the relevance of linguistics to literary studies'. She, like I, is very much convinced the doubters are wrong, and I think she gives the most persuasive demonstration yet that, in the hands of a sensitive and intelligent literary critic, linguistic tools are a magnificent aid to clarifying and articulating our best responses to literature.

Cluysenaar is not concerned with taxonomic stylistics, with the historical or synchronic classification of the style-prints of authors or genres. Nor is she concerned with what I would call diagnostic or interpretative or materialist stylistics and what I think she would call 'extrinsic' stylistics: namely the interpretation of stylistic traits as radical indices placing the author's consciousness in the context of the history of culture. Spitzer and Auerbach seem not to be mentioned in her text or notes. Rather, the book concentrates on stylistics as the technique of verbal analysis within practical criticism. Literary works (and their significant sub-parts, as the prose extracts she discusses) are seen as autonomous wholes. Each in its individuality is capable of surprising the reader and his society, creating a new and unique configuration of language structures; these in their turn promoting new experience with fresh particularity yet vast general significance. Cluysenaar's expectations of literature and of literary criticism are thus squarely within the individualist, organicist, empiricist, non-sociological New Critical tradition; the critics who have had most influence on her work seem to be the best British representatives of this movement, Empson, Davie and Nowottny. She shows herself capable of practical criticism of exemplary sensitivity and penetration, providing commentaries on the 'dominant structures', of pieces by Graves, Lawrence, Conrad, Lowry, Yeats, Day Lewis translating Valéry, Faulkner, Milton, Tennyson, etc. The high quality of the criticism certainly justifies her claim that linguistic analysis — without much technicality

---

* Anne Cluysenaar *An Introduction to Literary Stylistics: a discussion of dominant structures in verse and prose*

— has a positive function in literary study: in the classroom (including the teaching of creative writing) and in printed criticism.

'Dominant structures' are linguistic patterns made perceptually salient by their semantic/thematic importance. These patterns may involve features at any level of linguistic form, or cross-level patterns (as metre always is). Miss Cluysenaar is careful to dissociate herself from the extreme formalism of Jakobson and the Prague School (see pp. 61-2): linguistic patterning is not automatically self-justifying, but has to be made interesting through its semantic relevance, through the meanings which it has led us to perceive.

The aesthetic is familiar, and its practical demonstrations will please and impress teachers of literature. However, it might be felt that the congeniality of the practical criticism somewhat weakens the case that is being made for the specialness of the technique of stylistics. In general, linguistic technicality and terminology are kept to a minimum, and it is not always clear that anything more specifically technical than an extremely acute attentiveness to language is being practised. In a sense she has learned her lesson too thoroughly, absorbing the linguistic technique so well that it leaves too little trace on the surface. A detailed analytic notation is sometimes very revealing: for instance, the syntactic-metrical analysis of a passage from *Paradise Lost*, done in diagrammatic style (p.55), shows how Leavis misjudged the passage just because he lacked such an apparatus for precise analysis. More analysis of this degree of explicitness would have made a crucial point about linguistic stylistics: that the consistent use of a particular linguistic model gives the critic, not merely a way of looking closely at language, but a specific *kind* of perspective depending on the particular model chosen. Thus, it is probable that Miss Cluysenaar's focus on textual patterns which can be perceived (literally spatial patterning), and furthermore, her acceptance of a New Critical 'objective' aesthetic, is aided and encouraged by her scale-and-category ('systemic') linguistics: and that a freer recourse to transformations would have made it easier to fulfil her claimed (but not, I think, regularly achieved) aim of showing how dominant structures are perceived by the reader as they develop *in time*. In this case, a more eclectic use of models would probably have been more illuminating, and a more explicit discussion of the models themselves would have encouraged a more sceptical self-conscious criticism. Of course, I'm not suggesting that TG is always better than systemic for stylistics, but that students should be made aware of the filtering properties of the analytic equipment they use. A stronger version of stylistics than Miss Cluysenaar's would make possible the criticism of critical paradigms. Consigning the methodological and theoretical discussions to her (very copious) footnotes, in order not to alarm the literary student, is a kind of bowdlerization: it's not obvious from the text just how selective, even ideological, the (any) approach is.

The ideology that bothers me is that of practical criticism itself. I have never doubted that linguistic techniques for the analysis of verbal patterning could be readily assimilated into the practice of practical criticism, and have acted upon this assumption in my own classes and writings. It is splendid to have the correctness of this belief so ably demonstrated in Miss Cluysenaar's book. I do feel, however, that the very efficiency of her practical criticism implicitly compromises the linguistics she uses; linguistics has become so subservient that it cannot question the aims and methods of the criticism it accommodates itself to. It's time to go further: while criticizing the poem, we should also question the educational and social goals which this criticism seeks to promote. A linguistic criticism can be devised which has this analytic power.

(ii) Inclusive (sociolinguistic) versus exclusive (formalist) stylistics

Mr Hendricks' previous publications have shown his wide range of interests in linguistic stylistics and his broad knowledge of American and European traditions in linguistics, stylistics, and semiotics. His first book, *Essays on Semiolinguistics and Verbal Art* (1973) was much concerned with structuralist poetics and text-grammar; the present work* returns to more familiar preoccupations in the stylistics of individual authors and of groups, and may be regarded as an attempt to map out the theoretical status and relationships of some major concepts in the taxonomy of styles. The definition and delimitation of style attempted in this collection of papers seems to me to represent a disappointing contraction in the scope of stylistics as it has been emerging with the increasing methodological inclusiveness of recent years; and in reviewing this book I feel obligated to ask whether the theory it supports can really be justified in the contemporary critical and linguistic context.

Although the work under review articulates a single theoretical position, it has been written not as a unified theoretical monograph but as a collection of independent essays. This is not the most efficient format for a discussion which claims to clarify the intricate and perennially intransigent problems which surround the notion of style. Read as a whole book, this set of essays is rather repetitive, the same authors and issues tending to be approached repeatedly from perspectives that shift disconcertingly as the context alters. Hendricks goes round and round about such central preoccupations as paraphrase and style type, rather than confronting them squarely and explicating them by reference to a single unified theory. I have found it hard work to discern exactly where Hendricks stands on the crucial questions, and what linguistic or other theory he commits himself to as justifying his position. However, the ideas, once grasped, are simple and convincing enough. The question is whether they are really of any positive value.

Returning to the title, *Grammars of Style and Styles of Grammar*: the first part is an affirmation of the systematicity of style, a dismissal of the idea that style is merely a matter of free variation of structures against some normal or neutral pattern for the language: implicitly a rejection of Chomsky's pejorative unruly 'linguistic performance,' a rejection strictly analogous to Dell Hymes's appeal for a hypothesis of systematicity in the ethnography of language, but — crucially, from my point of view — lacking any recognition of the cultural or historical value of

* William O. Hendricks *Grammars of Style and Styles of Grammar*

systematic stylistic variation. The variation that Hendricks posits is, traditionally, variation of 'manner' of conveying the same 'matter' (cf. Ohmann's proposals within the early TG framework), though to this conventional and plausible assumption he adds the invaluable methodological and theoretical caveat that *paraphrase* is not a necessary condition in stylistics.

The second half of the title's chiasmus is, as Hendricks admits, somewhat rhetorical. There is no attempt at a review of grammatical models here (such would be outside the purpose of the book). The phrase refers to a suggestion that the (alleged) two major style types 'tight' and 'loose' are exploitations of two different properties of language, which might be captured in two different types of grammatical models, namely its 'hierarchical' and 'string' properties respectively. This is an original idea, but tendentious and presented in a highly oblique manner by a reinterpretation of some not very linguistic descriptions and claims by Francis Christensen and Walker Gibson.

Whatever the validity of these two 'style types', Hendricks comes close to maintaining that between them they exhaust the typology of styles (cf. p.180, 'only a few style types exist'). This classical-sounding reduction is supported by an argument to the effect that stylistic differentiation is possible at different levels of 'delicacy' (in Halliday's sense). The stylistic types are potentiated by a few very general linguistic universals; within these classes, numerous variant realizations are found, at a finer level of delicacy, answering to 'idiolects' in sociolinguistic or dialect description. In fact, Hendricks wishes to restrict the term and concept of 'style' to these two extremes of the taxonomy, to what he calls *group* and *individuating* styles. Of the two, group style is to him the more important, since it is controlled directly by the structural possibilities afforded by *la langue* and in turn sets the limits within which a writer can choose expressions of his originality.

The dual emphases on typology and on individuation leave us with a very rarefied, abstracted conception of the goals of stylistics. (That dreadfully barren statement of the goals of linguistic theory on the first page of *Aspects of the Theory of Syntax* comes to mind.) The author refers repeatedly to a host of structural variables that have to be 'factored out' before the analyst lays bare the object of stylistic description. In a sweeping dissociation, Hendricks excludes what he calls 'functional group style', that is, any variable that correlates with the sociological and historical standing of a text and its writer. Taxonomic terms like 'Baroque' or 'Ciceronian' are free of time and of historical causation; they simply reflect alternative realizations of the constant spirit of a language, available at any moment of time. Studies such as Paul Zumthor's accounts of the language of medieval French lyric poetry would be excluded from stylistics since they are founded on hypotheses about particular social structures, world-views, semantic organizations. Spitzer's work similarly would be classed as non-stylistic, as would Auerbach's, insofar as it explains expressive choices in terms of a historically determined psyche. A related exclusion is the rhetorical facet of linguistic variation: all features expressing writer-reader relationships — thus the traditional hierarchical division of high, middle, and low, and variants of that scale — disappear, likewise recent 'affective' stylistics such as the work of Stanley

Fish, and some of Riffaterre's. Outside stylistics also goes the study of literary techniques or devices: in an illuminating discussion, Hendricks argues that Halliday's famous study of *The Inheritors* describes not a style, but an instance of deautomization. Next to be cast out are all 'organic' patterns (i.e. linguistic organizations motivated directly by semantic structure) which are said to have the same status as phonetic symbolism: in effect, everything that a New Critic would delight in goes out of the window. Finally, neither textual macrostructure (e.g. theme, plot) nor intersentence cohesion (anaphora and the other connectives studied by Halliday, Hasan, and others) belongs to stylistics, and so a vast amount of contemporary European work in the structural analysis of plot and in text-grammar is excluded.

If I have presented these dissociations negatively, it is because Hendricks proceeds in just this reductionist way, delimiting the scope of stylistics by a set of exclusions. Certainly something very positive is intended: as we all know, the term 'style' is utterly promiscuous in common usage, and requires pinning down. Hendricks recognizes, correctly, that the structure of a text is multi-faceted. remarkably complicated; and so he proposes some very sensible divisions of labour for the description of these various complexities of diverse origins. Unfortunately, he is working not towards an inclusive array of the different structural features of texts but towards an exclusive concept of style in which all but 'group' and 'individuating' characteristics are regarded as unwanted noise. This filtration is as negative and disappointing as Katz and Fodor's way of determining the scope of a semantic theory, or Chomsky's idealization of the subject-matter of grammar to a constant, variety-free core.

Hendricks has shown that a theory of style is much less than a theory of text structure. Let us suppose that his definition of style is a useful working definition; we must certainly grant that this is a more workable definition than many that have been proposed in the past, since it involves a considerable reduction in scope and in diffusion. Having made such a concession, it seems necessary to question whether, even if the definition of style has been clarified, the discipline of 'stylistics' has been enriched. Hendricks' approach to style (in this book) is at best unfashionable and at worst trivial, limiting attention to marginal aspects of literary text structure. Perhaps authors possess individuating styles which can be measured by an examination of the linguistic structures (mostly syntax) he focuses on; the fact is that author-detection stylistics, which has a long history, has produced scant empirical evidence that this is the case. It seems much more likely that our intuition of the individuality of a writer is a response to typical text-features which go much deeper than 'style' in the traditional, and Hendricks', sense. Themes, narrative structures, ethical stances receive author-characterizing codings in language: Henry James is recognizable not just because he indulges in passives, nominalizations, state predicates, etc., but because these structures encode an analysis of a world peopled with alienated sensibilities. To say this sort of thing is *not* to retreat from the mechanical precision of strict stylistics to the impressionism of literary criticism. The theoretical terms of literary criticism — theme, narrative structure, ethical value — however vague among the critics, represent well-documented intuitions which critics have of text-structural conventions. They provide heuristic categories for theoretical linguistics, targets to be illuminated by the development of text-grammar and semiological poetics. Hendricks' attenuated definition of style discourages investigation of these broader and richer topics which are currently included in 'stylistics' in the looser sense. (Think of anthologies like Chatman's or Freeman's and consider how much of the contents would be excluded by Hendricks' definition.)

A bundle of related complaints against this conception of style emerges, then. First, by concentrating on sentential syntax conceived of as separate from 'content', it prevents access to major literary-critical preoccupations, including a sufficiently rich notion of the writer's uniqueness. Effectively, stylistics is severed from literary criticism; and while this is not an unusual conception of stylistics, it does militate against the increasingly varied practice of criticism and of textual description associated with the 'linguistic stylistics' of the last decade or so. Furthermore, this conception of style trivializes linguistics. It draws upon modern linguistics only to the extent of utilizing an early model of syntactic analysis working at the 'rank' of the sentence and below. One of the attractions of modern linguistic stylistics, to me at least, is that by juxtaposing, even confronting, linguistics and poetics, or linguistics and criticism, the 'stylisticians' have constantly enlarged the range of techniques and concepts drawn from a developing linguistics into the service of literary and textual studies: not only descriptive techniques such as the stress-assignment rules of generative phonology in metrics, but more fundamental proposals such as speech act theory within TG, thematization and information structure as microstructural cohesive devices and as controllers of the reader's attention, and deep semantic organization and its implications for *Weltanschauung*. The relationship between stylistics and linguistics in current interdisciplinary studies is reciprocally developmental. As stylistics, in the generalized sense I am advocating, diversifies and strengthens itself by drawing upon recent develpments in linguistics, so it also puts pressure on linguistics to meet the demands generated by criticism's bold yet poorly articulated theoretical categories. Two developments in contemporary European poetics come to mind. One is research into semantic macrostructures (e.g. themes, character traits, settings in fiction); another is text modality (e.g. point of view in narrative, rhetorical stance of personas, interaction of consciousnesses). Examples, respectively, are the work on generation of text from a semantic base by Zholkovsky and Scheglov, reported and demonstrated by L. M. O'Toole in my book *Style and Structure in Literature* (Cornell, 1975) and Genette's work on narrative discourse, or Seymour Chatman's (see his contribution to *Style and Structure in Literature* and cf. my *Linguistics and the Novel* [Methuen, 1977]). With respect to the people I have just mentioned, these researches are still at a primitive stage of development, but the problems encountered are very illuminating, drawing attention to previously unnoticed inadequacies in both linguistic and literary theory and encouraging repair of these deficiencies. This kind of dialectical juxtaposition seems to me most fruitful in 'linguistic stylistics', and of course it is excluded from Hendricks' stylistics.

Finally, Hendricks' taxonomic stylistics discourages *explanatory* statements about 'manner of expression' or about any other aspect of linguistic/literary form. 'Style as personality' is no part of his project; and, as he points out, we need to think in terms of personality types rather than individuals. 'Personality types', if admitted to the theory, would need to be translated into sociological terms, and ultimately regarded as a minor part of a materialist framework of argument. I have noted already that Hendricks regards his 'group styles' as synchronic, or, more exactly, free of history and independent of any historical aggregation of individuals. In my opinion, this decision impoverishes stylistics to the extent that it is of very little service to literary and cultural studies. Typological stylistics, as conceived of by Hendricks, might in a more developed version contribute to the theory of linguistic universals, but has nothing at all to offer to the history of literary forms, and nothing to our understanding of the reasons why dominant styles of writing emerge at certain moments in intellectual and material history. The history of literary forms manifests a series of structural revolutions (Chaucer, Wordsworth, Flaubert, Imagism, *nouveau roman*, etc. etc.) which are usually regarded as, at one level at least, transformations of the expressive (why not 'stylistic'?) potential of the genres in which these revolutions have occurred. Hendricks' orientation on style provides no motivation whatsoever for describing these major diachronic shifts; no apparatus for specifying the diversity of linguistic features transformed in these revisions (since he has reduced the methodology of stylistics to an elementary syntactic analysis); no way of enquiring into the *reasons why* individuals, or groups or writers, set off in new linguistic directions at specific points in the histories of their societies.

In brief, 'history' is neglected in two senses: the diachronic development of linguistic modes, and the relationship of language to social context. The exclusion of history in the sense of material context is particularly regrettable, since it denies stylistics access to some most promising developments in recent linguistics: namely, sociolinguistics (correlational and sociologically based as with Labov, but more particularly critical sociolinguistics as expounded by Dittmar) and functional theories of the motivation of grammatical structure (Halliday and the Prague School). Actually, since the dialectic is forfeited, the loss is multifold. The exclusion from stylistics of some major linguistic schools bothers me, but that worry is trivial compared with my concern that the linguistic study of literary form should be able to set literature in relation to its social origins, to explain linguistic choices as required by cultural determinants. Such a strategy of causal explanations is, of course, controversial in poetics and criticism as well as in linguistics: crudely, sociology of literature vs. 'litcrit' purism. It would be a pity if stylistics missed out on this dominant contemporary debate, particularly since an analogous debate lies at the heart of contemporary linguistics too. With the growing recognition that the human sciences have a compelling responsibility to offer a critique of society, progress in our academic field is likely to be in the direction of a sociolinguistic, inclusive stylistics. I regret that Hendricks' definition of style, though stringent and operational, encourages a counter-reforming programme of stylistic theory and description.

(iii) Against genteel poetics

'Our search . . . is for basic structures of poetic language, whether they are found in a Bantu riddle or a poem by Donne, in a Cherokee charm or a song by Shakespeare'*. The search is to be aided by some supposedly theoretical 'coordinates' drawn from 'modern poetics' and by reference to examples of 'primitive poetry'. The modern poetics is not that of Jakobson or French structuralism or any other serious scientific poetics. This neglect is surprising, since not only is Welsh's aim, as expressed in the above quotation, entirely compatible with Jakobson's, but in addition many of the 'poetic' structures which Welsh examines have a linguistic format which would respond well to Jakobson's technique of analysis. The 'modern poetics' is in fact the neo-Romantic poetics of Pound, Fenollosa, William Carlos Williams, and Valéry, with the added authority of some relevant parts of Northrop Frye's taxonomy. The 'roots of lyric' are techniques which 'charge language with meaning'. They are classified, following Pound, as *melopoeia*, *phanopoeia*, and *logopoeia* — Aristotle's and Frye's *melos*, *opsis* and *lexis*. *Melos* and *opsis* are of course musical and visual elements of poetic language; we will return to *lexis*, or *logopoeia*, shortly.

Welsh's thesis seems to be that lyric poetry has, has always had, and will always have, very important phonetic and visual devices. In this it is distinguished from other kinds of poetry — epic, etc. — although Welsh does not demonstrate the actuality of this generic difference. Phanopoeic (visual) tendencies are illustrated in four chapters on *riddle*, *emblem*, *image* and *ideogram*; melopoeia is divided up into *charm*, *chant* and *rhythm*. All these categories and their sub-categories are copiously illustrated with familiar examples ('At a Station of the Metro', 'Erce, Erce, Erce', Shakespeare's Sonnet 73, Wyatt for speech-rhythms, etc.), plus some old or exotic materials from the earlier history of European poetry and form modern anthropologists' collections. This material from outside the received canon of post-medieval lyric is for 'roots' or 'radicals'. Welsh maintains a truly poetic equivocation on the concept of 'roots', though he uses the term three or four times on every page. 'Roots' embraces (a) historical ancestry, (b) universal features, and (c) 'deep' features, all mixed up in a porridge of affirmations designed to impress by gesture rather than method. Since (a) there is mere citation of old texts without diachronic argument, the old texts are like the footnote references to Chaucer, Mandeville and Wyclif with which Mrs Gaskell dignifies the Northern dialect: they have no historical pertinence. As for (b), universal features might be empirical structures of language (e.g. parallelism, metaphor) but Welsh does not use his exotic materials to show this. As for (c), the book seems to suggest that the patterns of language are *basic* to lyric poetry, but lacking a decent theory of language the author cannot persuade us of this.

All he shows is that some features of the modern Romantic poets he admires (Pound, Williams, Dylan Thomas, Yeats, Hopkins) are found in some other selected texts of widely divergent provenance. It follows (for Welsh) that the poetic theories which have been articulated by these people and their favourites

*Andrew Welsh *Roots of Lyric: primitive poetry and modern poetics*

and associates to justify the practice of this kind of poetry are correct for all poetry. So he swallows hook line and sinker the most tendentious rationalizations, of which the most outrageous is Pound's/Fenollosa's justification of Images and Ideograms. Welsh is led by his devotion to this 'theory' to a naive and preposterous doctrine of Realism, a belief that there are Things sitting patiently in Nature waiting for the Poet to come along and reveal them to us by discovering the Right Word:

> Phanopoeia, then, is a power in language for accurate naming, and the poet's job is to make present to the reader's imagination all the visual precisions, the paradoxical structures, and the complex, 'caught-time' spaces that an accurate naming must include. *Hoc opus, hic labor est.* Perhaps it has been that labor which has led poets to dream of finding what they must now make: a language that reveals rather than conceals the right names for things, a language that is itself charged from the roots up with the powers of phanopoeia.

(p.99; cf. p.25 on the biblical Adam finding the right names for the beasts of the field, and pp.125-6 interpreting Fenollosa as claiming that 'the processes and structures of nature are the roots of language'.)

The above quotation is, alas, a perfectly representative sample of Welsh's prose style and mode of argumentation. Modern Romantics buffs may get a good feeling from phrases like 'a language that is itself charged from the roots up with the powers of phanopoeia', but such phrases are largely meaningless. Undefined terms like 'charged', slippery terms like 'roots', vacuous terms like 'powers' and sonorous classicisms like 'phanopoeia', tiresomely reiterated throughout the book create an incantatory blur which is surely close to the roots of academic writing.

What happened to *logopoeia* ('the dance of the intellect among words')? A good question, and Welsh poses it and disposes of it (p.20, lines 1-26). 'Frye points out, simply and neatly, that *lexis* covers *all* the language of poetry; it is what *melos* and *opsis* both ultimately become in a verbal art. . . . In talking about the roots of melopoeia and phanopoeia in the language of poetry, then, as we are about to do, we are also exploring the roots of logopoeia, or *lexis*.' So much for *lexis*: a mere medium, as in neo-Aristotelean doctrine.

The sad fate of *lexis* is highly significant. Welsh's infatuation with visual and musical elements in poetry, and his preference for poems that foreground such effects, lead him to ignore language and meaning (language as communication, language as language). The consequences of this neglect are disastrous. The disasters include the false generalization that all poems are basically imagistic and phonetic, and the absurd belief that poems present a true unmediated reality. Then, because the dislike for statement, for meaning, infects his *own* practice of writing, Welsh is led to write a profoundly anti-intellectual book. My observations about his modes of argumentation under (a), (b) and (c) above could be damningly expanded and documented. A form of reasoning which suits a haiku, or (to give a closer analogy) a Dylan Thomas lyric, is not suitable for a scholarly book. Definitions, arguments, documentation and technical knowledge are needed, and this book is appallingly defective in all these areas. (I refrain from a detailed criticism of the ignorance of linguistics and poetics, except to say that this ignorance is total: an astonishing situation since the book is about language.)

I am saddened by having to condemn a book so totally. I do not know Mr Welsh and therefore have nothing personal against him. I am all too familiar with the academic position he mediates, however, and I believe that this position is damaging and should be attacked. Reviewing, like writing and publishing, is a social practice. *Roots of Lyric* is an anachronistic expression of an anti-intellectual formalism which has dominated Anglo-American literary studies for over half a century. The ideology of literature and of literary education of which it is a part is based on a social structure which is now recognised as inimical to personal dignity and equality of opportunity. Anyone who is capable of reading the New Critics critically knows this: their writings are an apologia for a privileged and unproductive élite, they deny literature any social responsibility, they mystify the practice of writing. And neo-Aristoteleanism is a pseudo-science whose vacuous taxonomies serve the same mystificatory ends as their apparent academic rivals. In publishing *Roots of Lyric*, Princeton University Press helps perpetuate the theory of literature as unspeaking but sacred object and of literary study as inarticulate celebration of its mysteries; and it prolongs the hegemony of the group which employs the apologists for poetry. Young people are now disenchanted with this nonsense, and our English departments are becoming depopulated. Such books as *Roots of Lyric* are hardly likely to restore confidence in the validity of literary education.

(iv) For semiotics

According to semiotic theory, the world human beings live in is a material reality which is shaped into systems of significant forms by the process of communication and the intersubjective cultural conventions (codes) which generate communication. The basis of this theory is very familiar from the *Cours de linguistique générale* of Saussure, commentaries on that work (e.g. Culler), extensions and illustrations of it (Barthes), and convergent theories in linguistics (Hjelmslev, Whorf, Lyons) philosophy (Wittgenstein, Peirce, Morris), and structural anthropology (Lévi-Strauss, Leach). Fundamental principles of this theory include the arbitrariness of the sign (the word 'car' is nothing like a car), the part played by systems of other signs in establishing the meaning of the individual sign (the meaning of 'car' is defined by and helps define the alternatives 'scooter', 'truck', 'bus' etc. and their superordinates 'vehicle', 'transport', etc.), the power of signs in segmenting objective reality (Sapir, Whorf, Leach), the omnipresence of signs, and their existence in any number of media in addition to language (Barthes, Sebeok, and Eco himself*, on signifying systems such as fashion, architecture, music, gesture).

Semiotics is thus not just a theory of communication but a theory of

*Umberto Eco *A Theory of Semiotics*

communication which includes a theory of cultural organization, a theory of cognition and semantic memory, and a theory of perception. Critics of semiotics accuse it of intellectual imperialism or totalitarianism. There is indeed a problem of range, and anyone who pretends to competence in the discipline is extraordinarily vulnerable to attack by 'specialists'. I should make it clear that I accept the justification for a global, integrative, science of knowledge, social organization and interaction; professing oneself a specialized semanticist, logician, aesthetician, etc. seems to me an ungrateful rejection of a stimulating perspective and context offered by the hyperdiscipline. Of course, few can bring off the polymathic learning; Eco does.

There is a second criticism of established semiotic/structuralist theory, and this derives from the premises that signs are (a) organized into systems; (b) only arbitrarily connected to material reality. These principles (Saussure's) make it unclear how semiotics is to accommodate (i) historical motivation, (ii) change, (iii) creativity. So semiotics comes under fire from all sides — it is attacked by naive reflectionists, who want texts to be expressive of historical conditions, by dialectical materialists, who want texts to be both a result of and a part of social process and material conditions, by 'intrinsic' art critics, who want texts to have their own unique structures unsupported by external conventions, and by champions of individual creativity, who distrust any system.

The remarkable achievement of Eco's book is that it is an extremely full and reliable account of classical sign-theory which despite its fidelity to its sources (and vast learning across the range of those sources) embodies a critique of them which anticipates and answers the more sensible criticisms levelled at semiotics. In a short review, it is impossible to rehearse the argument of a complex theoretical book 350 pp. long. Readers should consult two long reviews by Teresa de Lauretis and by Sollace Mitchell in *PTL* 2 (April, 1977), 367-96, for detailed critical accounts of the content of the book. The first chapter is a survey of the field and the discipline of semiotics; the second, 'Signification and Communication', presents an elementary model of communication, with a concrete (hypothetical) example, and a preparatory set of definitions which includes the essential definition of a 'code' — a conventionally regulated set of correlations between a system of material signals and either a system of denoted ideas (a semantic system) or a system of conventional responses on the part of the recipient(s) of the signals. The next chapter, 'Theory of Codes', elaborates, clarifying the nature of the sign ('sign-function' when Eco is being terminologically careful), and explicating the concepts of expression and content and their relationship. The sign-function is a *transitory* correlation between a segmented material substance and a segmented plane of content. The plane of content does not consist of material things: Eco replaces reference and extension with 'cultural units' — categorizations answering to the values of a culture at a specific point of history. The Katz-Fodor semantic theory is reinterpreted in these terms (and analyticity and truth-conditional semantics somewhat summarily disposed of). The chapter explicates a number of basic semiotic notions, e.g. connotation, and ends with a brief account of the strategies involved in communicative interaction — an account which could be much improved by detailed treatment of the processes of conversational interaction as recently investigated by Grice, Searle and the ethnomethodologists.

The final substantial chapter is 'Theory of Sign Production'. As Eco has emphasized the materiality of the expression plane, here he stresses the labour of producing and receiving sign-functions. Instead of a typology of signs, he offers a typology of modes of sign production. This is a decisive move, resulting in a crucial and fruitful difference from both Saussurean and Chomskyan linguistics. Eco differs from Chomsky in giving performance precedence over competence; and from Saussure in returning to the sign-user some influence over the codes he utilizes. The latter point is of great importance for the theory of the artistic text (all too brief in this book). The artistic text is an open form (cf. Eco's earlier work; Barthes' 'scriptible'; Macherey), self-focussing on the expression plane (cf. Jakobson). It is the site of negotiation between source and addressee, and both possess innovative freedoms. The author enjoys code-changing creativity because, by convention, s/he may innovate on the expression plane and thus reorientate our perception of content, producing new knowledge; the addressee brings the old codes and thus needs to achieve a new decoding to attain a new perception of the world — at both ends of the chain of aesthetic communication, artistic form entails a labour of coding. The addressee may, alternatively, refuse to discard the old codes (so treating Magritte or T.S. Eliot or Schönberg as meaningless); or he may find fault with the artist for failing to transform the existing codes (Wordsworth on the inane phraseology of his predecessors, or the mid-twentieth century reception of Gounod).

Eco's account of the semiotics of art is excellent. But he gives art more privilege than his own theory of culture implies or requires. Eco grants to *all* semiosis properties which allow it to escape the alleged constraints of system: variation in the material expression of signs, code-changing creativity in sign-users, both senders and addressees, and consequently a historically transitory (his term) significance of sign-functions, a potential for all communication, not just art, to 'produce further knowledge' (p.274). It is not chance that Eco's last substantial section concerns ideological language and the subversive decoding of ideology. In an important footnote (p.150) he speculates on the possibility of a 'semiotic "guerilla warfare"': 'One can change [the] content [of messages] by acting on the circumstances in which the message will be received'. This is a freedom-giving and knowledge-producing function for art, for criticism aesthetic and political — and for *semiotics*, which Eco says 'should be a theory that permits a continuous critical intervention in semiotic phenomena' (p.29).

Cohesive, progressive, and localizing aspects of text structure*

Recent enthusiasm for the prospect of generative poetics springs from many different sources; happily, this is as yet far from a unified field of enquiry and the diversity guarantees vitality in current researches. Among modern grammarians, Halliday has maintained a continuous interest in features of linkage between co-occurring sentences, studies under the heading of 'cohesion' in his earlier work (Halliday, 1964a, 1964b; cf. Hasan, 1968) and the 'textual function' of the grammar more recently (Halliday, 1970, 1971). He has consistently taken the position that the distinction between facts 'below' and 'above' the sentence rank is not so absolute as to force the linguist to restrict his activities to lower-level phenomena — a position which has been valuable in helping keep alive the study of textual structure during a decade and a half of willed neglect. Textual coherence, if not textual structure, has also been assumed by modern stylisticians and sociolinguists interested in the hypothesis that style of discourse, or register, is consistent and predictable in its correlation with features of the communication situation (Enkvist, 1964 and 1971; Halliday, McIntosh and Strevens, 1964; Crystal and Davy, 1969; Fowler, 1970a, b; Hymes, 1964; etc.). In such work, which has its roots in traditional author stylistics and taxonomic stylistics (Ullmann, 1964; Wellek and Warren, 1963: Ch 14; Wellek, 1971), the assumption is that the surface structure of a text is distinctively homogeneous and constant: this stylistics is more concerned with the unity of the whole seen from a distance than the ongoing relationships of textual segments in concatenation. I should also mention another, and influential, body of scholars who have been concerned with 'unity' in a different sense, with the single text as articulated whole. Any single-text analysis which maps the work as a whole structure, a unity built as a matrix of relations among parts, is implicitly an exercise in text-grammarianship. The Jakobsonian analyses would be the prime examples (e.g. Jakobson and Lévi-Strauss, 1962; Jakobson and Jones, 1970) but one could cite scores of other instances cast in many different metalanguages (e.g. Sinclair, 1966; Hasan, 1971; Leech, 1965; Fowler, 1967).

Single-text analyses are unwittingly but implicitly generative, because the

---

*The text chosen to illustrate the theory in this chapter is James Thurber's 'The Lover and his Lass' from *Further Fables for our Time* (New York: Simon & Schuster, and London: Hamish Hamilton, 1956). The text is reprinted below (p.78) with the sentences numbered for ease of reference.

analysis of an individual text 'in its own terms' is a logical impossibility: one is really setting the text against the formal choices offered by some external system or systems. In the case of true Jakobsonian analysis, for instance, the systems within which the poem is located include, principally, the English or French language, the metrical conventions of the sonnet genre, and an assumed value-scheme which is positively realised by poems which manifest multiple co-existent binary oppositions in the relation of part to part ('couplet versus quatrains' etc.). It is best to bring such systems to the forefront of one's analysis, to make it clear that the text's coherence results from the convergence of several independent systems or *langues* at a hierarchically superordinate level of abstraction. Paul Zumthor's interesting use of the concept of 'register' in describing medieval poetic genres is an exemplary strategy to avoid the 'immanence fallacy' (Todorov, 1968), and he is led to raise explicitly the possibility of constructing generative grammars for the texts in his corpora (Zumthor, 1971; see also Zumthor, 1963, 1972).

The French *nouvelle poétique* is a far cry from the textual pragmatism of the British school, but the cases of Zumthor and Jakobson show that a bridge can be constructed. Zumthor's *registre* is not incompatible with Halliday's *register*, as Zumthor indeed acknowledges; although Halliday has not rigorously applied the concept of register to literature, yet the linguistic features which he mentions under 'cohesion' could undoubtedly be interpreted as registral factors (cf. Leech, 1969). Much of Todorov's work shows a strong interest in defining genres in linguistic terms (e.g. Todorov, 1967, 1969), and this endeavour is compatible with the classificatory research of Zumthor and would benefit by the adoption of Zumthor's theoretically scrupulous substitution of register-system for genre: generative poetics has no place for 'genre' as a primary logical category — the system should take precedence over the corpus. Jakobson's descriptive work is deceptively intratextual: in fact he has provided the French structuralists with a perfect slogan for generative poetics — 'Etudier la littérarité et non la littérature'; not the particular work but 'les virtualités du discours littéraire, qui l'ont rendu possible' (Todorov, 1967: 7, 8; 1968: 102; Genette, 1972: 10). According to this highly ambitious criterion, the programme for *poétique* approximates closely to the goals of generative linguistics: Chomsky at his apogee (e.g. 1965, 1968) asserted that the ultimate task of linguistics was the discovery of linguistic universals.

Manfred Bierwisch in 1965 (trans. 1970) proposed a modification of an *Aspect*-type grammar designed to generate poetic texts: the addition of a 'poetic system' *PS* which would rank the structural descriptions generated by a grammar on a 'scale of poeticality'. For two reasons, I am not attracted by the specific technique of his proposal. First, it is inseparable from a syntax-based grammar with an interpretive semantic component, and that grammatical model is now commonly agreed to be inferior to one with a semantic base; second, Bierwisch's examples suggest that his technique can cope only with two sources of 'poeticality' in language, ungrammaticalness (lack of conformity to *langue*) and poeticalness (conformity to mechanical conventions in cliché literary styles). But Bierwisch's general statement of the aims of generative poetics can be accepted:

[W]e must set ourselves the seemingly trivial questions of just what poetics must deal with and which facts it must describe and clarify. The simple answer, that the objects of poetics are literary texts, is only valid on first glance. The texts at hand are merely the observable material, the data from which poetics must proceed: the facts are of a completely different nature. The actual objects of poetics are the particular regularities that occur in literary texts and that determine the specific effects of poetry: in the final analysis the human ability to produce poetic structures and understand their effect — that is, something which one might call *poetic competence*. (1970: 98-99).

Text grammars, then, generate or enumerate texts in the established sense of 'generate' in linguistics: with the crucial difference of focus that the occurring 'particular regularities' to be explained by reference to an abstract system are not regularities within sentences but within whole texts. This is the assumption which has guided explicit work on the theory of text grammars (see van Dijk, 1971, 1972, and copious references therein) and in terms of which a great many other, less formal, studies (including the majority of those cited above) can be understood.

Readers will recognise Bierwisch's close dependence on Chomsky's exposition of the distinction between competence and performance, and the concomitant division between subject-matter and data in science: see Chomsky, 1964, 1965: Katz, 1966. If we are to take the project of generative poetics seriously, we must include the domain of 'textual' or 'poetic' competence. At first blush, this admission might seem to diffuse or confuse the programme, since we have the whole history of affective criticism to provide an awful lesson in the perils of reader psychology. But as I hope to show, the 'ideal reader' in poetics can be employed as a useful analytic tool, as the 'ideal speaker-listener' has been in linguistics. It happens that the ideal reader has been entertained in a variety of contexts recently, for instance in the anti-Jakobsonian analysis of Riffaterre (1966) and in the confessedly affective criticism of Fish (1970 and 1972). And just as the ideal reader is finding his way into recent criticism, so is his controlling principle, the *code:* we can only allow the reader's responses into the data of poetics insofar as they represent the realisation of poetic knowledge systematically coded in the appropriate culture. One of the priorities in generative poetics is to provide a procedure for distinguishing reader responses which are idiosyncratic and accidental from those which are communal and necessary given the structure of the work. Barthes' tour de force *S/Z* (1970) employs the notion of 'code' in a manner which is illuminating from the present point of view, and Riffaterre's recent essay (1973) makes extensive, if rather informal, use of the words 'code' and 'codal'.

I do not intend that the above should count as an organised description of the background to present-day generative poetics! It is incomplete (I have not mentioned discourse analysis) and because of brevity of citation it risks misrepresentation of the scholars to whom it alludes. I offer this potpourri of allusions in an attempt to suggest the enormous scope, and internal diversity, of existing scholarship from which generative poetics may legitimately draw fragmentary illuminations. The task of ordering and synthesis is colossal, but the richness of the sources promises eventual great explanatory power in the completed model.

I have another motive in beginning with a miscellaneous potluck of references: a cautionary motive. It would be very easy for a critic or a linguist to peep into the field of generative poetics, spot some specific activity within and claim 'If that's generative poetics, why, I've been doing it all along! There's nothing new here.' Many established linguists behaved in just this way in the early years of TG; and since Chomsky insisted that his grammar was 'traditional', in a sense they were justified. Of course the fallacy was that these linguists, though they studied areas of linguistic structure which overlapped the research preoccupations of the transformationalists, lacked both the exacting formalism and the powerful theory of the latter. Literary studies being an even more amorphous and reckless pursuit than modern linguistics, the danger of shirking or skimping theory is proportionately greater.

To lay my cards on the table: I regard the construction of an explanatorily adequate text grammar for a specified example of one type of discourse as a project of unattainable magnitude for the imaginable future, if the criterion is to be observed that a text grammar reflects readers' textual competence. We simply know too little about linguistic structure, the psychology of the reading activity, etc. On the other hand, I realised as soon as I was invited to contribute to this volume that an observationally adequate treatment of the highly-patterned given text would be an unsatisfyingly facile job. The median level of descriptive adequacy might be the appropriate aim — and that level of adequacy only for some chosen aspect of text structure. In this aim we would be following the example of research in generative linguistics over the last fifteen years, which has progressed by striving for descriptive adequacy in selected discrete areas well-defined in terms of the general structure of the model (pronominalization, relativization, stress-placement, etc.).

The usual way of proceeding is to adapt for texts the existing categories of description established in generative grammar for the sentence and its parts. In a sense, then, the text grammar project returns to the submerged scheme of discourse analysis, attempting to develop it from the point at which Harris's transformations were transformed by Chomsky. However, the return cannot be exact, since our conception of grammar has been so enriched since Harris's time. Approximate though the correspondence between discourse analysis and text grammar may be, the comparison is instructive. Informally, let us imagine an inward, compacting process taking place in the transition between discourse analysis and TG, and an outward, expanding movement as generative grammar is returned to the study of texts. Adapting Jakobson's terms (1960: 358) for the purpose, we could suggest that Chomsky's achievement in *Syntactic Structures* (1957) amounted to returning the principle of equivalence from the axis of combination to the axis of selection — so that the active-passive relationship, for example, was a transformational relationship in the syntagm for Harris, while for Chomsky this relationship is relocated within the paradigm, the system. In moving out again to study the text in its linear extension, we single out elements of the system, and 'equivalences' defined by the form of the system, to determine structural relationships among items syntagmatically concatenated. Ultimately, it may emerge that this opposition between 'system' and 'syntagm' is more profitable for discourse analysis than that between 'sentence' and 'text'. As Hendricks has shown (1967), the study of structure 'above the sentence' may appeal to the sentence-unit in several diverse ways. He distinguishes five, and of these only one makes reference to the sentence as a unit of determinate 'rank' (cf. Halliday, 1961): this is the hypothesis that a text can be represented as a hierarchical structure, in which the sentence would be an intermediate syntagm 'above' the clause and 'below' the paragraph, chapter, etc. If the recent history of linguistics is any guide, the hierarchical model of text structure is likely to prove as unrevealing, and as vulnerable, as IC analysis in the linguistics of the 1950s (see Postal, 1964, for an over-argued attack on IC analysis).

It has been widely assumed that linguistics takes as its upper limit for description the sentence, and that longer stretches of discourse do not fall within the province of linguistics. This limitation is defended either on the grounds that combinatorial possibilities 'above' the sentence are free and unstructured, or that the study of larger units belongs properly to some other discipline, as for instance stylistics or discourse analysis (Saporta, 1960: 87-88). The cut-off point is not generally defended by any argument as to the theoretical centrality of the sentence. It is true that generative grammar defines a language as a 'set of sentences', but in that definition 'sentence' is very much a surface concept — as it is when it is applied to the segmentation of texts. When we come to describe sentences, we find that they are a mixed bag of syntagms, of extremely diverse structure, having in common the characteristic that they may all be derived by application of transformations of known structural types to a stock of basic semantic structures. It might be argued that the defining constants of the linguistic system are *not* sentences but transformations and semantic structures, the latter being not syntagms but abstract configurations of roughly the following organisation:

1.

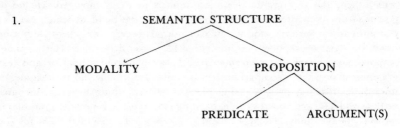

The transformational processes of English allow us to derive a range of surface structures (syntagms) from such abstract schemata, including, say,

2. *gray parrot* (with modality transferred to a higher syntactic node)
3. *Can you believe that?*

The latter is a sentence, the former not. The following is also a sentence:

4. But it was spring, and the lover and his lass were young, and they were oblivious of the scornful comments of their sharp-tongued neighbors, and they continued to bump each other around in the water, happily pushing and pulling, backing and filling, and snorting and snaffling.

The disparity between 3. and 4. emphasizes the weakness of the generalization 'sentence', and its unsuitability as a formal cut-off point between linguistics and discourse analysis. In the linguistic study of natural languages, 'sentence' is no more than a convenient grouping of a miscellaneous class of surface structures: simple or complex wholes realised by transformation of one or more semantic structures such as 1. above. If discourse analysis, or text grammar, complains against linguistics that the latter does not venture above the sentence, the complaint or the observation is more or less accurate but unimportant. It certainly should not be invoked as the defining difference between grammar and discourse analysis. More interesting, from the point of view of the theory of texts, is the fact that established grammar is unconcerned with some syntagms; and the fact that text grammars focus on syntagms (of various 'sizes') in distinctive ways. Prior to formalization, we know that a text grammar adequate for 'The Lover and His Lass' must be capable of offering significant statements about the macrostructure of the whole fable from title down to moral — even a casual reading suggests that this text is a single complex structure offered as a unitary reading experience, and familiarity with other pieces in Thurber's two collections of fables, or with the classical fable, encourages us to regard the text as a unified design. Bipartite syntax, and alliteration on /l/, associate the title and the moral, and 'frame' the body of the text. The text itself displays superficial symmetry, with four short paragraphs preceding, and four following, the long central paragraph, with sentences 2-7 and 13-15 containing dialogue, but not sentences 1 and 12. The discoursal continuity within each of these short dialogues needs to be described (they are in fact less alike than they first appear to be). Now except for this last question of the linkage and give-and-take of dialogue, linguistics has nothing to say concerning these broad structural matters. Note that the linguistic system provides some terms for elements which enter into the syntagmatic relationships (the phonetic reference points needed for describing alliteration, the syntactic categories appropriate to parallelism) but no terms for the relevant syntagms themselves. The same situation presents itself in textual microstructure (what might conventionally be called 'texture'). The fable is obviously densely patterned at syntactic, phonetic and semantic levels, and although the patterns can be recognised as moulded out of linguistic materials, we resort to the labels of rhetoric, or traditional stylistics, in order to pin-point the patterns themselves. Linguistics assigns no special status to syntagms which are significant at the level of text: 'disdain and derision', 'friends and neighbors', 'mocking and monstrous metaphors', 'hippopotamus ... hippopotama', 'waffled ... gurbled'. Note that these textually interesting syntagms are neither consistently 'below' nor consistently 'above' sentence-rank. Frequently they are subparts of sentences, and are involved in patterns which span sentence boundaries: one 'spanning' process takes in the text as a whole, since the alliterative patterns (e.g.) which unify particular sentences are pervasive and cohesive in the whole text. One excellent example of the independence of sentence and textual syntagm is the etymological, morphological and phonetic play which weaves in and out of the closing sequence:

5. hippopotamus ... hippopotama ... male hippopotamus ... female hippopotamus ... her inamoratus ... hippopotamuses ... hippopotamuses ...

It seems completely beside the point to enquire how this series relates to the sentence; it is a syntagm of no determinate grammatical rank: better to ask the more direct question of how it relates to the text's system.

Of course, we are led right back to the theory of Jakobson: 'the poetic function projects the principle of equivalence from the axis of selection into the axis of combination' (1960: 358). The axis of selection, in our terms, is the system: the multi-systemic set of relationships defining the language as an abstract form; the axis of combination, the syntagm. The poetic function — or, more neutrally, the textual principle — builds syntagms which are *not* fully specified by basic transformational rules, by setting up additional regularities in language in its linear extension. Since these additional regularities are formed by rules which have as their input units and relationships which are defined by conventional grammar, it would seem natural to regard text grammar as (at least in surface structure) a superstructure founded on the possibilities made available by the basic grammar.

Another way of putting it would be to say that discourse is generated by a system which includes the linguistic system and additionally other systemic components (these being, essentially, the rules for projecting paradigmatic relationships on to the syntagm). Varieties of discourse would be generated by variants of the discoursal system, probably by sub-regularities in a super-system rather than by choice among parallel systems stacked side-by-side. Thus, when we say that 'the grammar is used in different ways' in different 'styles' ('registers', 'varieties', etc.) we refer to the effect of distinctive choices among the super-structure rules, the syntagm-forming rules.

It follows that 'poetic competence' or 'textual competence' is knowledge of the conventions for forming discourses, on the foundation centrally of the grammatical system and additionally on the basis of various other systems of knowledge. I have maintained this multi-systemic explanation of communicative competence (ability to perform *appropriately* in language) previously: see Fowler, 1970a. The theory is highly compatible with other accounts of CODING processes in diverse styles of linguistic performance: see Barthes, 1970; Zumthor, 1971; Riffaterre, 1959 and 1973. Note that the orientation is radically different from that in earlier versions of TG, where all features pertinent to discourse structure, style, etc., were relegated to linguistic performance. At one stage it seemed that linguistic performance was being used as a sort of trash-can for disposing of all aspects of communication which were not readily explainable by the grammar — aspects which appeared to be random, probabilistic, idiosyncratic, etc. But it makes no sense to assign communication features to linguistic performance on the grounds that no explanation is forthcoming: every aspect of performance presupposes some competence (or incompetence!) It is much preferable to acknowledge that there are some qualities of linguistic performance which do not receive a grammatical explanation but which must be referred to other systems of knowledge. Among several advantages of this approach is the fact that, to the extent that we can systematize non-grammatical 'competences', we add to our understanding of the attributes of the grammatical system itself.

If we enjoyed complete understanding of the competence systems relevant to text structure, and of the relationships between them, we would be able to design schemata for the deep structures of various kinds of texts. Such knowledge would include familiarity with discourse transformations, and so we would be equipped to construct derivations for texts. It is obvious that text grammar theory is, as yet, a long way behind this ideal. So far, we may acknowledge some attractive proposals for deep structure categories — also some theories which, though not framed in this way, in effect amount to suggestions of systems bearing on deep structure: principally the formalist-structuralist analyses of narrative in the tradition of Propp (Propp, 1928, trans. 1968; cf. Todorov, 1967, 1969; *Communications* 8, 1966) but additionally such less formalized insights as the codes of Barthes (1970) which must be granted the status of approximations to underlying semantic structures. At the moment, we can boast no more than an incomplete and unstructured collection of partial and unformalized systems which may be part of the generative source for the deep structure (semantic, but including performatives and other non-cognitive elements: cf. Fowler, 1972) of texts. The most promising approach to these existing materials will be to compare them, and their organization, with the postulated structure of the generative semantic version of TG, which provides a framework for hypothesizing the status of the various recognised systems in generative poetics, and for predicting some yet unacknowledged systems bearing on textual deep structure. I am sure that other contributors to this volume will undertake such explorations; I am going to investigate the 'shallow' end of text structure.

Textual surface structure is not inherently less interesting than deep structure (and whether statements about one level can avoid bearing on the other is doubtful anyway); and as an object of study it has clear practical advantages. We are dealing with manifest, overt, aspects of text structure; and we are dealing with aspects of TEXT structure which link most intimately with traditional and familiar features of LINGUISTIC structure. That is to say, if we choose textual 'microstructure' as our point of entry into the construction of texts, we minimize the embarrassment caused by the theoretical opposition of 'text grammar' and 'sentence grammar' (see van Dijk, 1972, for this opposition). In many cases, the units we posit as formative elements in textual surface structure will correspond closely in scale with units already well understood in existing linguistic descriptions (sentence grammars): for example, the metrical units of some of the major European poetic forms (sonnet, pentameter, alexandrine, etc.) approximate sentence and clause structure to such a degree that we can plausibly suggest that the development of these line, couplet and stanza structures has been directly favoured by the grammatical possibilities afforded to poets by their languages. At least, from the critic's point of view, linguistic categories provide relevant access to significant elements of text, certainly at the microstructural level: obvious access for some of the more formalized genres, and a natural exploratory tool even in the case of literary kinds for which isomorphism of linguistic and textual structure cannot reality be demonstrated (e.g. extended prose works).

The study of linguistic surface structure is of immediate value in criticism based on a poetics which incorporates the idea of literary competence. For the notion of competence serves to return the reader to the forefront of critical attention: texts are to be described and interpreted in terms of the systems of knowledge which the adequate reader brings to them, and in terms of the process of decoding by which he 'realises' the structure and meaning of texts. This process of realization must be strictly controlled by the linguistic structure of texts; one might say that the linguistic code is a filter, or shaping mediator, for the more abstract systems which underlie the text. There can be no perception of poetic structure except in the form dictated by the overt structure of language as the reader encounters this in his text. The reader in a sense constructs a text — a version of a text — out of his own cultural knowledge, including his linguistic knowledge. the version he constructs is adequate to the extent that his competence is adequate, and (as every critic and teacher of literature knows) readers' versions vary considerably because readers vary substantially in the degree to which they are attuned to the cultural systems which ideally relate to the text. This cultural relativity produces, for the writer, an awkward obstacle to communication: for the student of literature, a suspicion that reliable, agreed interpretation may not be possible. But the author is by no means utterly at the mercy of cultural diversity and change; he can control the process of decoding through his deployment of the resources of the most securely institutionalized cultural system, language itself. He can assume that a responsible reading, at least by a contemporary, will retrieve surface structure in very much the form that he, the writer, arranged it; and that surface structure can thus be deployed to determine the perception of particular textual significances. These possibilities for the control of decoding follow from the extent to which linguistic competence (contrasted with competence in other semiological systems) is shared among the members of a community. It seems to follow that the structure of language *as the reader experiences it* — that is, the text's overt or surface structure — is a fundamental and indispensable object of study for the analyst of text structure. This principle is in fact so well established in stylistics (if not in the generative framework) that I will offer no further justification; for a consistent train of arguments virtually wholly compatible with my position, see the work of Michael Riffaterre, from whom I take the notion of the ideal reader and this general requirement: 'Une analyse de style devrait donc précéder toute tentative pour construire le modèle structural d'un texte' (1971, 'Le formalisme français': 285; cf. Riffaterre, 1959 — and an interesting French translation with author's annotations, 1971; 1966; 1973). For 'precede' one might substitute 'accompany', except that 'precede' has the advantage that it does reflect priority in the reader's decoding engagement with the text.

The three categories I mention in my title — cohesive, progressive and localizing aspects of text structure — refer to my selection of three ways in which a competent reader, controlled by the author's deployment of the surface organization of language, comes to realise the structural shaping of a text. COHESION has been extensively studied (Halliday, 1964a, 1964b, 1971; Hasan, 1968; Leech, 1965): it refers to linguistic patterning which contributes to the impression that a text 'hangs together,' that it is a single text and not an arbitrary concatenation of distinct sentences; nor, one might add, an assemblage of distinct texts — the Hallidayan discussions of cohesion concentrate on sentence-relationships, but as we have seen text grammar does not have to limit itself to the sentence as the primary constitutive unit.

The fullest discussion of cohesion is by Hasan (1968). She assumes, as I do, that a text may be cohesive by virtue of the arrangement of features at any level of linguistic structure, but she concentrates on a small range of syntactic features which lead to cohesion, under the headings of reference, substitution, ellipsis and conjunction. Her chief interest is in fact in pronominalization and in other cross-sentence features involving pro-forms. More specifically, the key to cohesion, for Hasan, is *anaphora*, which in this context means the use in one sentence of an item which has the same referent as, or substitutes for, an item in the preceding sentence (or in an earlier one if there is no intervening lexical material to which the anaphoric item could be taken to refer). Here are two of her examples:

6. (= Hasan 6) Wash and core six cooking apples. Put them into a fireproof dish.
7. (= Hasan (137d)) Is she watching television? She was doing, but she's gone out.

Cataphoric reference, where the pro-form points forward to a following item, as in *When he had finished, John paid the bill,* has no text-cohesive potential since it invariably points to an item within the same sentence as the pro-form and thus cannot serve to link sentences.

The details of Hasan's analysis are clearly expounded in her monograph. I would like to suggest a general characterization. She is concerned with those indispensable syntactic ties between sentences which ensure that a discourse is coherent in the ordinary sense of the word: that it maintains a clear focus on one topic, or signals transitions between topics; that appropriate responses are given to questions, rejoinders to assertions, etc. In short, cohesion for Hasan is the sum of the syntactic mechanisms which are prerequisites for the cognitive, narrative, etc., wholeness and fluency of a text. I will be using the concept of cohesion to cover a wider range of intra-text relationships; but it is easy enough to show that 'The Lover and His Lass' is cohesive in this basic sense. Clear sentence-linkage is guaranteed by several usually rather salient devices tying the sentences together, each one to its predecessor. In sentence (2) *He* and *her* relate to *a lover* and *his lass*; *Mrs. Gray*, and *you* in (3), somewhat more opaquely, to *his arrogant mate* and *an arrogant gray parrot*. (4) links with (3) by the response *No* to a 'yes/no' question. (6) develops from (5) by the repeated phrase *capsized bathtub* and the refuting exclamation *indeed!* (8), beginning a new paragraph, announces that this is not a new text by the use of *But*; and this evidence is reinforced by the prompt repetition of a phrase from sentence (1), *lover and his lass*; the use of the article *the* here, as opposed to *a* in (1), suggests the co-referentiality of the phrases, and allows one to deduce that the *sharp-tongued neighbors* are the parrots and not new characters. (9) links with (8) through the pronoun *they*. (10) implies the presence of (9) by its use of *however*. (11) is linked to (10) by *But* and by *they* (= *the Grays*). (12) is not closely linked to (11); but the word *that* requires that there should have been preceding, and directly relevant, co-text (contrast *Late one evening*) and the phrase *the hippopotamus and the hippopotama* declares that sentences (1) — (11) constitute appropriate preceding text matter. (13) relates to (12) by the word *hippopotamus*, as does (14) to (13) — additionally, (14) links with (13) by the phrase-pair *the male X/the female X*. *Her* in (15) refers to *the female hippopotamus* in (14), and the link is reinforced by the phonetic echo *hippopotamus/inamoratus*. (16) refers back, through the immediately preceding sequence including (15), to *the hippopotamus and the hippopotama* in (12). (17) repeats the major referents of (16): *the hippopotamuses* = *they* and *the Grays* = *gray parrot . . . gray parrot* (terminating the text by a link which also served to tie (1) and (2) together — a fact which an analysis of the kind offered by Hasan makes available but which, I suspect, would not be significant in her analysis).

The importance of these sentence-linking devices to the narrative and ratiocinative coherence of the text can easily be tested by removing or radically altering some of them. The text can readily be rendered extremely disjointed by interference with the pronouns, and it will appear inconsequential if the *buts* and *howevers* and *indeeds* are removed. Notice, though, that the sentence-links form a very small part of the total text; and substantial segments elsewhere in the text can be altered without destroying the overall structural cohesion given by the linking of sentences — e.g. we could introduce new characters by diversifying the noun phrases, we could predicate different actions of the existing characters, etc.; in short, change the content of the narrative within the same basic cohesive framework. Since so little of the text contributes to cohesion in Hasan's sense (though its contribution is fundamental and essential) and so much else is variable, we might ask whether this variable, non-framing, material contributes in some different way to textual cohesion. This certainly seems to be the case. If we examine the referential properties of the text generally, for instance, we detect strong restrictions on the subjects which are mentioned. The syntactic frame for cohesion does not dictate a limitation in the narrative participants to parrots and hippopotamuses; but if we examine those NPs which are animate, or can be construed as animate, including pronouns of unambiguous reference, we discover the following proportions:

8. NPs and pronouns referring to parrots: 20
   NPs and pronouns referring to hippopotamuses: 27
   Other animate: 6

(I have treated compound and complex NPs as single NPs: *any male in his right mind, the lover and his lass, etc.*) 'Other' comprises *any male in his right mind, a female that has no more charm than a capsized bathtub, enormous creatures who should have become decent fossils long ago*, all of which are used generically but refer by metaphor to the hippopotamuses; *the A.B.I., or African Bureau of Investigation*; and *their friends and neighbors* twice: in the first the *they* = the parrots, in the second the hippopotamuses. I have no comparative figures to prove my point, but I am confident that this restriction of animate NPs to such a small number of participants is exceptional.

A further measure of the domination of this text by NPs referring to the main protagonists is the ratio of words in these noun phrases to the word total of the text: 97:377 (counting articles, modifiers, etc. within these NPs; excluding title and moral). Finally, the NPs concerned are distributed evenly through the text. Every sentence contains at least one NP referring to one or the other of the pairs of protagonists or to an individual, all but two sentences refer to both groups of protagonists, and most sentences refer to one or both groups, or to individuals, several times. (This even distribution, difficult to describe in words, can be graphically displayed by circling or otherwise marking off the NPs concerned on a copy of the text.)

In claiming that these distributional properties of animate NPs contribute to the cohesion of the text, I am extending the Halliday-Hasan conception of 'cohesion'. For these authors, cohesion in a text is a product of linkage between successive sentences — a factor which I am happy to admit since it stresses the linear extension of the text in a way that formalist analysis generally fails to do. However, cohesion by sentence-linkage may be accompanied by cohesive features of a non-linear kind: by linguistic features leading to semantic and/or stylistic *consistency*. Allowing this second type of cohesion enlarges considerably the range of linguistic structures available for study. I have already shown how consistency of nominal reference contributes to this text's homogeneity; and there are many other features which have cohesive value, some of them much more palpable than the cohesion by sentence-linkage and by referential consistency already noticed. The two most salient pervasive qualities of style are alliteration (with other phonetic figures) and syntactic parallelism.

The title, with /l/ alliteration, indicates an alliterative style which is firmly established in the first sentence:

9. arrogant ... arrogant   /æ/   and rhyming word-repetition
   African afternoon   /Vf/   — the V will be the same in
                                              some dialects

disdain . . . derision	/dV/	— identical V for some dialects
lovemaking . . . lover . . . lass	/l/	— also links up with *listened* in the first clause
happened . . . hippopotamuses	/hVp/	

The text continues heavily marked with phonetic devices in great variety, usually variations on the alliteration/assonance types. I will merely illustrate some of the varieties; their pervasive distribution throughout the text is obvious. Ordinary alliteration, near-alliteration, assonance and vowel harmony are found throughout the text: *the lover and his lass* (sentence 8); *mocking and monstrous metaphors* (11); *surprised and shocked* (12); *snooky-ookums* (2); *entertain affection* (5). Sometimes alliteration is interestingly asymmetrical with superficial phrase-structure. Usually alliteration ties together words which are syntactically conjoined (*a lover and his lass*); but in (1) the /l/ alliteration extends backward to the subordinate predicate (*lovemaking*) and the main predicate (*listened*). *Mocking and monstrous metaphors* (11) resists the bipartite alliterative convention in the text: the two adjectives alliterate powerfully because of the identity of the following vowel, but they do not form a syntactically complete phrase and their claims to balanced unity are disturbed by the asymmetrically alliterating head-noun *metaphors*. In the same sentence, the conjoined NP *friends and neighbors* might (with other lexical choices) have been a candidate for alliteration according to the text's prevailing conventions, but instead *phone* and *friends* alliterate, segmenting the sentence across the grain of the syntax.

The text displays some more elaborate phonetic patterns, but based generally on an extension of the alliterative principle of sound-repetition. In *bumbling romp* (10) only /m/ is literally repeated; however, the close approximations of /ʌ/ and /ð/, /b/ and /p/, satisfyingly suggest equivalence of syllable structure. The most striking phonetic pattern of this kind is the last part of sentence (8): *happily pushing and pulling, backing and filling, and snorting and snaffling*. The first pair alliterates on /p/, the last on /sn/; *pulling, filling* and *snaffling* are linked by /l/ at the syllable transition; labials occur at the beginning of each member of the first pair of words (/p/); /p/ changes to /b/ and then to /f/ in the second pair; /f/ reappears in *snaffling*; /p/ in *happily* sets the sequence of labials in motion, while /l/ in the same word initiates the series of liquids (and note that /p/ and /l/ occur in *happily* in the same order in which they appear in the paired words — /p/ or another labial variant always precedes /l/); *-ing* unites the whole series. The prominent vowels also are patterned: *happily* presents a movement from low to high front, *pushing* and *pulling* start with a back mid vowel, *backing* and *filling* resume the contrast of *happily*, *snorting* and *snaffling* start with low back and low front, respectively.

These few examples will, I hope, be adequate to suggest the extent and the complexity of the phonetic patterning in 'The Lover and His Lass': it is highly characteristic of this text and pervasive through it, as it is in many others among the *Further Fables*. This phonetic patterning (particularly the strict alliteration) is extremely compatible with a repetitive and cohesive two-stress rhythmic pattern which in turn is the product of marked and consistent syntactic balance and parallelism, featured at every syntactic 'rank'. As with the phonetic and referential consistencies just noticed, syntactic parallelism is announced as a formative cohesive device in the very first sentence: *an arrogant gray parrot and his arrogant mate, in disdain and derision, a lover and his lass*. The conjoined phrases typified by the structure of the title establish the dominant constructional mode for the parallelism exemplified throughout the text. Examples are so easy to pick out that I will not list the numerous conjoined NPs. Interestingly, this syntactic (hence rhythmic) pattern is so marked that phrases which are not strictly in parallel are experienced as being so: *the scornful comments of their sharp-tongued neighbors, flowers in bud or green things opening* (disparate internal structure although theoretically parallel). NPs and VPs are drawn into pairs: *pushing and pulling, hard to comprehend and even harder to tolerate*, etc. Towards the end of the text, whole sentences are arranged in parallel (sentences 13-15), and also complex clauses — sentence (17) and the Moral. Off-beat parallelisms are also to be found, a fact which again recalls the alliterative patterning: *mocking and monstrous metaphors* once more, and such pseudo-parallels as *monolithic lovemaking by enormous creatures*, which are rhythmically plausible in terms of the 'metrical set' (Fowler, 1968b) which the text encourages but which are not strictly parallel.

The frequency and pervasiveness of syntactic (hence rhythmical) parallelism in this text does not need demonstrating. Any observationally adequate grammarian can display it by taking a soft-leaded pencil to the text. What has to be noted is the simple fact that it works for cohesion in just the same way that referential consistency and consistency of phonetic patterning do. In all cases we find cohesion by pervasion of surface-structure consistency, adding to the cohesion by linkage which the Hasan-Halliday method reveals.

One cohesive device which I have not analysed is cohesion by transformation; this has been thoroughly discussed, for other texts, by Harris (1952, etc.) and cf. Fowler (1966c).

I would like to make three general points about cohesion, briefly. First, textual cohesion and ungrammaticalness are not incompatible. Utterances which might be judged deviant from the point of view of a sentence grammar can, if their deviance is consistent, become text-grammatical; and the consistency of type of deviation gives rise to textual cohesion (cf. Thorne, 1965). Second, textual cohesion may be claimed in some instances where the text is NOT characterised by continuously homogeneous or repetitive linguistic structure. There is, that is to say, a linguistic correlate to the general aesthetic principle of unity in diversity. Regular modulations in style can be shown to be integrative rather than divisive; and even severe disjunctions of style may, in great works, conspire to create unity where the transitions and oppositions are truly functional. *The Waste Land* and *Ulysses* are spectacular examples of this effect (if one judges them successful) but more easily demonstrably cohesive texts (yet incorporating marked stylistic disparities) are, for instance, *A Portrait of the Artist as a Young Man* and *The Great Gatsby*. In *Gatsby* there are two dominant, and distinct, stylistic modalities:

the commonsense, linguistically aphoristic, mode of Nick Carraway the upright Mid-Western observer of the decadent East; and the florid romantic mode, heavy with symbolism, of Nick the participator, attracted to the life of Daisy and Tom, participating by contagion in Gatsby's sensuous idealistic dream. The two sets of linguistic consistencies are functionally distinct and yet functionally related. If (as I believe) the text of this novel is aesthetically cohesive, then its LINGUISTIC cohesion assumes hierarchical structure at the textual level — rather than being linguistically 'flat' with some feature(s) unvaryingly foregrounded throughout, the text manifests segmental sub-cohesions which are gathered into a cohesive relationship at some higher level of text structure. Finally, it must be pointed out that the surface structure features which are scanned for cohesive structure may be put to critical-descriptive use in several ways, for several motives. I am concerned with cohesion as it contributes to an impression of the singleness of the text — a strictly limited interest. Cohesive devices may also be studied for other purposes: e.g. as contributing to the consistency of an author's style or a period style; as communicating thematic or other significance within a text (cf. Lodge, 1966).

We turn now to the PROGRESSIVE dimension of text structure. A text is progressive if its structure leads the reader onwards, projects him forward from one segment of text to a succeeding one. I am not referring only to dramatic effects in the rhetoric of expectation and suspense (this is the area in which Stanley Fish mostly works) although suspense is indeed a part of progressive structure. Progression has to do with the whole stock of language features which contribute to a text's logical and temporal ongoingness: sequence of tenses and time adverbs, logical and temporal connectives (*although ... nevertheless*; *when ... then*, etc.), order of introduction of lexical items — a text which introduces referentially fresh words is likely to be more progressive than one which practises elegant variation. The impression of progressive structure always depends on the intersection of several of these linguistic features. For example, Isaac Babel's very short text, 'The Cemetery at Kozin' (Babel, 1960: 107) should be progressive in terms of the continuous introduction of new lexical material (including a string of proper nouns) but is so only towards the end; the syntax of the first two paragraphs, based on non-finite verbs, gives an overall static, fragmented, impression.

I would like to make progressive structure responsible for one other characteristic of texts in addition to their projective or ongoing quality: the recognisability of beginnings and ends of internal sectionalisations. An indefinite article with a noun of unknown reference is a conventional way of beginning a story: in this way the author can discourage presuppositions about the protagonist introduced, and hint that information will be supplied as the tale proceeds. Correspondingly, there are linguistic signals of finality, as we shall see in *The Lover and His Lass*. When I introduced cohesion above, I was careful to speak of 'the single text': completeness is a function of progressive, singleness of cohesive, structure.

The Lover and His Lass illustrates some of the linguistic circumstances which are productive of progressive structure, but it is in fact not a strongly progressive text. (We have seen that it *is* highly cohesive; but it must not be suspected that progression and cohesion are antagonistic qualities.) This fable is minimally narrative and minimally argumentative — two conditions which are characteristically associated with progression and which are reflected in surface structure in typical sequences of predicates and temporal expressions, and logical connectives, respectively. But the skeletal apparatus of progression is present here; the text could not be rearranged in another order without sacrificing its linear significance. Not only would the sentences be linked nonsensically in such a rearrangement (they would form a non-cohesive text), they would also be patently in the wrong order: the signals of progression within the sentences would contradict the new ordering of the sentences.

The text opens, in a conventional way, by giving all three major narrative constituents, time, place and personae, in a manner which indicates that the reader is supposed to be innocent of these contextual circumstances at the outset: the NPs *an arrogant gray parrot*, *a lover* and *one African afternoon* are indefinite, a sure signal that this is the opening of a text or at least a new distinct section (e.g. chapter) within some longer whole. Progression from this opening position is marked by definitization of NPs with established referents: definite personal pronouns in the first three sentences, proper names in the second, fourth and sixth. Of course, the hippopotamuses and the Grays have to remain definite for the rest of the fable, so no further progressive force can be derived from this particular source.

One possibility for progression within the text is not exploited: the introduction of new characters within the established spatio-temporal fiction. Neither the A.B.I. nor either set of friends and neighbours enjoys a second mention, an agent role or a finite verb. The transition from indefinite to definite cannot be made for these characters, and in turn they cannot be used to advance the narrative.

Narrative progression is commonly managed by the sequencing of new predicates (*Veni, vidi, vici*) and of temporal expressions. The predicates which secure this progression are

10. listened   (sentence 1)
    said   (2)
    said   (4)
    exclaimed   (6)
    continued   (8)
    said   (9)
    thought of calling   (10)
    decided ... to phone ... [to] describe   (11)
    were surprised and shocked to hear   (12)
    wuffled   (13)
    gurbled   (14)
    said   (15)
    called up   (16)

discussed	(16)
stopped criticizing	(17)
fell asleep	(17)
stopped maligning	(17)
retired	(17)

I have picked out those verbs which imply a train of actions performed by the protagonists, or a sequence of states in which they find themselves. Certainly there is a narrative sequence; one might also comment that the predicates concerned are semantically 'weak' in some way that is appropriate to the style of this fable (nothing much happens, it's all attitudinal, and the lexical choices bring this fact home) but that is beside the point of the present discussion. A narrative progression of sorts can at least be extracted from the text.

This fragile but ordered temporal thread given by the predicates is strengthened by a consistent but minimal apparatus of explicit phrases indicating time:

11.	one . . . afternoon	(1)
	late that evening	(12)
	long after midnight	(17)

(Perhaps one ought to include also indications of the passing of time, as well as references to points of time: *continued* (8), *for a time* (10).) In the last sentence, the third temporal phrase, *long after midnight*, coincides with a dense cluster of predicates signifying cessation of action: *stopped criticizing, fell asleep, stopped maligning, retired*. The end of the discursive part of the text is thereby signalled.

I have concentrated on that part of textual progression which relates to narrative sequence; that is to say, on those features of surface structure which guide our retrieval of more abstract structures of linear sequence. Two questions of supreme importance for text grammar are raised by this part of the discussion; both emerge from the general problem of the relationship between microstructure and macrostructure, which may be expressed, for exploration, as a problem parallel to that of the relationship between surface structure and semantic structure in modern generative sentence grammars. Structuralist poetics posits that texts are formed on a deep structure of abstract formatives which, as research proceeds, are gradually emerging: e.g. the cultural codes proposed by Barthes, one of which, the actional, is presumably the same as the conventions of narrative structure revealed in analyses in the tradition of Propp, Todorov, etc.; conventions of modality, performatives, which are presumably responsible for the rhetorical aspect of texts; and so on. Very little research has been done into the transformations or textual realization rules which carry these abstract elements into surface structure[1]. Barthes (1970) ignores the problem by dumping the stylistic (microstructural level, and in *S/Z* he declines to show how his proposed codes (macrostructure) are attached to the *lexies* which he segments out of Balzac's text; yet there is more than a suspicion that the *lexies*, formalized, could be seen to EXPRESS, in their textural details, the abstract elements which constitute the codes (see Chapter six, for comments on the expression of the referential code). The two major questions to be raised with reference to the relationship of textual deep and surface structure are: how does the text grammarian describe the process of realization — what sorts of transformations does he need? How does the reader realise textual deep structure on the basis of his encounter with the surface? It is beyond my present project to tackle these questions; I raise them at this point because we know more about narrative structure than about any other aspect of textual deep structure, so that the microstructural reflexes of narrative organization might be a promising point of entry into discussion of the more general problem. Obviously, *The Lover and His Lass*, being minimally narrative, is not a rewarding text for this exploration.

'Progression', like my other two terms, is a psycholinguistic concept. It refers simultaneously to the linear character of the reader's experience and to the linguistic features which (in a responsible reading) presumably control this experience. I have limited my discussion to those aspects of the textual surface which relate to narrative in deep structure, but in fact any aspect of the textual surface structure may contribute to, or alternatively inhibit, our experience of the text's progressiveness. Elementary syntactic factors such as, for example, preference for SVO ordering (in English), avoidance of inversion, avoidance of a suspensive syntax, guarantee progression; consistent inversion, etc., leads to an impression of non-progressiveness.

Now it should be clear that progression has its direct converse, non-progression. The notorious 'later style' of Henry James is continuously non-progressive: the style (syntactically controlled) is consistent, and exactly the features which are consistent conspire to obstruct the reader's progress through the text. (I do not say that this is bad, or unmotivated.) This possibility — and actuality — of *continuous* resistance to progression encourages me to distinguish anti-progression or non-progression from the third of my analytic categories, LOCALIZATION. Textual surface structure may be said to be localizing when it operates to hold up the reader's attention at a specific place in the total syntagm. Language, at one place, becomes different from the ongoing textual norm. Inevitably, the immediate impact of localizing structure is to interrupt progression and to disturb cohesion.

Numerous types of linguistic construction are available to effect localization; but what is available in a given case depends upon the context. Localization is departure from a norm — not from an absent, implicit norm outside the text, but a concretely present textual norm carried through to the immediately preceding text segment and often resumed in the succeeding segment. It can be produced by, for example, a long or complex sentence where the ongoing norm is short or simple sentences; by a sudden morphological or lexical departure (e.g. polysyllables, or scientific words, against the background of prevailing short words or a casual vocabulary); by unexpected phonological foregrounding (e.g. unanticipated alliteration or withdrawal of alliteration); and so on. It may also be — and perhaps most frequently is — produced by a combination of different linguistic circumstances, all conspiring to effect a local deformation of the ongoing linguistic conventions.

The immediate norm of *The Lover and His Lass* has been sufficiently described under 'cohesion' and 'progression' above: a balanced, paratactic style based on parallelism at each syntactic rank reinforced by alliteration. The texture shows pervasive phonetic play; lexical selections and collocations are continuously and appropriately witty; the narrative progresses smoothly through a sequence of undramatic predicates and a minimal temporal scheme. Cohesive/progressive structure is broken at two particular points of localization: sentences (7-8) and (10-11). The dominant style is sufficiently cued in the first sentence, and the second fails to disturb it: notice that Mrs. Gray's short speech is, through not balanced, syntactically symmetrical, with a short sentence on each side of 'said Mrs. Gray'. But (5) is immediately non-symmetrical: the monosyllabic 'No' in (4) is matched by a moderately long and syntactically complex utterance almost lacking in syntactic balance and phonetic patterning. Syntax is hypotactic, right-branching from *I don't see ...* with a variety of embedded clause structures (nominal; relative; relative; comparative); and syntax is foregrounded over lexical choice here by the use of the compound *entertain affection* instead of one of the many available simple verbs. But Gray's scornful comment culminates in a lexical device which reappears in other localized segments, the mocking and monstrous metaphor *capsized bathtub*, taken up indignantly by Mrs. Gray in sentence (6) and replaced by the laborious and grotesque *coastwise fruit steamer with a cargo of waterlogged basketballs*. Hippopotamuses are perhaps vulnerable to such comparisons, but here one metaphor is piled on another in an unmotivated way: the cargo of waterlogged basketballs is a gratuitous appendage which has no force to add to the already blatant coastwise fruit steamer. The combination is in effect tautologous, and tautology, in Jakobson's scheme (1960; cf. Riffaterre, 1973) is a prime case of language drawing attention to itself by means of the processes allowed under the 'poetic function'. And as these metaphors pile up, another aspect of the language becomes foregrounded: syllabic prominence. By the time we get into sentence (7), the rhythm of paired phrases, established early on by parataxis and phrase conjoining, has been broken by the intrusion of a complex hypotactic syntax. Stresses now tend to cluster unpredictably rather than to stand in balanced pairs. The density of stresses is also a product of lexical choice; the nouns and adjectives which form the basis of the mocking and monstrous metaphors contain many non-reducible vowels bunched closely together (*capsized bathtub*, *coastwise*, *waterlogged basketballs*); there are few lightly stressed functional words; heavy syntactic premodification in noun phrases leads to the juxtaposition of strong vowels (*coastwise fruit steamer*, etc.). Some of these characteristics recur in the second localized passage, which starts in the middle of sentence (10). The first part of the sentence is cast in the re-established binary rhythm of (8-9: *the bumbling romp of the lover and his lass was hard to comprehend and even harder to tolerate*. Then the syntax becomes subject to right-branching and nesting. Vestiges of balance are illusory: *monolithic lovemaking by enormous creatures* appears initially to be a case of parallelism, but is not so at all — the succeeding material (*who should have ...*) must be read within the same intonation contour as *enormous creatures* to prevent the relative clause being interpreted as non-restrictive (appositive). At the end of sentence (11) we find two more instances of fake parallelism: *mocking and monstrous* is unbalanced by its head noun *metaphors*; and the two phrases *skidding buses on icy streets* and *overturned moving vans* are quite dissimilar in their internal structure. (Notice that the abundance of modifiers recalls the metaphoric phrases in (7-8).) I have commented above on the asymmetry of syntax and alliteration in *phone their friends and neighbors.*

The localizing effect of (10-11) is not as dramatic as that of (7-8); the syntax is more diffuse, the metaphors are less densely compacted and do not disturb the prevailing stress-pattern so severely as, for example, the ones at the end of sentence (7) do. But the two passages quite patently relate to each other in the kinds of linguistic devices employed to interrupt the reader's experience of the prevailing cohesive/progressive norm. In both cases a complex of similar syntactic, phonetic and lexical strategies conspire to disrupt the comfortable rhythm of the reader's linguistic experience of the hippopotamus' amorous universe. The similarity between the two passages is of course predictable from their meanings: in both places the parrots give voice to sharp-tongued and preposterous comments on the habits of their neighbours. The act of thus commenting is picked out by Thurber's use of localizing structure at the two significant points in the text. At a third place (sentences (13-15)) the hippopotamuses take their turn, and revile the parrots: a conversational interchange similar to (2-7), and positionally balanced against that sequence, ends with the grotesque metaphor of the garden shears. But the sequence does not have the effect of the other two localized passages, for it is too securely cocooned in a patterned syntactic/phonetic framework consistent with the dominant style of the text. It is perhaps for this reason that the hippopotamuses seems to come off best; although the moral, and indeed the content of the tale, insist that both parties are equally guilty of intolerance towards the natural practices of their neighbours, the voices of the parrots are much more clearly isolated in the structure of the text; and the verbal world of the hippopotamuses, generally the norm against which the strictures of the parrots are foregrounded, remains sympathetic — *normal.*

I do not intend to elaborate on the interpretation of the tale; that would go beyond the aim of this paper. But if the interpretation is at all plausible, it demonstrates the availability of localizing surface structure for the cueing of 'deeper' structural polarities in a text. In this case, a contrast in life-styles between the hippopotamuses and the parrots is suggested by the localization of the parrots' pronouncements only, leaving the hippopotamuses in control of the textual norm and in enjoyment of its stylistic connotations. This opposition could not be predicted from the apparent summative statement of the text's meaning, the Moral. But a great deal more research, particularly into the nature of the semantic categories implied here, is necessary before we can state in formal terms the textual processes involved.

Notes

1. But see Scheglov and Zholkovskii (1975) and O'Toole (1975).

The Lover and His Lass

(1) An arrogant gray parrot and his arrogant mate listened, one African afternoon, in disdain and derision, to the lovemaking of a lover and his lass, who happened to be hippopotamuses.

(2) 'He calls her snooky-ookums,' said Mrs. Gray. (3) 'Can you believe that?'

(4) 'No,' said Gray. (5) 'I don't see how any male in his right mind, could entertain afection for a female that has no more charm than a capsized bathtub.'

(6) 'Capsized bathtub, indeed!' exclaimed Mrs. Gray. (7) 'Both of them have the appeal of a coastwise fruit steamer with a cargo of waterlogged basketballs.'

(8) But it was spring, and the lover and his lass were young, and they were oblivious of the scornful comments of their sharp-tongued neighbors, and they continued to bump each other around in the water, happily pushing and pulling, backing and filling, and snorting and snaffling. (9) The tender things they said to each other during the monolithic give-and-take of their courtship sounded as lyric to them as flowers in bud or green things opening. (10) To the Grays, however, the bumbling romp of the lover and his lass was hard to comprehend and even harder to tolerate, and for a time they thought of calling the A.B.I., or African Bureau of Investigation, on the ground that monolithic lovemaking by enormous creatures who should have become decent fossils long ago was probably a threat to the security of the jungle. (11) But they decided instead to phone their friends and neighbors and gossip about the shameless pair, and describe them in mocking and monstrous metaphors involving skidding buses on icy streets and overturned moving vans.

(12) Late that evening, the hippopotamus and the hippopotama were surprised and shocked to hear the Grays exchanging terms of endearment. (13) 'Listen to those squawks,' wuffled the male hippopotamus.

(14) 'What in the world can they see in each other?' gurbled the female hippopotamus.

(15) 'I would as soon live with a pair of unoiled garden shears,' said her inamoratus.

(16) They called up their friends and neighbors and discussed the incredible fact that a male gray parrot and a female gray parrot could possibly have any sex appeal. (17) It was long after midnight before the hippopotamuses stopped

criticizing the Grays and fell asleep, and the Grays stopped maligning the hippopotamuses and retired to their beds.

(18) Moral: *Laugh and the world laughs with you, love and you love alone.*

CHAPTER FIVE

Literature as discourse

I would say that syntax is a significant, if shifty, index of a writer's perspective on his subject-matter. In this light, please consider the syntax of my title. It is two nouns connected by a logical term, 'as'. On one version of the programme for this lecture series, the word 'as' is misprinted as 'and', this makes a big difference. A simple conjunction of two nouns, 'Literature and Discourse', would suggest that I accept the meanings of the two words as stable, unanalyzed. The connective 'as', however, is intended to announce that this juxtaposition of the two noun terms is an *analysis* of the two nouns, particularly the first — an examination of the nature of the first term in the light of the meaning of the second. The aim of this analysis is basically methodological: I want to argue that viewing literature in this unusual light — as discourse and thus as communication rather than as object — produces some unusual insights. Thus it is an argument about procedure in literary criticism. Because the idea of 'discourse' is to be defined in linguistics, it is an argument about the scope and aims of linguistics too. But beyond these methodological considerations you should sense an implicit political, or at least educational, goal also: the approach I recommend is designed to make the institution of literature more accessible, to attack an artificial and polemic barrier that has been built between literature and other modes of discourse.

Adopting a linguistic approach to literature, as I do, it is tempting to think of and describe the literary text as a *formal* structure, an object whose main quality is its distinctive syntactic and phonological shape. This is a common approach, adopted by, for instance, the most famous of the linguistic stylisticians, Roman Jakobson (see Jakobson, 1960; Jakobson and Lévi-Strauss, 1962; Jakobson and Jones, 1970). It also happens to agree with the dominant formalist tendency of the more conservative schools of modern criticism. I argue that linguistic formalism is of limited significance in literary studies, and educationally restrictive. As an alternative I shall employ some linguistic techniques which emphasize the *interactional* dimensions of texts. To treat literature as discourse is to see the text as mediating relationships between language-users: not only relationships of speech, but also of consciousness, ideology, role and class. The text ceases to be an object and becomes an action or process.

This anti-formalist approach is pretty much at odds with received opinion in conventional literary aesthetics. Among my heresies, from this point of view, are willingness for literary works to be kinetic; denial of their alleged formal autonomy; acceptance of the relevance of truth-values to literature. It is not my purpose in this paper to argue a collision of linguistics and aesthetics, however — as I said, my immediate object is methodological. Furthermore, I shall assert, without offering any formal justification, one other assumption implicit in my position — that is, that no plausible essentialist or intrinsic definition of literature has been or is likely to be devised. For my purpose, no such theory is necessary. What literature is, can be stated empirically, within the realm of sociolinguistic fact. It is an open set of texts, of great formal diversity, recognised by a culture as possessing certain institutional values and performing certain functions. (Of course, 'recognition' in this context doesn't mean that members of the society are capable of describing these values and functions accurately or willing to acknowledge them truthfully.) The values are neither universal, though they are subject to a small range of types of historical explanation, nor stable, although they change slowly. They derive from the economic and social structures of particular societies, and I am sure you can think of any number of Marxist and historicist interpretations which illustrate the causal process to which I refer. My aim here is not to promulgate Marxist explanations, but to suggest that once we start looking at literature as a part of social process then texts are opened to the same kinds of causal and functional interpretations as are found in the sociology of language generally. (For readings in sociolinguistics, see Giglioli, 1972; Hymes, 1964; Laver and Hutcheson, 1972; Pride and Holmes, 1972.)

Now I must talk a little bit about linguistic metatheory. It is obvious that my approach requires what might be called a 'functional' theory of language. Not all schools of linguistics pay any attention to linguistic functions, to the various kinds of work language performs in actual communicative situations. Notably, transformational grammar has no interest in the functions of language, and the way it looks at language implies that only one function is to be attributed to language, the so-called 'referential' function, that is, the channelling of propositional meanings through the medium of sound. For Chomsky, linguistics is the study of sentences, or the theory of sentences, and a sentence is, in his terms, essentially a syntactic construct responsible for pairing what he calls a 'semantic interpretation' with a 'phonetic representation' (e.g. Chomsky, 1967, 1968). Transformations are neutral operations for mapping meanings on to phonetic signals. For instance, active sentences and their passive counterparts are said to have the same meaning, despite the fact that their surface structures are very different and that they tend to be used in different situations. A functional grammar would be concerned to pose and answer the question *why* languages like English provide a choice between *John threw the ball* and *The ball was thrown by John* as different ways of talking about the same event. One explanation seems to be that active and passive equivalents tend to be used in texts and situations with different information structures. *John threw the ball* seems an appropriate answer to the question 'What did John do?' whereas *The ball was thrown by John* responds to 'What happened to the ball?'. Also, it has been suggested that the passive provides for deletion of agency in descriptions of transitive events — *The ball was thrown, The window was broken*. Such deletion could occur for any of a number of reasons: anonymity, impersonality, mystification, ignorance. It is clear that a rich set of motivations could be supplied for the active/passive choice, that it is not a case of arbitrary syntactic variation. Similarly, the functionalist would claim, all other aspects of linguistic structure are to be explained by reference to their communicative purposes. This is the position of the Prague linguistic school and of the English linguist M.A.K. Halliday:

> The particular form taken by the grammatical system of language is closely related to the social and personal needs that language is required to serve.
> (Halliday, 1970: 142)

Now the functionalist is after something more powerful than a mere list of *ad hoc* connections between details of linguistic structure and points of social usage. He proposes that, although the particular sociolinguistic institutions of cultures differ considerably, they may be referred to a small number of global functional categories. Halliday posits three functions, which he calls *ideational, interpersonal* and *textual*. The ideational function has to do with the transmission of a world-view, a structuring of experience; the interpersonal, with communicative intercourse, the establishment and maintenance of personal and group relationships; the textual, with the completeness and shape of a communicative unit, a text or utterance, within its context of situation. Textually, we recognise that a piece of language is a well-formed communication rather than inconsequential gibberish; interpersonally, that it is addressed by our interlocutor to us, that it is a question or an assertion, etc., that it signals the interlocutor's status relative to us, and so on; ideationally, that this discourse is a series of propositions conveying structured judgments on some topic or topics. Each of these functions relates to some definite aspects of language structure. The ideational function explains such structural features as the distinction between nouns and predicates, the semantics of quantification, logical connectives between propositions, etc.; interpersonal structures include questions, imperatives, person distinctions among pronouns, and many other aspects of language which I will mention below; the textual function is reflected in all those structures which preserve continuity of discourse, for instance anaphoric cross-reference by pronouns across sentence boundaries: *John threw the ball. It bounced against the fence.*

Whether or not you accept the validity of Halliday's three functional categories (they seem to me commonsensical at least), and whether or not you adopt his descriptive terminology (I prefer the metalanguage of the generative-semantics version of transformational-generative grammar), his grammar evidently has considerable potential scope and power. It is broader, more inclusive, in its conception of what counts as linguistic fact than are traditional syntax-centred linguistic theories such as TG; and it calls for bolder and more socially relevant explanations of linguistic structure.

Note that Halliday's three functions of language are conceived of as *simultaneous*, not *alternative*: any complete piece of language working in a communicative context is structured to serve all three needs. There is a trivial sense in which one can talk about alternative linguistic functions: you can use language to write to the bank manager, to pray, to urge on manual work, to write an advertisement, to abuse the wife, to write *Paradise Lost*, etc., and surely the style will vary enormously from one use to another, so there is a form-function correlation of a sort. But this is just a list. The list becomes a bit more interesting if the categories are made more general, as in the sociolinguistic theory of 'register'. But when you reach an extremely high level of generality, alternativity of function becomes implausible. I.A. Richards's 'two uses of language', 'scientific' versus 'poetic', otherwise 'referential' versus 'emotive', provide an excellent example of the absurdity of exclusively alternative general functions (Richards, 1924: Ch. 34). A purely scientific, inexpressive language is as absurd as a contentless poem of total expression. And I don't think it helps to make it a relative, more-or-less, choice, as Roman Jakobson tries to do.

Jakobson's famous paper 'Linguistics and Poetics' (1960) will help us return to the main topic. You will recall that Jakobson derives his six functions of language from a scheme of six 'constitutive factors' of any speech event. I reproduce his diagram of the six factors as Fig. 1:

CONTEXT

ADDRESSER   MESSAGE   ADDRESSEE

———————————————

CONTACT

CODE

The *addresser* and the *addressee* are source and target of the message, respectively: considered intentionally, the voluntary emitter and the desired receiver of the communication. The *code* is the language in which the message is constructed, English or Russian or whatever natural language (or, presumably, some other semiological system; see Barthes, 1967). *Contact* is physical channel, sound waves or light waves. *Message* seems to mean, in Jakobson's system, the palpable surface structure of the communication (e.g. phonetic substance). *Context* is not simply the immediate or wider situation of the actual communicative act (not 'context of situation' as in Firth, 1957) but the non-linguistic world as it is treated by language, ie. the subject of discourse. Jakobson comments on the functional relevance of these communicative factors, as follows:

> Each of these six factors determines a different function of language.
> Although we distinguish six basic aspects of language, we could, however,
> hardly find verbal messages that would fulfill only one function. The
> diversity lies not in a monopoly of some one of these several functions but in
> a different hierarchical order of functions. The verbal structure of a message
> depends primarily on the predominant function. (1960: 353)

So six functions, and six types of verbal organization, are derived from the constituent factors. Jakobson puts these into an isomorphic diagram, Fig. 2:

REFERENTIAL

POETIC

EMOTIVE   PHATIC   CONATIVE

METALINGUAL

Again, the terms are not entirely conventional, but the purport is clear. The *emotive* function, perhaps better called 'expressive', is found in language devoted to highlighting the character and state of the speaker. Conversely, *conative* language is directed at the addressee; it has 'perlocutionary' designs upon him — e.g. advertising language. The *metalingual* function involves language *about* language, commentary on the code, from the language of scientific linguistics to regulatory utterances like '*i* before *e* except after *c*'. *Phatic* utterance is communication designed to establish interaction within the selected channel: routine vacuities like 'Hello', 'It's a beautiful day', 'I love you'. The *referential* function is the outward-directed function of language, minimizing speaker, hearer, channel, etc., focusing impersonally on subject-matter: what Richards and others have called the 'scientific' use of language. Finally, the *poetic* function demands heightening of the physical texture of the message, patterned objectivication of the phonic surface; the influence of Shklovsky's 'art as device', Mukařovský's 'foregrounding', is clear (Shklovsky, 1965; Mukařovský, 1964). The next stage of Jakobson's argument is a proposal and demonstration of a structural mechanism by means of which is achieved the foregrounding of linguistic surface structure which he claims typifies the poetic use of language. It's irrelevant to my purpose to investigate this in detail, except to report that its effect is, in Jakobson's words, to 'promote the *palpability* of signs', to make form more important and salient than content. Needless to say, Jakobson is strongly oriented towards a quite limited, although historically important, tradition of highly patterned, phonetic, lyric verse.

Despite his concession that no linguistic event obeys only one function of language, Jakobson's theory implies a potent suppression of functions other than the one chosen for designating a particular text or corpus. The practical analyses of poetry which he has published bear out this impression. Jakobson has decided that poetry is dominated by phonetic and syntactic features of repetition, parallelism and antithesis, and his analyses concentrate on the way these features contribute to the concreteness, perceptibility, of the texts discussed. Other aspects of language are neglected. In his analysis of Shakespeare's sonnet 'Th' expense of spirit . . .', for instance, semantic interpretation consists only of one page of free paraphrase, and nothing is said about the kind of speech act performed by the poem, the relationship between its implied interlocutors (see Jakobson and Jones, 1970). The vast body of critical literature on the Sonnets shows that a much wider range of response to their language has seemed appropriate to other commentators: there is plenty to say about referential, interpersonal and metalinguistic aspects of this corpus of poetry (cf. Fowler, 1975). I think it is clear that Jakobson's concentration on formal structure is determined not by the nature of the material but by his decision to treat it in such a way. This decision has its causes and its consequences. The causes I would locate historically in Jakobson's own intellectual maturation during the high period of European modernism, and, more specifically, Russian formalism. Jakobson's definition of literature is in fact a way of looking at literature which reflects the classicist and formalist goals of the precisely historical culture within which he was educated. The consequences of his definition are to perpetuate the values of that culture, to insist that literature is a contained, quiet, socially unresponsive object outside of history.

One can see the attraction of these values to a society which favours stability and closure above change and openness. Such predilections are prominent in both Jakobson's culture and our own. But our culture is also — as Jakobson's was also — a society of verbal violence — advertising, abuse, rant — and verbal intimacy — the solidarity of shared class languages. To define literature as patterned form is to cover one's ears against the presence of these actional and kinetic potentialities in all language. Literature isn't exempt from language's general responsibility to work in the real world of conflicts and sympathies. Being language, literature can't shed its interpersonal function. The theorist and critic, obeying his ideology, may choose (without knowing he is choosing) to downgrade the interpersonal in favour of the less committing formal-textual-poetic function. I choose, perhaps for equally ideological reasons, to redress the balance by drawing attention to the inevitable and important interpersonal-interactional-discursive dimensions of literary texts.

I now make my way toward analysis by way of a little more theory. John Searle's revision of Austin's speech acts is relevant to my thesis and for my present audience will provide a familiar entry into the material (Austin, 1962; Searle, 1969). Austin divided speech acts into performative and constative utterances, and concentrated on the latter. Searle, though still much interested in performative speech acts like promising, maintains what seems to be the correct general position, namely, that every utterance is simultaneously three language acts. It is a locutionary act, that is, an utterance in the words and sounds of English. French, etc.; it is a propositional act, i.e. it attributes a property to a referent outside of language; and it is an illocutionary act, e.g. an act of stating, promising, questioning, marrying, or whatever. The theory of illocutionary act and illocutionary force is quite easily incorporated into a transformational grammar with a semantic base, and there have been a number of proposals to that effect. In technical terms, the highest predicate in a sentence will be an illocutionary verb with a first-person subject. See Fig. 3, which is a schematic diagram for the semantic structure of *Brutus killed Caesar* (cf. Seuren, 1974 for discussion and references).

$$\text{state}_I$$
$$\text{past}_S$$
$$\text{cause}_x$$
$$\text{become}_y$$
$$\text{not}_y$$
$$\text{alive}_y$$

x = Brutus
y = Caesar

Of course, the set of illocutionary verbs is as yet undetermined; but presumably it will include STATE, DENY, NEGATE, COMMAND, ENQUIRE, GENERALIZE, and so on as well as the more obvious PROMISE, MARRY, REFUSE, UNDERTAKE TO, etc. Next, the illocutionary verbs must be accompanied by a set of realization rules. In most cases realization involves deletion of the illocutionary verb, its first person subject and its present tense. So *I state that Brutus killed Caesar* becomes the unmarked *Brutus killed Caesar*. Other transformational processes include the deletion of, additionally, a second-person subject when the illocutionary verb is COMMAND (*Kill Caesar!*), and the assignment of extra heavy stress to a dummy auxiliary when the illocutionary predicate is AFFIRM (*Brutus DID kill Caesar*). These transformations yielding marked modal constructions are well understood in linguistics. As far as literary criticism is concerned, the priority is to investigate the implications of both marked and, particularly, unmarked illocutionary determinants of the discourse structure of texts. The stylistician Richard Ohmann has already begun this study, concentrating on illocutionary situations which are either marked or deviant or both (see Ohmann, 1971, 1972, 1973). To give a quick example of my own, a poem so familiar that I don't even need to put the text in front of you, consider William Blake's poem *Tyger*. The text is dense with morphological and punctuational indicators of illocutionary actions — exclamations and questions — so a speech act approach is *prima facie* appropriate. Application of the Austin-Searle theory is immediately rewarded. Felicity conditions are obviously and functionally broken. In general, the requirement of a normal communicative channel is not fulfilled. You can't expect a civil answer if you put questions to a tiger, and if you don't expect an answer, it is arguable that you are not asking a question at all. There are also more specific infelicities; the speaker asks, among other things:

> What the hammer? what the chain?
> In what furnace was thy brain?
> What the anvil? what dread grasp
> Dare its deadly terrors clasp?

No creature, cat or man, can be expected to give a reliable first-hand report on the circumstances of its creation. These unanswerable questions bounce off the tiger towards the implied reader of the poem, and so a discourse is established. The reader recognises rhetorical questions which are really directed to persuading him of the terror and the inscrutability of power and beauty. Speech act theory in this case initiates a formal explanation of our recognition of the force of the questions, our creative disorientation in the face of a battery of infelicitous illocutions. These facts about illocution (which could be elaborated) do not take the critic very far towards an interpretation, but an understanding of them is prerequisite to interpretation.

> Slowly the poison the whole blood stream fills.
> It is not the effort nor the failure tires.
> The waste remains, the waste remains and kills.
>
> It is not your system or clear sight that mills
> Down small to the consequence a life requires;
> Slowly the poison the whole blood stream fills.

They bled an old dog dry yet the exchange rills
Of young dog blood gave but a month's desires
The waste remains, the waste remains and kills.

It is the Chinese tombs and the slag hills
Usurp the soil, and not the soil retires.
Slowly the poison the whole blood stream fills.

Not to have fire is to be a skin that shrills.
The complete fire is death. From partial fires
The waste remains, the waste remains and kills.

It is the poems you have lost, the ills
From missing dates, at which the heart expires.
Slowly the poison the whole blood stream fills.
The waste remains, the waste remains and kills.

A more delicate example is William Empson's poem 'Missing Dates'; above. The illocutionary problem, I mean, is more delicate. You cannot readily see what illocutionary act is being performed, and so, just as the syntax of the title is ambiguous between a transitive and an intransitive meaning of the verb 'missing' (like Chomsky's 'the shooting of the hunters'), there is a radical ambivalence or uncertainty of tone which may produce misreadings. This ambivalence begins with the tense of the very first verb, 'fills', and continues with other present-tense verbs in the poem. In English the present tense serves a number of functions, so there is always a potential for ambiguity. The first line of the poem, for instance, is in principle ambiguous between two different speech acts, present tense narration or simultaneous commentary on the one hand, and timeless generalization on the other. You can make the first sentence work as narrative present if you fit the words to some plausible reference, e.g. consider them as a voice-over commentary on some gruesome medical documentary on TV. But this illocution isn't appropriate. The noun phrases in the poem are so diverse in reference that they obviously can't be acting as definite descriptions within any continuous narrative: the poison, and old dog, Chinese tombs, slag hills and so on. Deciding to read these nouns metaphorically, we are also deciding to read the illocutions as timeless generalizations. However, the general truth asserted by the first sentence is not transparent. The inversion of the verb and the object noun phrase reminds us that this is a line in a poem and thus likely to require a metaphorical interpretation: also the dislocation of word order interferes with our perception of the intonation contour of the sentence, making it difficult to decide where the information focus is. If we read on to lines 2 and 3, though, we realise that line 3 is a paraphrase of line 1: poison may be waste matter in the blood (e.g. alcohol), waste kills, waste means also lost opportunity or unproductive activity or unfilled time, thus connecting with the title. So line 1 means something like 'the cause of the spiritual death I'm talking about is a process which may be likened to the action of poison slowly polluting the blood stream'. The first line doesn't mean, for instance, 'It is in the nature of this specific poison to slowly fill the whole blood stream'. Now I'm not concerned here with the exact correctness of the paraphrase, but rather with the route by which we arrive at it, and, further, with the consequences of this route for our perception of illocutionary structure. Using line 2 in order to interpret line 1, we realise that 'poison' is affirmed as the cause of death in a context which denies the validity of other, specified, causal explanations. 'If x is a class of events, the cause of every token of x is a and not b or c'. The illocutionary act is, therefore, not simply affirmative generalization, but affirmative generalization incorporating denial of competing generalizations. Of course, the structure 'not b, nor c, but a, is the cause of x' becomes explicit and repeated in the syntactic surface structure:

It is the Chinese tombs and the slag hills
Usurp the soil, and not the soil retires.

The relevance of this illocutionary analysis to my presentation of literature as discourse is this: the strategy of the speech act is to create a specific type of reader, a second voice, and include him within the communicative format of the poem. This particular reader is in a conflict relationship with the author, and he is a pre-defined loser in this dialogic battle: he holds false beliefs, that is, the author presents the implicit addressee's beliefs as false, and the implicit reader can't refute this since his beliefs can only be presented through the author's voice. (For 'dialogic' analysis see Bakhtin, 1973; Uspensky, 1973; Vološinov, 1973).

The belittled and berated addresseee surfaces as 'your' and 'you' in stanzas 2 and 6. This is a personalized 'you', not the impersonal and general 'you' of 'You pays your money and you takes your choice'. The cap is meant to fit. I said earlier that there was an ambivalence of tone in this poem, but I think that the tone is resolved on an accurate reading of the author's speech act. The reader constructed by this poem, if he is not irrelevantly lulled into a mood of complacent melancholy by the reassuringly repetitive metre, has a distinct feeling of being *got at*. He is the source of the rejected false explanations. Although he is only mentioned in the two 'yous', he can don the cap at many other places in the poem. One striking characteristic of the syntax is the deletion of noun phrases in agent and patient cases: *whose* blood stream? *who* makes the effort? *who* fails? *who* gets tired? *who* wastes *what*? *who* is killed, and *who* kills *whom*? These slots are open to be filled by the 'you' of the poem: he suffers, and it's his fault and responsibility. The title is transitive, after all: dates don't go missing by themselves any more than the soil retires; you lose them, just as you usurp the soil by building tombs and piling up industrial waste.

My next passage is taken from George Eliot's *Middlemarch*.

. . . Was he not making a fool of himself? — and at a time when he was more than ever conscious of being something better than a fool? And for what end?

Well, for no definite end. True, he had dreamy visions of possibilities: there is no human being who having both passions and thoughts does not find images rising in his mind which soothe the passion with hope or sting it with dread. But this, which happens to us all, happens to some with a wide difference; and Will was not one of those whose wit 'keeps the roadway': he had his bypaths where there were little joys of his own choosing, such as gentlemen cantering on the highroad might have thought rather idiotic. The way in which he made a sort of happiness for himself out of his feeling for Dorothea was an example of this. It may seem strange, but it is the fact, that the ordinary vulgar vision of which Mr. Casaubon suspected him — namely, that Dorothea might become a widow, and that the interest he had established in her might turn into acceptance of him as a husband — had no tempting, arresting power over him; he did not live in the scenery of such an event, and follow it out, as we all do with that imagined 'otherwise' which is our practical heaven. It was not only that he was unwilling to entertain thoughts which could be accused of baseness, and was already uneasy in the sense that he had to justify himself from the charge of ingratitude — the latent consciousness of many other barriers between himself and Dorothea besides the existence of her husband, had helped to turn away his imagination from speculating on what might befall Mr. Casaubon. And there were yet other reasons. Will, we know, could not bear the thought of any flaw appearing in his crystal: he was at once exasperated and delighted by the calm freedom with which Dorothea looked at him and spoke to him, and there was something so exquisite in thinking of her just as she was, that he could not long for a change which must somehow change her. Do we not shun the street version of a fine melody? — or shrink from the news that the rarity — some bit of chiselling or engraving perhaps — which we have dwelt on even with exultation in the trouble it has cost us to snatch glimpses of it, is really not an uncommon thing, and may be obtained as an everyday possession? Our good depends on the quality and breadth of our emotion; and to Will, a creature who cared little for what are called the solid things of life and greatly for its subtler influences, to have within him such a feeling as he had towards Dorothea, was like the inheritance of a fortune.

George Eliot was writing at a time when the rhetorical status of the implied author was becoming a critical issue in the development of European prose fiction. Flaubert had pronounced for impersonality in narration, and from 1850 novelists went through all kinds of linguistic contortions to seem to erase their personal voices from their fiction. The disappearing author is a major crisis in the recent history of narrative discourse, and the linguistics of affected impersonality is of immense interest. The goal of Flaubert, Joyce, James, Hemingway was the technically impossible one of constructing texts without modality, chains of propositions without illocution, addresses without addressor or addressee. I am not going to talk about the linguistics of self-effacing discourse this evening, though I wish I had time to do so (see Fowler, 1977a on this and related aspects of fictional discourse). Rather, I quote George Eliot to illustrate the explicit signals of modality, of narrative discourse, in an author who was aware of the crisis and chose not to erase her own and her reader's voices but to dramatize them in full dialogic intercourse. For my taste, the effect is magnificent: a kind of highbrow but passionate version of Henry Fielding's authorial persona. In this passage, she simultaneously presents her own and Will Ladislaw's reflections on his motives for situating himself close to the not-yet-widowed Dorothea. When I say 'presents', I want you to remember that the verb 'present' is relational, transitive: *a* presents *b* to *c*. *a* is George Eliot, *b* Ladislaw, *c* the reader, so there are discourse relationships between three separate vocalizable consciousnesses.

The presence of the author, and her discourse relationships with her subject and with her reader, are signalled by the variety and shifts of illocutionary acts in the passage, and particularly by some specific speech acts. *Questions* are plentiful, especially at the beginning and towards the end of my excerpt. A question strongly implies a questioner and a questioned: being a marked illocutionary act, it reminds us of its participants more strongly than does, say, a plain statement. Notice how the first questions — 'Was he not making a fool of himself?' etc. — place all three parties to the discourse in a complex of dynamic relationships. These questions occupy a triple situation in the structure of discourse. They are George Eliot's questions, relating her to the reader as questioned and to Will as topic. Second, they are George Eliot's questions addressed to Will, part of her moral interrogation of him; the reader undertakes jury service, and listens. Third, we have been told that Will is reflecting on his position, so these questions may well be indirect free thought (see Chatman, 1975, and references): he is questioner and subject, his questioners simultaneously himself, ourselves and the author. Then, the sentence 'Well, for no definite end' stabilizes the discoursal position. Considered as speech act, it is an *answer*, and it is unambiguously the author's answer; she uses it to assert her control over the voices in the discourse. Another illocution I would like you to look at is *generalization* (see further, Chapter six). George Eliot's prose is full of generic sentences, often verging on a proverbial style of syntactic construction: 'Our good depends on the quality and breadth of our emotion'. Now, the universalizing generic is a quite distinct speech act from the act of plain narrative report carried by the past tense. When George Eliot writes 'he had dreamy visions of possibilities', she claims only that Will from time to time entertained certain vaguely realised versions of the future. But the shift to the generic present of 'there is no human being . . .' transforms the scope of claimed validity. We are no longer in the finite realm of particular events; in the second part of the sentence the author generalizes over an open set of cases, predicting the applicability of this 'truth' to a range of instances outside the scope of her fiction. The scope of the prediction makes the speech act salient, draws attention to the essentially ethical and authoritarian quality of the voice in control of the narrative. Insofar as the speech act signals the stance of a lofty sage, it may be experienced as alienating, particularly within the context of the more modest claims of narrative report. George Eliot has several ways of coping with this danger. Although her generalizations often sound proverbial, she avoids the stark canonical form of the generic sentence, rarely saying things like 'All men are mortal'. Instead she couches her generalizations in a great variety of syntactic constructions, usually of some complexity, drawing the reader into the constructive syntactic process of formulating the generalizations. Just as proverbs convey folk-wisdom, George Eliot's generalizations suggest that they are the reader's wisdom as well as the author's. She insinuates the continuity of her own, her readers' and her characters' experience through generalizations attached to the first-person plural pronoun 'we': 'Our good . . .' 'Do we not . . .' First and second person pronouns are, of course, a very direct realization of the interpersonal function of language, strong indicators of the structure of discourse. Here the strategy of the discourse, through these pronouns and other means, is to build a community of sympathy, to implicate the reader in the author's judgements.

Pronouns are extremely significant in the discourse of my last example, W.H. Auden's poem 'A Communist to Others'.

> Comrades who when the sirens roar
> From office shop and factory pour
>   'Neath evening sky;
> By cops directed to the fug
> Of talkie-houses for a drug
> Or down canals to find a hug
>   Until you die:
>
> We know, remember, what it is
> That keeps you celebrating this
>   Sad ceremonial;
> We know the terrifying brink
> From which in dreams you nightly shrink
> 'I shall be sacked without,' you think,
>   'A testimonial.'
>
> We cannot put on airs with you
> The fears that hurt you hurt us too
>   Only we say
> That like all nightmares these are fake
> If you would help us we could make
> Our eyes to open, and awake
>   Shall find night day.
>
> On you our interests are set
> Your sorrow we shall not forget
>   While we consider
> Those who in every country town
> For centuries have done you brown,
> But you shall see them tumble down
>   Both horse and rider.

O splendid person, you who stand
In spotless flannels or with hand
    Expert on trigger;
Whose lovely hair and shapely limb
Year after year are kept in trim
Till buffers envy as you swim
    Your Grecian figure:

You're thinking us a nasty sight;
Yes, we are poisoned, you are right,
    Not even clean;
We do not know how to behave
We are not beautiful or brave
You would not pick our sort to save
    Your first fifteen.

    . . . .

The worst employer's double dealing
Is better than their mental-healing
    That would assist us.
The world, they tell us, has no flaws
Then is no need to change the laws
We're only not content because
    Jealous of sisters.

    . . . .

Comrades to whom our thoughts return,
Brothers for whom our bowels yearn
    When words are over;
Remember that in each direction
Love outside our own election
Holds us in unseen connection:
    O trust that ever.

(stanzas 1-8, 16, 22)

This was first published in 1933 but later dismissed and disowned by the author along with a few other poems about which he has said 'Mr. W.H. Auden considers these five poems to be trash which he is ashamed to have written'. The poem is quite long, technically confident, maintaining its complex metrical pattern for 22 stanzas. But it suffers from an embarrassing and I think ultimately disabling insecurity of tone. 'Tone' is a crucial consideration in this work, which is an apostrophe to a variety of addressees in different ways involved in the political argument Auden is proclaiming. In a poem about division and solidarity, the lines of sympathy drawn by the language must be clear; and they are not. The title contains an ominous equivocation: does 'other' mean 'other communists' or 'people other than communists'? Is the title divisive or sympathetic? Even if the title is meant to suggest community — 'A Communist to Other Communists' — its binary, dichotomous syntax hints at division. The question is, of course, whether the persona's asserted solidarity with the proletariat is genuine. The discourse of the poem, particularly its pronominal structure, is likely to be a good index to the reliability and strength of the speaker's feelings. The persona of the poem is implicitly singular, an 'I' figure. This must be the case with any speech act except choral singing and dramatic choruses. The singularity is confirmed by the title of this poem. '*A* Communist to Others'. But the persona never speaks directly as an 'I': throughout, he presents himself as a spokesman, consistently and frequently using the pronoun 'we'. Such is the rhetoric of the poem that 'we' is always opposed to a category 'you', but the referent of 'you' shifts as the poem proceeds. 'You' is initially the proletariat; then it is the idle aristocracy, the priest, and a succession of other privileged oppressors. Now the pronoun 'we' has two distinct meanings, 'inclusive we' and 'exclusive we'. The inclusive meaning embraces the speaker and his addressee or addressees, the exclusive meaning opposes the addressee on the one hand and the speaker and some third party on the other. Wherever 'we' is used in a speech act which also contains 'you', then the 'we' must be exclusive, and this is so throughout most of Auden's poem. The pronouns signal opposition rather than solidarity. The exceptions are stanzas 16 and 22. In sixteen, an inclusive 'us' and 'we' is possible through the use of the third person for the party opposed to the 'we'. In the final stanza, the 'our' of line 5 and the 'us' of line 6 are inclusive, appealing to the unity of the poet and the brothers through love. The extreme awkwardness of this conclusion is not due entirely to sentimentality, but to the shift from exclusive to inclusive use of the word 'our' in the last stanza. This shift is accompanied by a *referential* movement: the final 'our' and 'us' refer the poet and the proletariat, the two immediately preceding 'ours' refer to the poet and some unspecified body not the proletariat. The pronouns tell us, in effect, that Auden is not really with the proletariat, and the ending is either optimistic or hypocritical. The seeds of this alienating outcome are in fact present in the opening stanzas. Who are the 'we' of stanzas 2, 3 and 4? This is the exclusive 'we', and Auden is addressing the workers at this stage, so he can't mean them to be included. They are, we must conclude, fellow-communists (other than the workers) or fellow liberals (other than the intellectuals he castigates later in the poem). This unspecified 'we', excluding the workers, hangs over the poem vaguely and patronisingly, so frequently are they invoked. In these circumstances, the meaning of the 'Others' in the title becomes opaque, and, in stanza 6, the exclusive 'we' which can only mean 'the poet and the workers' becomes false and alienating.

So far I have concentrated on those linguistic patterns which are manifest signals of discourse: pronouns, illocutionary devices. Briefly, let me add to these *modals*, which are overt indicators of the speaker's attitude to his material. Just glance at stanza 3 of the Auden poem. The first four lines are confident assertions with only a hint of dubiety in the 'cannot'. The 'we' delivers an eye-opening truth to the 'you': the nightmares are false. The next line, however, produces a conditional putting the 'you' in control: 'if you would . . .' Then in the last line the conditional is ungrammatically completed with the assertive modal 'shall' instead of the hypothetical 'should' or 'would' that is required here. This confusion of modals suggests to me an uncertainty about authority-structure, which if I had time I would go on to investigate in relation to structures of agency and causation in this perplexed stanza.

Finally, I want to illustrate the fact that discourse structure can be inferred from elements of language other than the overtly interpersonal ones. In the Auden poem, the suspect loyalty of the persona is mirrored in an extremely off-putting jarring of stylistic levels. Already in the first stanza there is something uneasy about the language. The proletariat are identified as the workers in offices, shops and factories, and they are assigned a low, slang vocabulary: office, shop, factory, cops, fug, talkie-houses, drug, canals, hug. If this is patronizing, it is doubly so when contained within a metrical frame blatantly parasitic on the formal conventions of the highest of high poetry. The high-literature words ''Neath', 'ceremonial' and 'testimonial' are absurd in this context, more so because the last two are picked out by the artificial form of metrical style. I think the divisive implications of this discord of registers are obvious and need no more comment.

I will sum up very briefly. I have tried to demonstrate the value of analysing texts in a way which differs from the emphasis on objective, formal structure found in received literary education, and which yet stays close to actual regularities of language. A text is treated as a *process*, the communicative interaction of implied speakers and thus of consciousnesses and of communities. So we focus on those features of language — usually suppressed in criticism — which signal the interaction of consciousnesses, the awareness by a speaker of the voice of another. The consequences of this approach, for literary criticism, are very considerable. Literature seen as discourse is inevitably *answerable, responsible*; it cannot be cocooned from an integral and mobile relationship with society by evasive critics' strategies such as 'implied author', 'persona', 'fiction'; or 'stasis', 'objectivity', 'depersonalization', 'tradition'. This is *not* to deny the applicability of such concepts in the analysis of literature, of course; only, to demand that they should not be invoked as compositional principles setting literature aloof from other communicative transactions. They are generally relevant to linguistics and semiotics and social psychology at large. For instance, 'persona' is commonly appealed to in criticism to excuse the 'real author' from making political or ethical judgements (Wimsatt and Beardsley, 1946), yet as Goffman has shown (1969), the construction of a persona is an inevitable strategy (usually not conscious) in the management of one's public and 'private' presentation of 'self'. Similarly with 'fiction': the Crocean tradition of sceptical historiography (Croce, 1941; Carr, 1964), substituting for 'fact' in history the idea of a processing and ideologically dynamic dialectic between present and past, provides a definition of fiction which it is hard not to extend to the process of what is called narrative fiction. As for 'objectivity': *of course* poems have a tangible physical dimension, but so too do all texts — we do not generally say that the surface structure of language is designed to stand in the way of semantic apperception, and if we say this about literature, as Jakobson and the Russian formalists do, we most likely want to preserve literature as an empty routine outside the normal political and sexual commitments of our times. To preserve a mode of discourse resistant to institutional change: counter-revolutionary, if you like. 'Practical criticism' actually devoted to those ends perverts both of the words 'practical' and 'criticism'.

The above polemic is far from original. Originality, if I am justified in claiming it at all, resides in the use of a certain kind of linguistics to explicate the actional dimensions of literature, treating it as accessible and committed just like other forms of discourse: the linguistic of *modality, illocution,* the *interpersonal function.* It happens that, linguistics until recently being a rather conservative and socially negligent institution, these concepts are still in need of technical development. It is pleasant to predict that, if work in this spirit continues, we shall enjoy the mutual enrichment of a linguistic criticism and a critical linguistics.

CHAPTER SIX

The Referential Code and Narrative Authority

Stylistics is emerging from an era of constricting domination by a formalist linguistics, a formalist literary criticism, and a formalist poetics. This paper is intended to assist that emergence by exploring some modal/illocutionary aspects of one type of literary discourse: I examine some linguistic constructions which are of particular importance to 'point of view' in fiction. The main focus is on description of the form and the rhetorical and ideological functions of 'generic sentences,' a category of utterances about which linguists know very little. The use of generics in narrative is discussed in such a way as to throw new light on the problem of the 'intrusive author' in the tradition of bourgeois realist fiction from the eighteenth through the twentieth centuries. The same problem is alluded to in respect of history writing, and both fictional and historical discourses are considered in the broader epistemological context of bias in the interpretation of narrated content. These ideas are referred, speculatively, to the hypothetical structural categories of a suitable text-grammar. The paper assumes a less formal starting point, beginning with an interpretation of the 'referential code' in Roland Barthes's *S/Z*:[1] this 'code' overlaps with some of the discourse phenomena discussed in my paper, but it is treated by Barthes in an allusive and somewhat incoherent way.

Five years after its publication, *S/Z* remains an admirable and often puzzling work. As a piece of writing, it is technically brilliant, this unconventional analysis of Balzac's story *Sarrasine*: the ingenuity of its format and typography, the inventiveness — playfulness even — of its style, are splendid gestures against the monotony and solemnity of most academic writing. However, the style of the book makes interpretation both necessary and difficult. Barthes willfully deprives the mechanisms of *S/Z* of any explicitly announced intellectual context, and to make public sense of them the reader is forced to rewrite the book so as to connect its theses with the metalanguages of appropriate familiar backgrounds of ideas: Proppian narrative analysis and its modern French developments; Barthes's own departure from classical analysis of *récit* in his theory of *indices*; the ur-semiology of Saussure and Barthes's theoretical reorientation of it in *Elements of Semiology*; the applied cultural criticism of his *Mythologies*; the classical French linguistics of syntagm and paradigm, generative linguistics, both for its own anlaysis of language and as providing models for generative poetics and for literary competence; a socio-economic model of a producer-consumer relationship for bourgeois literature. The *travail* of reading-rewriting *S/Z* is a convincing instance of the very reading process that the book celebrates.

In Barthes's model, texts — even limited 'classical' or *lisible* texts — attain a plurality of connotative meanings as the reader applies his appropriate textual competence in the act of reading. *Sarrasine* is shaped as a counterpoint of five 'voices' speaking in five 'codes'. To put it another way, connotations cluster in five areas of meaning. The codes are systems of literary knowledge possessed by the reader, inscribed in the literary community to which he belongs, and realized in the experience of the language of texts. Barthes enumerates them as *hermeneutic, semic, proaïretic* or *actional, referential* or *cultural,* and *symbolic.* The hermeneutic code, 'voix de la Vérité,' concerns all aspects of a text which have to do with 'absolute' truth — riddles, questions, lies, clues real and false. In *Sarrasine* the dominant enigma is the identity of the old man who causes a stir in the *salon* of the Lanty family; the narrative develops and finally solves the riddle. The hermeneutic code is, of course, the primary structuring device in the classical detective novel. The semic code, 'voix de la Personne,' collects attributes of character and setting, e.g., the signs of ostentatious luxury in the Lanty household and the behaviour of its members. (Two or more codes may emerge in one piece of text: the luxury of the house connotes semically and also hermeneutically, since conspicuous consumption raises the question of the source of the wealth.) The actional code is expressed in conventional sequences of narrated events which fall, according to Barthes, into set types: 'murder,' 'promenade,' 'declaration of love,' etc. The cultural or referential code, 'voix de la Science,' covers all citations of traditional, familiar wisdom — for example, artistic allusions and proverbs, vulgar ethnic stereotypes, etc. The symbolic code, finally, mythologizes the meanings coded in other dimensions of the text. For instance, castration is a narrative actuality in *Sarrasine,* the old man being the Italian castrato Zambinella, and castration is also a powerful term in the symbolic systems life: death and human: non-human.

Barthes's analytic method is simple. He divides Balzac's story into 561 syntactically arbitrary linear segments which he calls 'lexies'. They range in length from single words to long sequences of sentences, and their linguistic arbitrariness reflects Barthes's disregard for strictly linguistic or stylistic analysis.[2] Each *lexie* is annotated in turn, according to the types of connotative meaning furnished by the five codes. One code, or all five, or some intermediate number, may express itself in a single *lexie.* The result is a rich and complex commentary, justifying the metaphors of polyphony and stereography which Barthes invokes to depict his mode of analysis.

Unfortunately, the particular codes Barthes proposes are neither empirical nor systematically related. They are unempirical in that they are merely assigned to the *lexies* of *Sarrasine* without formal definition, without announcement of the criteria for assignment, without being tested on any other text, and without any kind of subjection to counter-examples or counter-explanation. The absence of formal criteria makes it extremely difficult to make assignments of codes to new texts or to resolve disputes about Barthes's assignments. Lamentably, Barthes deliberately ignores the best source of empirical criteria, the observable recurrences in linguistic structure which correlate with regularities in codal structure: it is these linguistic cues which I will appeal to in the later, reconstructive, part of this paper.

The lack of system among the codes is particularly worrying in a descriptive mechanism which claims to reflect semiological systematicity. Barthes refuses to order the codes in any hierarchy or system of precedence,[3] although, as Kermode has pointed out, he bestows different valuations on their messages: the linear, horizontal codes (hermeneutic and actional) are associated with the lower form of the novel, the *lisible* or classical, while the symbolic code can redeem the classical novel by mythologizing its vulgar elements, making it more eloquent and freeing it from its time. But the lack of an *evaluative* scale is not the disabling fault of the system, merely an inarticulacy in Barthes's exposition of his Darwinist history of the novel. The real handicap, in a semiological approach which ought to take a linguistic model, is the failure to indicate a logical or 'derivational' order among the codes. This disability might have been avoided if Barthes had not abandoned his hypothesis of 1966:

> postuler un rapport homologique entre la phrase et le discours, dans la mesure où une même organisation formelle règle vraisemblablement tous les systèmes sémiotiques, quelles qu'en soient les substances et les dimensions: le discours serait une grande 'phrase' (dont les unités sauraient être nécessairement des phrases), tout comme la phrase, moyennant certaines spécifications, est un petit 'discours'. (*Communications*, 8, 1966, p.3)

Here he proposes a homologous relationship between the structure of narrative and that of the sentence: 'homologous,' essentially alike through kinship, rather than 'analogous,' similar and perhaps only fortuitously similar. We possess some very sophisticated models for the relationships between components in sentences, and if the codes, *qua* semiological systems, obey the laws of linguistic structure — if texts, as significant cultural artifacts, are sentence-like — then it should be enlightening to apply the mechanisms of linguistic analysis to the structure of texts.[4] Linguistic application to text structure is thus of two kinds. The surface structure of texts is a sequence of sentences (other types of units are possible, as Barthes allows), and linguistic analysis can be applied to them in the ordinary way — this is 'micro' analysis, and I will be using it when I come to scrutinize the forms of expression of the referential code. Texts also need to be discussed in terms of elements other than sentences, for sentences are only the expressive (surface structure) constituents of texts,[5] and there are deep-structure components which are yet to be properly understood. 'Macro' analysis explores the hypothesized homology between these elements and the underlying components of sentences. I take it that Barthes's 'codes' are a contribution to the deep-structure analysis of texts. Relationships between the codes could have been profitably explored by reference to the analytic categories employed for sentences: by, for example, expressing the actional structure as a grammar of predicate-noun relationships, the nouns in different cases, formalizing the 'actantiel' theory of Propp-Bremond-Greimas-Todorov[6] in terms derived from a Fillmorean case-grammar;[7] by submitting the 'semes' which make up the particularity of characters and settings (though drawn from a culture-wide set) to componential analysis as it is applied to the senses of lexical items;[8] by establishing a hierarchy of distinctive features so that the 'symbolic code' can be understood as a higher or more general *level* of semantic content, abstracting thematically from the features of character and setting; by formalizing the transformations, or post-semantic processes, which are responsible for arranging narrative predicates in sequences and for realizing underlying features of content as actual text-sentences. Some of these formalizations have already been explored by others: by Barthes' own colleagues such as Todorov, by text-grammarians such as Van Dijk, and by the new generation of Russian structuralists.[9] The task of formalization is, of course, essential not only in relation to Barthes's codal model but generally for all interested in questions of the abstract structure and the derivation of the narrative text.

Barthes's codes are, on the whole, de-formalized developments of earlier structuralist work on the structure of content, or *histoire*, or — in sentential terms — proposition. One of them, the 'referential code,' seems on the other hand to concern expression, or *discours*, or modality. This is actually a plurality of cultural codes, as Barthes makes clear: he marks as REF those lexies which cite generalizations, cultural stereotypes, those attitudes to human behaviour and values which Balzac's society might have accepted as valid in a number of fields — medicine, psychology, the arts, assumptions about sex and money, etc. According to Jonathan Culler,[10] the sum of these diverse citations of 'common knowledge' forms the foundation for the 'cultural *vraisemblance*' of the work, that element which allows Balzac's readership to accept the story as depiction of a society regulated according to conventions and principles which, however arbitrary, they have institutionalized as the evaluative frames through which they are conscious of their own lives. Now the relativity, or arbitrariness, of a society's presentation of its 'reality' to itself seems beyond question; it seems correct that a particular, partial, social ideology is one of the things which Balzac analyzes out of *Sarrasine*. Beyond that, however, the referential codes have a specific discourse function within the compositional structure of the story: they contribute to our perception of the values and preoccupations of the narrator (and behind him, Balzac) as an individual voice and personality. I am encouraged in this view of REF as part of the presentation of a specific discourse stance — point of view — by the fact that its citations are cast in a consistent stylistic mould, accompanied by recurrences of linguistic structure, especially in the syntax. Because Barthes has dismissed the stylistic facets of this text, he misses those discoursal regularities, as perhaps Culler does. The recurrent constructions in question, and the rhetorical posture they signal, are of considerable historical and esthetic importance in the formal development of the novel in the eighteenth and nineteenth centuries; and they are, more widely, relevant to some other genres of representational writing seen, more widely still, within the framework of an epistemological discussion of the relativity of the transmission of knowledge. Before we discuss these broader issues, however, let us look in some detail at Barthes's analysis of his referential codes; we may begin with the first instance he notes in *Sarrasine*, lexies (2)-(3):

(2) *J'etais plongé dans une de ces rêveries profondes* ... (3) *qui saisissent tout de monde, même un homme frivole, au sein des fêtes les plus tumultueuses* .... La phrase n'est que la transformation de ce qui pourrait être aisément un proverbe: *'A fêtes tumultueuses, rêveries profondes.'* L'énoncé est proféré par une voix collective, anonyme, dont l'origine est la sapience humaine. L'unité est donc issue d'un code gnomique et ce code est l'un des très nombreux codes de savoir ou de sagesse auxquels le texte ne cesse de se référer; on les appellera d'une façon très générale des *codes culturels* (bien qu'à vrai dire tout code soit culturel), ou encore, puisqu'ils permettent au discours de s'appuyer sur une autorité scientifique ou morale, des codes de références (REF. Code gnomique). (*S/Z* , p,25)

Les codes culturels enfin sont les citations d'une science ou d'une sagesse; en relevant ces codes, on se bornera à indiquer le type le savoir (physique, physiologique, médical, psychologique, littéraire, historique, etc.) qui est cité, sans jamais aller jusqu'à construire — ou reconstruire — la culture qu'ils articulent. (p.27).

In lexies (2)-(3) the narrator indicates his situation within the action and simultaneously connects that situation with an experiential observation alleged to be generally valid in the world outside the narrative, thus making the situation accessible to the reader and inviting him to agree with the authority implied in the general claim. The sentence is derived by transformational reordering and fusion of two separate series of deep structure propositions, which might be represented informally thus:

(a) Je me trouvais à quelque fête tumultueuse; j'étais cependant plongé dans une rêverie profonde, quoique je sois homme frivole.
(b) Des rêveries profondes saisissent tout le monde, même un homme frivole, au sein des fêtes les plus tumultueuses.

Only (a) is essential to the setting in motion of the action and to the locating of the narrator within it; (b) is a trivial proverbial sentiment of no actional significance, and its incorporation within the text is a pure feature of discourse. This discourse component does not expand on the nature of the festivities referred to, nor does it provide content or cause for the narrator's reverie. Like an idiosyncrasy of speech, but ideological rather than physiological, this 'reference' begins to characterize the narrator as a *speaker*: sententious, with a penchant for socio-psychological wisdom. It turns out that the narrator is contemplating, cynically, the juxtaposition of the vivacity of the *salon* and the melancholy symbolism of death in the snow-covered garden just outside the window near which he is sitting. He rapidly establishes himself as an ironic observer submitting the people and events of the *fête* to the judgments of a cynic from their own world. The great majority[11] of instances of the working of the cultural codes identified by Barthes in the first few pages of the story serve to construct the universe of values from the viewpoint of which the narrator presents the 'content' of the narrative. In lexie (8), for example,

Les arbres . . . ressemblaient vaguement à des spectres mal enveloppés de
leurs linceuils, image gigantesque de la fameuse *danse des morts.*

The reference to the dance of death lends to the narrator the authority of
someone versed in traditional artistic culture (here claiming distance from the
vulnerable immorality of the Paris socialite); his credentials are similarly stressed
by his many other references to the arts, to historical figures, and to legend: 'le
conte de *la lampe merveilleuse*' (20), Byron (25), Malibran and others (20),
Antinoüs (22), Metternich and Wellington (24), Vespasian (26), Anne Radcliffe
(27), Faust and Robin Hood (53), etc. It is easy to see how these are 'references'
and 'cultural': a certain relevant culture is created (romantic, artistic,
fashionable, privileged, socializing) to be shared by the narrator and his
appropriate reader — a reader for whom these citations have a coherent
significance. They are literally citations — footnote references to a selected world
outside the fiction. The narrative stance created by the invocation of these
cultural codes joins narrator and reader in a compact of knowing superiority.
From this base the narrator can claim general acceptance of the judgments he
makes on the world within the story. Three classes of judgments are densely
footnoted: stereotypes of national psychology; sexual psychology; and the traits of
social groups, particularly Parisian socialites. M. de Lanty is 'sombre comme un
Espagnol' (24); Germans are naive (34); southern women are ravishing (139-40).
Two guests at the *salon* speculate on the Lanty fortune; they belong to 'cette gent
curieuse qui, à Paris, s'occupe exclusivement des *Pourquoi? des Comment? d'où
viennent-ils? Qu'y a-t-il? Qu'a-t-elle fait?*' (15); the inquisitive are also called 'ces
gens qui tiennent à savoir dans quel magasin vous achetez vos candélabres, ou qui
vous demandent le prix du loyer quand votre appartement leur semble beau' (28).
The narrator can hardly mention a woman without generalizing on the attributes
of the sex or of some type of woman. Of Mme. de Lanty: 'Avez-vous jamais
rencontré de ces femmes dont la beauté foundroyante défie les atteintes de l'âge
. . .?' (21); Mme. de Rochefide has 'une de ces figures aussi fraîches que l'est celle
d'un enfant' (59); she knows 'cette craintive curiosité qui pousse les femmes à se
procurer des émotions dangereuses' (73, cf. 96); she silences the narrator with 'cet
air imposant et railleur que toutes les femmes savent si bien prendre quand elles
veulent avoir raison' (106).

In all these, and many similar, instances, the narrator is doing something more
complex than telling us what the people in the story are like; he tells us in such a
way as to display his own authority for their characterizations, and also invites our
complicity by assuming that we share the values he announces. The purpose of the
rhetoric is to create an in-group, an audience (including Mme. de Rochefide) who
are 'in the know,' sharply distinguished from the naive, of whom the archetype is
of course the fatally innocent Sarrasine (cf. *S/Z*, p. 190, 'mourir d'ignorance').
The values of the in-group are worldliness, mature sexuality, hedonism, *savoir-
faire*, scepticism, selfish irony. Through the particular preoccupations of his
references under the cultural codes the narrator 'authorizes' this world-view. In
view of the content of the actional, semic, and hermeneutic codes in this story, the

references to the psychology of women and to national characteristics have special functions: the inexperienced Sarrasine's grasp of the psychology of women is so much less adequate than 'ours' (the narrator's implied norm) that he deludes himself as he tries to make Zambinella's behaviour connote femaleness; and he would have escaped his fatal infatuation altogether had he known what every cultured Frenchman ought to know about the Roman theatre: 'D'où venez-vous? Est-il jamais monté de femmes sur les théâtres de Rome? Et ne savez-vous pas par quelles créatures les rôles de femmes sont remplis dans les Etats du pape?' (468-69). If the narrator's rhetoric has succeeded, we ought to be titillated by the story of Sarrasine but still feel the cruel amusement of superiority. But as participant the narrator has misjudged his discoursal universe, for Mme. de Rochefide rejects him and his values. This rejection is, of course, a trick of Balzac's, a 'sting in the tail,' but the action does justify an observation which Barthes misses. For Barthes it is 'the text,' 'the discourse,' which achieves the accreditation of a world-view through cultural citations; for Culler, it is the ambient society. Now Barthes's 'text' is determinedly impersonal, silent, and uncommitting; hence his slogan: 'dans le texte, seul parle le lecteur' (p. 157). This is true in the sense that the reader recreates the text on the basis of linguistic cues; but what he constructs includes, according to traditional fictional theory, a voice or voices 'in command' of the discourse — various species of narrators, implied authors, and the like. It is important to the nature of the story *Sarrasine* that it is put into the mouth of a participant narrator, one who figures within his own narrative to the extent of a disappointed seduction at least. In this way the narrator can be seen as a dramatized, personalized, rather than passively recording, consciousness. By the same means he can be treated ironically: the unsuccessful seduction indicates the fallibility of the values to which the narrator appeals. The ironist is the implied author, a shadowy Balzac-figure who has at best an ambiguous relationship to the values he ascribes to his narrator — he dissociates himself from his narrator only by a structural trick at the end of the story, failing to make the ironic distance clear in the texture of the language.

It seems that the referential or cultural codes need to be considered in relation to traditional concepts of 'point of view' — rhetorical and ideological stance.[12] The linguistic structures which Barthes labels REF are, as he says, citations of *savoir, science, sapience, sagesse,* but they are partial and motivated citations. He speaks of 'une voix collective, anonyme, dont l'origine est la sapience humaine'. Now it is clear, even from the fragments I have quoted so far, that the citations picked out by Barthes are not timeless truths which all human spirits must and will always acknowledge, but rather the prejudices of a precisely historical culture — filtered through a functional narrator. The stereotypes of female behavior and female sexuality in which the narrator indulges grate against the less patronizing assumptions general to the public consciousness of the 1970s (of course, the liberated dispositions of *our* culture are no more absolute!). The 'voix collective' of the citations is actually either the voice of an individual within the story — the narrator as presented by the implied author — with his own motives of self-interest, or the voice of a temporally and socio-economically restricted culture filtered through the Balzacian consciousness. In which of these frames one chooses to 'locate' the voice will depend on one's interest in analysis: 'participant narrator' finds a locus within a traditional fictional point-of-view system; 'culture' — Culler's emphasis — finds a historical and semiological locus in the process of ideological analysis of linguistic connotations. The two emphases are compatible. In either case, what Barthes has really diagnosed is a set of linguistic forms of expression by which a voice within a text accredits itself by claiming gnomic validity for partial valuations. The next stage of my argument will entail study of the linguistic mechanisms by which this rhetorical sleight-of-hand is accomplished.

There is a sense in which every text continuously provides its own references: the lexical items in the text, by generalization of reference, connect with you experience outside the text. The words *rêveries* and *fêtes* anchor the first sentence of *Sarrasine* to categories of known experience; and so on with all other lexical items, by the same principle. What is special about Barthes's REF is that it is an explicit mode of footnoting which openly sets about restricting the text's connotations for the reader by announcing judgments on the world and inviting the reader's connivance. This is done by means of a characteristic, identifiable set of linguistic structures. The most blatant syntax for this rhetorical process would be absolutely general statement in generic sentence form ('Gentlemen prefer blondes'); the first sentence of *Sarrasine* might have been 'Des rêveries profondes saisissent tout le monde, même un homme frivole, au sein des fêtes les plus tumultueuses.' The rhetoric of *Sarrasine* is somewhat less direct than that, but still relatively overt. Generic sentences, of claimed universal application, are the basis of the technique, but as in the actual first sentence of the story, they are embedded within actional sentences and so removed from the foreground of the language. The typical syntax is a relative clause with a verb in generic present attached to a noun qualified by a demonstrative:

2-3 une de ces rêveries profondes qui saisissent tout le monde . . .
13 ces deux tableaux . . . qui . . . rendent Paris la plus amusante et la plus philosophique . . .
15 cette gent curieuse qui . . . s'occupe exclusivement . . .
21 ces femmes dont la beauté foudroyante défie les atteintes de l'age . . .

This structure is repeated over and over again; expression of the general 'truth' in a full sentence rather than a relative is very rare (see the fourth and fifth sentences in lexie 26, and cf. 83 and 348). If embedding by relativization, with attachment to an *NP* containing a form of *ce*, is the foregrounded superficial syntax, the semantic or illocutionary centre is the modal of the predicate — generic present tense, contrasting regularly with the past definite and with the imperfect.[13] The verb form permits the reader to interpret the *ce* paradigm as generic in this context, contrasting with the particularizing demonstrative *ce*. The following sentence from lexie (20), part of the characterization of Marianina, mixes generic and particular meanings of *ce*; I have italicized the generics:

Cette fille était le type même de *cette* poésie secrète, lien commun de tous les arts, et qui fuit toujours *ceux* qui la cherchent.

As in English, the French articles and demonstratives can both be used to make either particular or universal reference, and the preferred form here is *ce*, corresponding to English *that/those*, and by its association with generic modality on verbs, coming to mean something like 'that well-known type of. . . .' The meaning may be thought of in terms of presuppositions: the particularizing *ce* presupposes a sentence in the preceding co-text mentioning the individual referred to by the head-noun ('Qui n'aurait épousé Marianina, jeune fille de seize ans . . .') whereas the generic presupposes an unspecified class of sentences in the *context* applying the predicate to other nouns ('X s'occupe exclusivement . . .' 'Y s'occupe exclusivement . . .' etc.). The generalizing claims are often reinforced by universalizing quantifiers (*tout*, cf. 20), noun phrases (*tout le monde*, 3), and adverbs (*toujours*, 20). In this text, the head-noun to which the relativized generic sentences are attached is very often a taxonomic word: *type* (20), *sorte* (21), *gens* (28), *espèce* (33). This combination of taxonomic nouns and generic modality stresses the appeal to an allegedly established categorical analysis of society, and is interestingly consonant with, perhaps symptomatic of, Balzac's goal of setting down through his fiction a typology of human species in society analogous with biological classifications of the animal kingdom.[14] (The appropriateness of the narrator's syntax to Balzac's world-view is in my opinion a major piece of evidence for the thinness of the irony.)

A second linguistic form associated with REF is simile: 'sombre comme un Espagnol' (24), 'ce génie familier . . . apparaissait au milieu des salons comme ces fées d'autrefois qui descendaient de leurs dragons volants . . .' (44), cf. (57), (66), (73), (82), etc. Simile requires belief in general propositions implied in the vehicle (the right-hand side of the comparison) — the habits of Spaniards and dragons, etc. Often a generic assertion can be transformed out of a simile just as it can from the relativized forms discussed above: 'Les Espagnols sont sombres.' Though simile is a syntactically recognizable mode of expression, it is an oblique or disguised manner of philosophizing, since the requisite transformation allows deletion of the giveaway generic present. A rather clever indirection of a different type is the offering of straightforward statements which appear to be actional but which will transform into generic propositions by minute adjustment. When the narrator says (34)

il se rencontrait çà et là des Allemands qui prenaient pour des réalités ces railleries ingénieuses de la médisance parisienne

we may take a contextual hint (as it happens, there aren't any Germans in this story) that the sentence should be read us

Les Allemands prennent pour des réalités les railleries ingénieuses de la médisance parisienne.

This, like the relativized forms, is a sort of attitudinal name-dropping, one more prejudice against another out-group to add to the system of valuations the narrator asks us to build up. *Literal* name-dropping is a further mechanism for activating REF: the significant mentioning of proper names from outside the cast-list of the fiction — historical, literary, artistic, and legendary figures suggesting the repertoire of socio-cultural templates with which the narrator wants his own and the reader's stock of valuations to be matched. The opening pages of *Sarrasine* are packed with such references.

So the narrator, with the pretence that his partial values are universal, seeks to get them accepted by his readers by presenting them as familiar and unexceptional: syntax suggests that the reader can regularly supply presupposed sentences out of his own experience. In view of this reader-oriented function, it is not surprising that what Halliday calls the 'interpersonal' function of language, Jakobson the 'conative,'[15] is prominently foregrounded in the narrator's rhetoric. While it fulfills the purpose of conveying information in the form of propositions, making reference to the world outside of itself, language simultaneously functions to establish or maintain the parties to a communicative event in an appropriate relationship. Certain linguistic constructions — questions, commands, first- and second-person pronouns — are especially influential in controlling relationships between interlocutors. In *Sarrasine* the pronouns *nous* and *vous* are used to suggest community of experience and attitudes between narrator and reader at places where questions of value are implied by the citation of a cultural code. *Nous* is the 'inclusive *we*,' assuming that the reader habitually concurs with a judgment; *vous* is a personalizing version of *on*, meaning 'everyone, including specifically the person addressed.' Here are some examples:

13 un de ces vents coulis qui vous gèlent une moitié du corps . . .

21 Avez-vous jamais rencontré de ces femmes . . .? Et voilà pourquoi peut-être les aimons-nous si passionément!

26 Pourvu que la haute société sache le chiffre de votre fortune, vous êtes classé parmi les sommes qui vous sont égales, et personne ne vous demande à voir vos parchemins . . .

83 Quelques vieillards nous présentent souvent des portraits plus hideux . . .

The above examples are found in the opening section of the story, preceding the inner narrative addressed specifically to Mme de Rochefide. The narrator seems to be personalizing an antecedently anonymous readership — creating an implied reader. The discourse, far from being the cold silent structure which Barthes's a-stylistic approach alleges, contains, on examination of the evidence of Barthes's own analysis, a distinct and moderately complex rhetorical act. The narrator of the story of Sarrasine attempts to construct a community of readers sharing a *Weltanschauung* which will find the moral force (a particular sexual cynicism) of Sarrasine's story agreeable. The rhetoric can be traced in the linguistic regularities which I began to analyze — generic propositions transformed as distinctive surface structures, mingled with certain 'interpersonal' usages designed to implicate the reader, to suggest that the ideal reader is likely to sympathize with the narrator's prejudices. Scrutiny of the type of transformation to which the generic sentences have been treated seems to indicate a further rhetorical dimension: Balzac is perhaps closer to the position of his narrator than his superficial irony might imply. So in this aspect of the discourse structure of *Sarrasine* there seems to be, in addition to the plurality of Barthes's codes, a rhetorical polyphony of at least three voices: Balzac or his second self, the narrator, and the implied reader.

Where do these observations lead? Barthes's code REF in itself is useless as an analytic instrument because of the lack of formalization, the neglect of stylistic patterns, and the refusal to claim generalizability or transferability mentioned earlier. We must abandon REF and attempt to establish instead the status of the phenomena I have extrapolated out of it. Constraints of space, and the incomplete development of the relevant disciplines, force me to be sketchily programmatic in the following remarks, but at least three fairly elementary comments which might be developed come to mind: (1) we are examining a cluster of linguistic regularities, occurring in only some of the sentences of a text and describable within the boundaries of each single sentence, at deep and at surface levels; (2) these constructions seem to contribute to a consistent rhetorical function — a relationship between implied author, narrator, and implied reader — which would be discussed under 'point of view' in literary criticism; (3) this 'point of view' must have a theoretical correspondent in a formal account of text-structure (a formal text-grammar).

It is not my intention now to articulate, let alone substantiate, a hypothesis concerning the third observation; only some brief comments can be indulged. In a sentence-grammar a basic distinction is made between *proposition* and *modality* as the two constitutive elements of the semantic (deep) structure of a sentence. Proposition is, roughly, 'content' or cognitive meaning: a reference to some phenomenon in the world outside of language, e.g., an agent performing an action or an object undergoing a process. Linguists usually analyze the proposition into two components, a *predicate* on the one hand and a *noun* or nouns on the other. Thus we could say about the propositional structure of the sentence 'Did Bob throw the ball?' that it is based on the action predicate *throw* accompanied by the agent noun *Bob* and the object noun *ball*; 'agent' and 'object' are *cases*, semantic roles. This accounts for only one dimension of the meaning of the sentence. It is also a question, and 'question' is a different kind of meaning; also, it is in *past tense*; it is *active*; it characterizes the action as *momentary* or *single*. Such aspects of meaning are subsumed under the modality component. The definition and the analysis of this component are quite problematical in both linguistics and logic. Crudely speaking, modality covers all aspects of the speaker's stance in 'situating' himself in relation to the proposition and its communicative context: temporally vis-à-vis the time of the speech act and the time of the described event; in terms of belief commitment (the speaker here claims to have no knowledge of the factuality of the event); in relation to the interlocutor or reader or audience — the speaker's utterance presupposes prior knowledge of the identity of the ball and of Bob in both himself and his addressee. These 'orienting' aspects of the speech act are as yet poorly understood; there are still major theoretical issues to be worked out; for example, whether we should distinguish a separate category 'performative'[16] from 'modal' — should we distinguish a speaker's action (here perhaps 'threatening' rather than 'questioning') from his orientation on the proposition, distinguish it to the extent of admitting a separate performative element in the semantic base of the sentence?[17] The resolution of such problems is of very considerable importance to the area of text-grammar on which this study focuses, for it is fairly clear that if we are to apply the structural categories of sentences to texts, on the basic semiotic premise of sentence-text homology, then such concepts as 'point of view' and *discours* must be elucidated by the notion of modality.

If the theory of modality in sentence-linguistics were fully worked out, we could appeal to it as a source of clarification for the theory of modality generally in texts — point of view in fictional esthetics. A more modest procedure is called for. Generic sentences and their transforms are clearly one important set of constructions among a number of types of structure which are particularly significant for point of view, and we can begin to assemble a list of such constructions. In starting this list we will be assisted by what we already know about the expression of modality and performatives in the sentence, even if we do not fully understand the deep structure categories involved: we can focus on modal verbs such as *may* and *might*; modal adverbs such as *probably*, *certainly*; personal pronouns; deictics; verbs of external conjecture (*seem*); verbs of intimate knowledge (*feel*), etc. Point-of-view theory in literary criticism may help us notice relevant linguistic structures, but not without interpretations: classic books in the Anglo-American Jamesian tradition make little reference to actual linguistic structures, although works in the more empirical Russian tradition do.[18] This necessary act of interpretation must juxtapose text-modality, point of view, and sentence linguistics, putting them in what it is hoped will be a reciprocally illuminating dialogue.

Before re-examining generics in this spirit, I shall digress to a broader epistemological context, and a different class of texts, in order to suggest that the phenomena we are considering have much wider philosophical and linguistic significance than has been indicated so far.

The distinction between proposition and modality in texts is cognate with, or on a stronger argument the source of, a whole series of dualisms in epistemology, perceptual psychology, communications theory, esthetics, the philosophy of science, and related disciplines: object and subject, fact and interpretation, *signifié* and *signifiant*, content and form or expression, subject-matter and composition, stimulus and schema, phenomenon and observation, etc. To proliferate the terms induces confusion, so I will narrow the discussion to two fields where the respective versions of this dichotomy are a necessary preoccupation and in both of which *text*, and *the activities of writing and reading*, are central factors: historiography and the theory of point of view in fiction (or one part of the latter: authorial judgment and interpretation in narrative discourse). My intention is to suggest that modal aspects of narrative texts can be profitably studied, in a powerful communicative and epistemological context, via the analysis of some specially significant linguistic structure, and that the applicability of the approach in both history and fiction adds to the power of the theory. It seems to me that the issues transcend, and are not dependent upon, the esthetics of fiction. My discussion will tend to suggest, but not attempt to prove, that 'history' and 'fiction' are both corpora of narrative writings to which the same principles of textual structure apply, though they occupy different positions in traditional Western culture and enjoy different valuations and study perspectives. In this paper I will stay with the English versions of the constructions found significant in Barthes's version of *Sarrasine*. In subsequent work I hope to investigate this integrative hypothesis by exploring a wider range of syntactic and modal structures in different narrative genres.

Nowadays a sceptical, relativistic view of history writing is encouraged. In concurrence with the revolt against empiricism in science generally, and in implicit particular agreement with the hypothesis of perceptual psychology that perception depends not on objective properties of the perceived but on schemata internalized by the perceiver, historians reject the idea of history as conclusions from objective facts, and stress the editorial, selective, interpretative role of the writer of history. In this century an articulate tradition of sceptical historiography has grown up, its formative spokesmen being Croce, Collingwood, and (ambiguously) Butterfield, and its most influential and lucid popularizer E.H. Carr.[19] Carr's warm account of this tradition in his book *What is History?* is well known and easily accessible, and its terms are quite suggestive for the study of narrative discourse; so I will refer to this exposition. He begins by claiming that 'the belief in a hard core of historical facts existing objectively and independently of the interpretation of the historian is a preposterous fallacy' (p.12). Facts are made historical by the historian, who chooses to make them significant. He quotes Barraclough: 'The history we read .... is ... a series of accepted judgements' (p.14). These are not to be seen as personal, deliberately individual, judgments; the historian interprets his materials according to his situation as a man living in a society at a particular time (different from that of his subject matter) and within a particular scheme of values (again, different from those of the culture he writes about, but inevitably used to interpret that culture). 'History consists essentially in seeing the past through the eyes of the present and in the light of its problems' (p.21, paraphrasing Croce). So the reader of history must be aware of the circumstances of writing which gave rise to the 'interpretation' in the writing (the date and place of publication as well as the author's name, p.42 — and presumably all that that broadening of context implies); and the reader of history written at a time culturally distanced from the time of reading will learn as much about the culture which produced the historical account as about the period chronicled: 'Grote's *History of Greece* has quite as much to tell us today about the thought of the English philosophical radicals of the 1840s as about Athenian democracy of the fifth century B.C.' (p.37).

Various responses to this analysis of the situation of history writing are possible.

The history teacher may encourage his students to read Carr, and interpret the book as a dire warning to be on one's guard against 'bias' in the writings of historians ('Whigs' and 'Marxists' are notorious bogey-men). This is either sensible advice or a misunderstanding of the thesis — the latter if it is believed that objective history can actually be filtered out of the cloudy distortions of its interpreters and that this filtration is the proper hygiene in the reading of history. Next, there is a defeatist scepticism which complains that history cannot be written if the past is continuously subject to revision. Finally, historians who intend to go on writing welcome the dynamism of this dialogue between present and past, the educative function of seeing one's own ideology relating to that of other minds situated in other cultures.

All this is commonplace in modern historiography and is discussed with much greater sophistication than my brief summary has managed. I mention these standard arguments for two reasons. First, they can be illuminated by linguistic theory and analysis. Second, these views about the rhetorical and ideological intervention of the writer of history intersect interestingly with some arguments of the nineteenth and twentieth centuries concerning point of view and the responsibilities of the author in narrative fiction. The question of 'narrative authority' or 'author's intervention' is common to both sets of arguments, and in both historical and literary texts we should be able to study this manifestation through language structure as we did the world-view of the narrator in *Sarrasine* and its relation to Balzac's world-view.

I mentioned that the thesis of relativity of historical judgment might be illuminated by linguistics. In fact, *it is strictly speaking a linguistic theory*. When Carr talks about the relation between 'facts' and 'interpretation' (e.g., p.29), arguing that facts become history only through the mediation of interpretation, it is natural to remark that, if history is a kind of text or discourse, the theory can be expressed in text-grammatical terms: propositions (facts) cannot be communicated without modality (interpretation). As there is no sentence which does not imply a speaker taking a certain stance, so there is no text in which the content has not been filtered by an author who has selected and expressed the propositions and so set himself in a certain belief posture towards them. Interestingly, at a crucial point in his argument Carr claims that interpretation happens, or is formed, during the actual process of writing: see pp. 28-29, including, e.g., 'The reading [of sources] is guided and directed and made fruitful by the writing: the more I write, the more I know what I am looking for, the better I understand the significance and relevance of what I find.' The use of his language determines his perspective on his material, the construction he puts on it, even his construction *of* it. And using language commits the historian to a valuation posture derived mainly from his location in the cultural system of his speech-community, if (as has often been claimed) a distinct world-view reposes in the language of a community. Writing or speaking, one perforce uses a medium shaped more by the community than by oneself; one is not entirely in control, but performs according to the conventions of the culture which are shaped in the language — the 'codes' which bind linguistic communities together and which are built into their structure of discourse.[20] (When I speak of 'communities' here I mean less than the whole set of speakers of a given natural language: ideologically and thus linguistically defined sub-communities, so that there can be radical and conservative historians, for example.) I assume that this process whereby one inevitably expresses oneself and one's values (as an individual and as a member of a social and ideological group) in the act of discourse, as well as communicating content or propositions, must be common to all acts of linguistic performance in speech or writing, whatever goal they may be directed toward. It was obviously essential for historians to recognize clearly and to acknowledge openly the influence of this process on the practice of their discipline. Critics of fiction have also discussed the issue, independently and somewhat differently.

'Point of view' theory in criticism is concerned with relationships among three or four parties to the communicative act which is mediated by a narrative text: (1) the implied author, (2) the narrator, (3) the characters, and (4) the implied reader. The different relationships in this network of fictional voices can all be discussed in terms of distance, irony, status, community, or solidarity (cf. the common parameters for interpersonal relationships in sociolinguistics), these relationships being supported by empirical study of conventional aspects of the language of novels and groups of novels. In the last hundred years there has been an immense amount of refined speculation on the esthetics of these rhetorical relationships, but a dearth of empirical work on the linguistic structures which control them — to cite a spectacular example, Percy Lubbock's enormously influential *The Craft of Fiction* (1921), which talks endlessly of craft, shape, design, and technique, contains no analysis of language and does not even quote more than half a dozen fragmentary phrases from the whole set of great novels discussed. It is only by systematic linguistic analysis that these relationships, and the various compositional theories they are called on to support, can be evaluated.

It happens that the constructions which I extracted from the 'referential code' — generic sentences and interpersonal constructions — provide an entry into one of the most important and controversial aspects of point of view: the degree of 'presence,' and the authority, of the implied author or narrator as a source of judgments on the content of a novel. The interpersonal, pronominal usages suggest a community relationship between implied author and reader and foreground the presence of both, making explicit a primary rhetorical relationship; the generics are a vehicle for author's or narrator's evaluations. Together, these linguistic features contribute to the rhetoric of a whole tradition of authors who were until recently condemned as 'intrusive,' 'unobjective,' or 'undramatic' in the received dogma of the English, European, and American 'realistic' novel. Henry Fielding, with his essayistic digressions and his appeals to the reader, became the villain of this style of writing quite early in the nineteenth century; comments made by Sir Walter Scott in 1827 foreshadow the growth of a severe esthetic later in the century which could not tolerate his sort of too-visible and too-demanding presence:

. . . Fielding pauses to explain the principles of his art, and to congratulate himself and his readers on the felicity with which he conducts his narrative, or makes his characters evolve themselves in its progress. These appeals to the reader's judgement, admirable as they are, have sometimes the fault of being diffuse, and always to the great disadvantage, that they remind us we are perusing a work of fiction; and that the beings with whom we have been conversant during the perusal, are but a sort of evanescent phantoms, conjured up by a magician for our own amusement.[21]

The doctrine which condemned Fielding (and later Thackeray and Trollope) is a demand for 'objectivity,' 'impersonality,' 'authorial silence'; in the later nineteenth and earlier twentieth centuries the authority most cited for this esthetic program was Flaubert, particularly some remarks in his correspondence:

One mustn't bring one's own personality on to the scene. I believe that great Art is scientific and impersonal.

It is one of my principles that one must not write oneself into one's work. The artist must be in his work as God is in creation, invisible yet all-powerful; we must sense him everywhere but never see him.[22]

James Joyce allows Stephen Dedalus to paraphrase the latter formulation in a famous passage in *A Portrait of the Artist as a Young Man*,[23] and it is thought that Joyce tried to hold to the principle in his own early work. Conrad, Ford Madox Ford, and Henry James argue the necessity of impersonality, and attempt to put the aim into practice. The *Portrait* shows a clear reduction in authorial judgment compared with its early version, *Stephen Hero*. Conrad shifted the responsibility of narration to a first-person narrator. James wrote in the third person, but went through the most intricate stylistic contortions to give the impression that the world of the novel was being presented and judged by the consciousness of one of the participants. Hemingway's technique (restriction of the range of modals and adverbs in the implied author's or narrator's voice) is different again. These various stylistic practices proliferated in popularity and ingenuity as the theory which accompanied them spread outward from the esthetics of high literature to be accepted as the working principles of any narrative writing — even, as Booth has shown, being taken up as dogma in commercial handbooks on hack fiction writing. Lubbock's *The Craft of Fiction* established the value-terms which became commonplace when people spoke with approval of the 'objective,' 'impersonal' mode of writing: presentation must be *dramatic*; the characters and events must be placed before us like actors on a stage, without authorial commentary. The author must *show* the world of his novel, he must not *tell* us about it. In the words of that classic vulgarism, the world of fiction must be shown 'like it IS,' without the intervention of the author's eye. The analogy with drama is dubious (the author hardly ever appears on the stage, but doesn't he have other ways of manifesting himself?) but the intention is clear: all discursive, evaluative elements associated with the author's point of view must be banished. It is a plea for propositions without modality, content without interpretation.

To someone standing outside this system of esthetic goals and techniques, two thoughts occur. First, assuming that this program were achievable, it seems likely that those writers who tried hardest to efface themselves would be successful in inverse proportion to the intensity of their stylistic efforts. Witness James and Hemingway:[24] the styles employed to deflect attention from the author are so saturated with consistent syntactic restriction (very different for each, of course) that, willy-nilly, these are two of the most recognizable writers in English fiction. Second, authorial silence is an unattainable goal in any circumstances. This should already be obvious from my theoretical discussion so far, and the way I have applied it to historiography: there can be no text which is not modalized, which does not imply the presence of a speaker with a determinable set of habits of mind reflected in his style. To rephrase the observation on Hemingway: the posture of effacing oneself as an author is itself an authorial stance. The practical impossibility of authorial silence has been fully argued by Booth in a literary-critical context, and I need report nothing further on the treatment of the issue in literary theory.

The literary-critical discussion of the author's point of view in fiction, although for some part based on false assumptions about what can and cannot be done in language, is of considerable interest to the linguistic investigator of fiction, since it provides a folk typology of modalities in narrative; and the informants who supply this framework are major novelists in our culture, accompanied by their most sensitive commentators. The novelists have worked deliberately toward the various effects afforded within the framework, adopting distinctive linguistic strategies which are a very proper subject for description for those who, like myself, work to close the chasm between text-linguistics and literary criticism. These fiction writers belong to definable linguistic sub-communities, and these sub-communities have their values — world-views — which they convey either with easy authority or slyly, through various transformational disguises. I will conclude this paper with an illustration of the use of just one structure, generic sentences, in 'authorizing' a narrator's or author's values.

My informal account of generic sentences[25] may as well begin with one of the best-known examples in all fiction, the first sentence of Jane Austen's *Pride and Prejudice* (1813):

It is a truth universally acknowledged, that a single man in possession of a good fortune, must be in want of a wife.

Contrast this with the third sentence of the same work:

'My dear Mr. Bennet,' said his lady to him one day, 'have you heard that Netherfield Park is let at last?'

These sentences differ in at least three significant ways. (1) The first is present tense, the second past. (2) The modalities differ: the second relates an individual event, the first claims universal validity for a general assertion. (3) The quantification on the chief nouns differs: Mr. and Mrs. Bennet are identified individuals, whereas 'a single man' can be instantiated by *any* man who is single and wealthy, including individuals unknown to the speaker.

Some syntactically simpler sentences which I would call 'generic' are:

All men are mortal.
The whale is a mammal.
A knife is for cutting.
Adjectives qualify nouns.
Cats eat meat.
Some people are left-handed.
Most gentlemen prefer blondes.

Evidently there are a lot of variables *within* this postulated class of generics, and it is quite difficult to specify the necessary and sufficient common features of the class, or those of its sub-types, with any certainty.[26] Let us look at the three features distinguishing the two sentences from *Pride and Prejudice* pointed to above. First, tense. In English, present tense is the usual medium for generics — understandably, since most of the interesting judgments one would make on the state of the world are interesting to the extent that they apply to one's present situation within it. But present tense doesn't necessarily mean present time. Strawson points out that present tense in general statements may mean a disjunction of different times, or timelessness.[27] Furthermore, present tense is by no means the only way of expressing judgements which are relevant to the present. If generics can refer to time-spheres other than the present (while retaining relevance to the present), it seems probable that the usual morphological markers of time-distinctions may be employed where appropriate, including markers of past tense. We may say 'Mammoths are quadrupeds,' since the zoological classification is still current, or 'Mammoths were quadrupeds,' if we want to stress that the beasts no longer exist. Contrastively, 'The automobile used to have inadequate brakes' presupposes that the automobile, unlike the mammoth, still exists but that the technology of braking has changed. A similar interplay of present and past time-spheres can be observed in such sentences as 'Millions of year ago, we lived in the ocean,' or, from George Eliot's *Felix Holt* (1866),

Why was it, when the birds were singing, when the fields were a garden,
and when we were clasping another little hand just larger than our own,
there was somebody who found it hard to smile?

The transformed generics here attach judgments on the psychology of childhood to a purely notional past — the childhood of 'we' which is an 'empathic' present to be appropriated by the reader to the time-sphere of reading (so that the 'past' of the sentence has now been shifted to a time about a century later than the 'now' of George Eliot's writing). Finally, future generics are possible — 'Women will be free by 1984' — and also temporally ambiguous generics (not the same as timeless): the following could be uttered in either 1975 or 2075: 'If it hadn't been for the energy crisis, we would all have been legless by the year 2000.' Thus, generics need not be present tense, though it is generally possible to relate them to a present time-sphere by tenses on presupposed sentences or by perfect aspect.[28] I will return to tense and generics in fiction below; for the moment, I shall suppose that, although present tense is a feature of surface structures expressing the canonical form of this structure, it is not actually a necessary condition for generics.

The necessary, and perhaps sufficient, conditions relate to comments (2) and (3) above. There is a modal condition: the speaker believes and asserts that the predicate attributes an essential and immutable quality to the subject-noun (within some relevant world): 'Water boils at 100°C (at sea level),' 'A single man with a good fortune needs a wife (in Mrs. Bennet's world).' The qualification on 'belief' will accommodate irony and scientific scepticism. Thus, a generic statement is a particular kind of illocutionary act which we will call, tentatively, *universalization*. This act will be contrasted with others such as *relation, question, command, promise, commentary* — the set of speech acts and their names is not properly established yet. Second, there is a quantificatory condition: the predicate is affirmed to apply to all members of the class designated by the subject, but essentially without specification of the individual members of that class (so that generics predict new instances of their application). Thus a generic is a particular type of propositional act. The following sentences, although they use the predicates to make generalizations, do not belong to our type because they identify the subject specifically and allow no extension of the range of referents of the subject:

(a) John travels by bike.
(b) He is always smiling.

Note that generics contain subject-*NP*s with a range of determiners: *a, the, Ø, all, many, some*, etc.[29] It is particularly important to be aware that universalization can involve an *NP* containing words like *some* and *many* which would be denied universal quantifier status in logic on the grounds that they necessarily circumscribe a sub-set. In (c) 'Many people go to Majorca every year,' the set of 'many people' is less than the set of 'all people,' but it is still an open set, since the membership is not specified; cf.

(d) The Joneses go to Majorca every year.

But (d), and (e) below, add a complication.

(e) The third boy from the right in the first row cheats.

These appear to be comments on the habitual behaviour of specified individuals, not generalizable to other. However, they are ambiguous, because they can be interpreted as universalizations. We might normally assume that the Joneses are the Bill, Sally, and the two kids who live at No 27; but the sentence could mean 'all people called "Jones" . . . . ' And (e) can be rendered generic by the assumption of a universal quantifier '(x)' in the deep structure: 'whoever is sitting there.'

Examples of such ambiguities can easily be multiplied — cf. the important type represented by 'The cat drinks milk' which is triply ambiguous: 'Anything which is a cat drinks milk'; 'Our cat, Fred, is in the habit of drinking milk'; 'The particular cat which I am at the moment looking at and telling you about is in the act of drinking milk.' The first interpretation is generic; the second cannot be, since the subject is an identified particular; the third is a speech act of present-tense commentary on an occurring event, not generalizable even to Fred's future drinking habits, let alone those of anything and everything which is a cat. These ambiguities do not in the least invalidate the concept of generic sentence or universalizing speech act; they derive not from any deficiency in the notion, but simply from a general condition of linguistic structure, the non-isomorphism of expression and content.

When I speak of a class of 'generic sentences' I do not construe it as a class of surface structures, even though there are canonical forms. Properly speaking, it is a type of speech act rather than a type of sentence: the voicing of a generalization with the predicate ascribing a property to all and any of an open set of potential designata of the subject-*NP*.[30] I have called this 'universalization,' but I am not completely satisfied either with the term or with my first tentative definition of it. The awkward term 'universalization' is chosen to avoid 'generalization,' which I suspect should be reserved for a superordinate class of speech acts. Almost certainly one would want to establish a set of distinctions among types of generalization according to their different illocutionary functions and their referential extension,[31] but I cannot undertake that task here.

The study of universalization in narrative has to be integrated with an account of tense; there has already been some theoretical and a little descriptive research into the latter topic, but much more needs to be done.[32] Among the various combinations of generalizing and narrating modalities, three are of especial interest: past tense relation + present tense universalization; past tense relation + past tense universalization; present tense relation (commentary) + present tense universalization. Other combinations are possible; I will discuss only the first two of the above.

The combination of past relation and present universalization is the crucial one with respect to the question of the author's authority, his right to generalize beyond the bounds of the narrative he relates. If we juxtapose examples of the canonical forms of relation and universalization in these tenses, we can see that they convey saliently different speech acts:

St George slew the dragon.
Dragons capture princesses.

Repeated, continuous, use of either form rapidly builds up an illocutionary posture diametrically opposed to that produced by the other:

Another cause of the gaiety and sprightliness of the dwellers in garrets is probably the increase of that vertiginous motion, with which we are carried round by the diurnal revolutions of the earth. The power of agitation upon the spirits is well known; every man has felt his heart lightened in a rapid vehicle, or on a galloping horse; and nothing is plainer than that he who towers to the fifth storey is whirled through more space by every circumrotation, than another that grovels upon the ground-floor. The nations between the tropics are known to be fiery, inconstant, inventive, and fanciful; because, living at the utmost length of the earth's diameter, they are carried about with more swiftness than those whom nature has placed nearer to the poles; and therefore, as it becomes a wise man to struggle with the inconveniences of his country, whenever celerity and acuteness are requisite, we must actuate our languor by taking a few turns around the centre in a garret. (Dr Johnson)

The door of Henry's lunch-room opened and two men came in. They sat down at the counter.

'What's yours?' George asked them.

'I don't know,' one of the men said. 'What do you want to eat, Al?'

'I don't know,' said Al. 'I don't know what I want to eat.'

Outside it was getting dark. The street-light came on outside the window. The two men at the counter read the menu. From the other end of the counter Nick Adams watched them. He had been talking to George when they came in.

'I'll have a roast pork tenderloin with apple sauce and mashed potatoes,' the first man said.

'It isn't ready yet.'

'What the hell do you put it on the card for?'

'That's the dinner,' George explained. 'You can get that at six o'clock.'

George looked at the clock on the wall behind the counter.

'It's five o'clock.'

'The clock says twenty minutes past five,' the second man said.

'It's twenty minutes fast.'

'Oh, to hell with the clock,' the first man said. 'What have you got to eat?'

'I can give you any kind of sandwiches,' George said. 'You can have ham and eggs, bacon and eggs, liver and bacon, or a steak.'

'Give me chicken croquettes with green peas and cream sauce and mashed potatoes.'

'That's the dinner.

'Everything we want's the dinner, eh? That's the way you work it.'

'I can give you ham and eggs, bacon and eggs, liver —' 'I'll take ham and eggs,' the man called Al said. He wore a derby hat and a black overcoat buttoned across the chest. His face was small and white and he had tight lips. He wore a silk muffler and gloves. (Hemingway, *The Killers*)

Choosing these passages, I have exaggerated the contrast, but the contrast itself is not contingent on my choice but inherent in the modal regularities employed by the two writers. Johnson's essay is of course frivolous, but it is offered with the air of a man who believes in the universal application of the propositions he advances. The thesis of the inspiriting effects of rapid circular motion is not justified by any citation of specifics, but simply asserted as being true in a series of general situations; different NPs in the sentences concerned are all quantified to apply to open sets: all dwellers in garrets, every man who has ever been in any rapid vehicle or on any galloping horse. The conclusion is applied to any man who pretends to wisdom, including any reader ('we'). The style is characterized by a strong authorial presence and a strong appeal to the reader: the writer tells the reader that the latter already accepts these preposterous assertions, their validity being 'well known,' 'plain'. Within the canonical forms of the generic sentence the writer employs various devices to emphasize the consistency of his modality and of his universal quantifications on NPs and he involves the reader in his assertions by, on the interpersonal level, regularly using the inclusive sense of the first-person pronoun 'we'.

The Hemingway extract consists entirely of reports of actions and speeches, and descriptions of physical appearances. All verbs which can be attributed to the author are past, finite. There is only one copula, 'was' in the last but one sentence, and the adjectives it introduces are strictly quantitative, physical. All nouns governed by predicates of the author's uttering designate particular individuals — people and things — with no generalization, no reference to open classes. The refusal to generalize is only one of a set of related restrictions on the Hemingway discourse. The author refuses to pass judgment, so there are no evaluative adjectives or adverbs. Modal adverbs like 'probably' cannot appear (as they do in Johnson) because they are direct signals of the author's presence. The same goes for predicates such as 'feel' and 'seem,' which would express, respectively, the author's privileged view of his characters' inner lives and his speculative interpretation of appearances. Any of these linguistic structures — generics, sentence-adverbs, evaluative adjectives, predicates of knowledge or of interpretation — would disturb Hemingway's narrative pose as an uninvolved, unprivileged mere recorder of events. As we have seen, his avoidance of comment is itself a distinct modal stance. How this posture would be transformed by other modal structures can be imagined by inventing some sentences which *might* have been used immediately after the extract:

(a) Gangsters always dress this way.
(b) You know how these gangsters dress.
(c) He was probably very hot.
(d) He seemed nervous.
(e) He felt nervous.
(f) He was repulsive.

All raise questions about the status of the speaker who utters them. Each signals the presence of a discourse participant doing something other than just 'relating': (a), universalizing, gives the reader a general premise from which he can deduce that Al is a gangster; (b)'s interpersonal words appeal for the reader's agreement; (c) speculates on Al's physical sensations but indicates ('probably') that this is speculation — the effect is like that of (d), in which 'seemed' announces a consciousness external to Al's; (e)'s 'felt,' on the other hand, explicitly professes an internal view, a window to Al's consciousness; (f) openly declares a judgment and contributes to the characterization of an implied speaker who would pass such a judgment. These constructions, eschewed by Hemingway in his third-person narratives, are all conventional devices contributing regularly to modal positions in contrasting strands of modern fiction. How they are used, in what combinations and with what rhetorical effects, is a subject for major stylistic description.

Generics form a sensitive area of narrative technique because not only is attention drawn to the presence of the implied speaker who transmits the discourse (any of the structures just illustrated can do that) but also propositions are implied concerning fields of experience outside the content of the discourse. A literary culture which supports the ideals of a Flaubert or a Hemingway is bound to find fault with an author who indulges in explicit universalization on one of several grounds: time-wasting or digression or moral impertinence or pomposity, etc. The practice is both functionally and ideologically vulnerable in an unsympathetic critical atmosphere. Of course, there are valid functional justifications to be argued in particular cases: for example, universalization by generics may be employed in the ironic characterization of a narrator, as in *Sarrasine* or *The Great Gatsby*. It is part of Nick Carraway's make-up that he protects himself by self-righteous citation of the moral aphorisms of a society intolerant of the permissive East. His embarrassed and defensive preamble to his tale constantly props itself up by invocation of generics whose wording verges on the biblical and proverbial:

> In my younger and more vulnerable years my father gave me some advice that I've been turning over in my mind ever since.
>
> 'Whenever you feel like criticizing anyone,' he told me, 'just remember that all the people in this world haven't had all the advantages that you've had.'
>
> He didn't say any more, but we've always been unusually communicative in a reserved way, and I understood that he meant a great deal more than that. In consequence, I'm inclined to reserve all judgments, a habit that has opened up many curious natures to me and also made me the victim of not a few veteran bores. The abnormal mind is quick to detect and attach itself to this quality when it appears in a normal person, and so it came about that in college I was unjustly accused of being a politician, because I was privy to the secret griefs of wild, unknown men. Most of the confidences were unsought — frequently I have feigned sleep, preoccupation, or a hostile levity when I realized by some unmistakable sign that an intimate revelation was quivering on the horizon, for the intimate revelations of young men, or at least the terms in which they express them, are usually plagiaristic and marred by obvious suppressions. Reserving judgments is a matter of infinite hope. I am still a little afraid of missing something if I forget that, as my father snobbishly suggested, and I snobbishly repeat, a sense of the fundamental decencies is parcelled out unequally at birth.

One of the reasons the 'intrusive' author has been found objectionable is the dependence of his discourse on (among other constructions) the present tense generic sentence, a speech act most obviously different from past-tense narrative relation. When the novelist universalizes, he manifestly performs a speech act at odds with his primary act of narration. Now a man who passes a general judgment ventures more than one who merely reports a single fact; and the transition between the two activities confronts the reader with a marked shift of the scope of claimed authority. Whoever says 'Love is a transient emotion' is putting his authority and credibility further at risk than someone who claims only that Amelia Sedley loved George Osborne: he thrusts himself forward as a man claiming more wisdom than pragmatic specific experience would supply. The 'thrusting forward' may be heightened by a foregrounding of interpersonal linguistic structures: questions, exhortations, vocatives ('madam,' 'dear reader'), or first and second person pronouns. Authors in the Fielding tradition combine the assertiveness and argumentativeness of the essayist —

> In return to all these concessions, I desire of the philosophers to grant, that there is in some (I believe in many) human breasts, a kind and benevolent disposition, which is gratified by contributing to the happiness of others. That in this gratification alone, as in friendship, in parental and filial affection, and indeed in general philanthropy, there is a great and exquisite delight. That if we will not call such disposition love, we have no name for it. That though the pleasures arising from such pure love may be heightened and sweetened by the assistance of amorous desires, yet the former can subsist alone, nor are they destroyed by the intervention of the latter. Lastly, that esteem and gratitude are the proper motives to love, as youth and beauty are to desire; and therefore though such desire may naturally cease, when age or sickeness overtake its object, yet these can have no effect on love, nor ever shake or remove from a good mind, that sensation or passion which hath gratitude and esteem for its basis. (*Tom Jones*, Bk. VI, Ch. 1)

— with the intimate jocularity of the familiar:

> We are now, reader, arrived at the last stage of our long journey. As we have therefore travelled together through so many pages, let us behave to one another like fellow-travellers in a stage-coach, who have passed several days in the company of each other; and who, notwithstanding any bickerings or little animosities which may have occurred on the road, generally make all up at last, and mount, for the last time, into their vehicle with chearfulness and good-humour; since, after this one stage, it may possibly happen to us, as it commonly happens to them, never to meet more: (*Tom Jones*, Bk. XVIII, Ch. 1)

The presence of the author-persona, and his dialogic interaction with the implied reader, are a positive feature of the rhetoric. Generics, although common in Fielding and George Eliot, are not essential to this narrative stance; they are less frequent in Thackeray and Trollope, whose intimate strategies to ensure 'that the author and the reader should move along together in full confidence with each other' have thoroughly offended the precious sensibilities of the defenders of artistic purity.[33] Fielding establishes his universalizing, essayistic, but un-serious posture in the introductory chapters of each book of *Tom Jones*. The irony is mild and works agreeably at his own and the reader's expense. There is another personal assertiveness in Fielding which does not spring from generics: the personal presence of the *histor* who dramatizes himself as someone with a life independent of his characters, who has sometimes privileged and sometimes defective knowledge of their actions and motives.[34] The independent life of the Fielding-type narrator asserts itself sometimes by claims or disclaimers concerning the accuracy of his material, sometimes by universalizing interpolations. He is assertive, or apologetic, always present. The persona is so fully dramatized that the reader comes to accept the constant shifts from relation to universalization: both illocutionary modes issue from a thoroughly self-conscious narrator who has established himself as our 'friend' and who indulges in generics with our toleration. We tolerate Fielding as we tolerate the flippancy of the essayist (cf. Johnson) who we know is playing at universalization: even when the essayist pretends seriousness (Sir Thomas Browne, Bacon), we do not actually engage in serious dispute with his generalizations; we grant him the license of one speaking within a conventional, stylized, illocutionary genre. This is tolerance for the mock-serious, a specialized mode of discourse whose voice is strongly determined by generic constructions. This tolerance is not easily extended to the novelist who is determined to be seriously philosophical, whose intention to offer generalizations that matter breaks the tongue-in-cheek contract protecting the Fielding-figure. The clearest and greatest seriously philosophical adaptation of the Fielding stance is found in the novels of George Eliot, who continuously weaves into her past-tense narrative general reflection connecting the experiences of her tragic heroes with the sentiments and fates of mankind in general:

> I share with you this sense of oppressive narrowness; but it is necessary that we should feel it, if we care to understand how it acted on the lives of Tom and Maggie — how it has acted on young natures in many generations, that in the onward tendency of human things have risen above the mental level of the generation before them, to which they have been nevertheless tied by the strongest fibres of their hearts. The suffering, whether of martyr or victim, which belongs to every historical advance of mankind, is represented in this way in every town, and by hundreds of obscure hearths; and we need not shrink from this comparison of small things with great; for does not science tell us that its highest striving is after the ascertainment of a unity which shall bind the smallest things with the greatest? In natural science, I have understood, there is nothing petty to the mind that has a large vision of relations, and to which every single object suggests a vast sum of conditions. It is surely the same with the observation of human life ... (*The Mill on the Floss*, Bk. IV, Ch.1)

George Eliot's intense moral and psychological concern finds constant expression in aphoristic generalizations often making very direct appeal to the reader's concurrence. In her own time this style was readily admired, though the response is vulgarly sentimentalized in such productions as Alexander Main's collection of *Wise, Witty and Tender Sayings Selected from the Works of George Eliot*, which was first published in 1873 and reached its 450-page eighth edition by 1889. There is an interesting study of the cultural history of language to be done, in which the contemporary acceptability of George Eliot's aphorisms would be an important focus. And there is the esthetic, rather than historical, question of the integral contribution of universalizing generics to the quality of George Eliot's narrative discourse. Some critics find the aphorisms incidental or objectionable;[35] others realize that they are an indispensable determinant (with other factors, such as certain characteristic metaphoric usages) of her style.[36] The acceptability of George Eliot's generics to the sympathetic reader is due, I think, to the variety of their transformations away from canonical forms, along with a corresponding variety in the forms of interpersonal appeals and with great metaphoric inventiveness. They are not meant to be passed over quickly, or swallowed whole; the reader is syntactically manipulated into involvement with the formulation of these sayings, which retain something of the ratiocinative and exploratory. Perhaps they are the sort of thing Bacon had in mind when he required that 'knowledge that is delivered as a thread to be spun on, ought to be delivered and intimated, if it were possible, in the same method wherein it was invented.'[37] To demonstrate how the surface structure of the discourse is arranged to sharpen the reader's engagement with the thought would require a lengthy transformational analysis, for which I have no space here.[38]

I promised to say something about one further narrative situation in which generics are of particular interest: past-tense generics within past-tense narration. Without going into detail on the complicated subject of time in narrative, I suggest that the past time of narrative is of two kinds. There is, first, 'immediate past' or 'zero past,' in his experience of which the reader annuls the temporal gap between the time of reading and the time of the related events, experiencing them as occurring in a kind of undated immediate yesterday. If he reflects on technological indices contained in the narrative, the reader may date the events as contemporaneous with Aeneas or Napoleon or Disraeli, and thus distinct from his own experience. But the speech act doesn't encourage him to posit a definite dating. What matters is not the 'pastness' of the events but their 'happenedness,' their vouchsafed actuality. The experienced immediacy of the past may, let it be noted, perfectly well characterize a reader's engagement with some historical novels. But there is, additionally, a narrative past, which we may call the 'historic past,' in which the reader experiences the events related as having occurred in a time-sphere determinately distanced from the present of reading. Markers of temporal contrast (now/then) and the regular citation of a historical chronology are natural devices for distancing the narrated content. The use of past generics is also an important method for creating the illusion of an estranged or superseded past: they can be used to characterize a time of which the values and the practices have been abandoned and replaced by others. Putting a universalization into past tense is an act of radical annulment or veto, a claim that passing time has brought irrevocable change. An assertion about one's own time is implied: ('People used to go to church every Sunday' implies 'People do not now go to church every Sunday'; 'People used to believe in witches' hints 'But that was a false belief'. Speaking in this mode, one simultaneously evokes two time-spheres, each with its own set of values, the earlier eradicated, surpassed, by the qualities of the later. The dialogue between present and past that distinguishes this discourse gives rise to the impression of a disjunction between the depicted events and the time of writing/reading, an impression of an estranged past: 'things are not like that now'. The effect is well illustrated in the opening paragraph of *Silas Marner*, in which George Eliot looks back from the vantage point of 1861 to a period perhaps fifty years earlier. The impression is given of a benighted, superstitious age; and the passage may also be felt to display a tone of patronizing superiority which is a pitfall of this technique:

In the days when the spinning-wheels hummed busily in the farmhouses — and even great ladies, clothed in silk and threadlace, had their toy spinning-wheels of polished oak — there might be seen, in districts far away among the lanes, or deep in the bosom of the hills, certain pallid undersized men, who, by the side of the brawny country-folk, looked like the remnants of a disinherited race. The shepherd's dog barked fiercely when one of these alien-looking men appeared on the upland, dark against the early winter sunset; for what dog likes a figure bent under a heavy bag? — and these pale men rarely stirred abroad without that mysterious burden. The shepherd himself, though he had good reason to believe that the bag held nothing but flaxen thread, was not quite sure that this trade of weaving, indispensable though it was, could be carried on entirely without the help of the Evil One. In that far-off time superstition clung easily round every person or thing that was it all unwonted, or even intermittent and occasional merely, like the visits of the pedlar or the knife-grinder. No one knew where wandering men had their homes or their origin; and how was a man to be explained unless you at least knew somebody who knew his father and mother? To the peasants of old times, the world outside their own direct experience was a region of vagueness and mystery: to their untravelled thought a state of wandering was a conception as dim as the winter life of the swallows that came back with the spring: and even a settler, if he came from distant parts, hardly ever ceased to be viewed with a remnant of distrust, which would have prevented any surprise if a long course of inoffensive conduct on his part had ended in the commission of a crime; especially if he had any reputation for knowledge, or showed any skill in handicraft. All cleverness, whether in the rapid use of that difficult instrument the tongue, or in some other art unfamiliar to villagers, was in itself suspicious: honest folks, born and bred in a visible manner, were mostly not overwise or clever — at least, not beyond such a matter as knowing the signs of the weather; and the process by which rapidity and dexterity of any kind were acquired was so wholly hidden, that they partook of the nature of conjuring. In this way it came to pass that those scattered linen-weavers — emigrants from the town into the country — were to the last regarded as aliens by their rustic neighbours, and usually contracted the eccentric habits which belong to a state of loneliness.[39]

Past generics, and their dangers, are a matter of interest in historical ('non-fictional') narrative. The social or intellectual historian, for example, may employ them to give a generalized impression of a period which he wants to present as a discrete (cf. 'estranged') span of time. But there are two traps into which the technique may lead him. As we have seen, the past generic rather actively implies other general assertions, indicating the values of the present; and, in historical discourse, the qualities of the preceding past as well. The social historian, generalizing about the characteristics of a period anterior to his own, necessarily engages in an interpretation from the standpoint of his own situation within the semiological and ideological matrix of the present. Thus he characterizes himself as well as his material, and stands in danger of 'dating' himself, of giving his account built-in obsolescence. I think that the use of past generics can be analyzed as a direct demonstration of the Crocean thesis that all history is contemporary history. Next, the historian using past generalizations to suggest the individual essence of a period may suggest its separateness not only from his own time but also from the time that preceded it. Insofar as it is virtually impossible to eliminate evaluation form generalization, this implicit juxtaposition of three time-spheres may result in a teleological orientation: 1920 was an improvement on 1900, but still not as good as 1950. ... I can't show this in detail without an exhaustive analysis of a long piece of text, but at least the interplay of three time-spheres may be seen in this extract from a popular social history of the 1930s, published in 1971[40] and, I believe, displaying an implicit consciousness and valuation of the 1920s and the 1960s:

> The vogue for motor-cycles had in fact reached its zenith; the adventurous young men with slicked-back hair and goggles who scorched up the roads on motor-bikes in the twenties had now presumably graduated to the two-seater or small family car. The 'quality car' which had dominated the market in the twenties was now being overtaken so far as numbers were concerned by the small cheap car sold at prices within reach of the less affluent middle class. Thus in 1931 the world-famous Austin Seven was selling at £118, a Morris Minor two-seater at £100. That was the price when new; a second-hand car of sorts could be bought for much less.
>
> Horse-drawn traffic was disappearing fast; yet though some new roads were being built, most were still more suitable for horse-drawn than for motor vehicles. They were badly surfaced, badly lit, narrow and full of sudden blind corners. All the same, motoring had compensations which were never to come again. For you could still 'get away from it all'; unspoilt countryside and unbroken rural solitude seemed just a little way away; the first few who were taking holidays with a caravan on a trailer had no difficulty in finding empty fields to camp in and friendly farmers to supply milk.

The value-scheme is obvious: a love-hate relationship with technological progress, nostalgia for a pastoral golden age now disappeared, support for the lower middle class (in its 'adult' manifestation!). How these values attach to the three time-spheres that are simultaneously held in consciousness could be shown, in a full analysis, by reference to the shifting tenses and time-adverbs that accompany the generics. Perfect aspect, and such collocations as 'was now,' are particularly crucial and interesting.

I don't intend to summarize an already long paper; only to indicate informally some of the directions in which this type of analysis might be developed. My starting point, the incoherent but stimulating *S/Z*, encourages reflection on a number of topics which are excluded from traditional stylistics: the constructive role of the reader; the coded, or generatively conventional, nature of the components of text; the text's reliance on ideological touchstones drawn from a defined culture. One priority for theoretical research is the construction of a formalized text-grammar — Barthes's disinclination to sort out the logical relationships among his components just won't do. Within a text-grammar framework, the discourse or modality component is of particular interest, and nothing is, at present, more mysterious in linguistics or poetics. The linguistic/ rhetorical structures I have concentrated on fall under such a component, but they are only a fraction of the relevant constructions which need detailed study. (Some others happen to be illustrated in (a)-(f), p.117 above.) I speak negatively of 'formalist' approaches in linguistics and in criticism, on both of which my analysis is a definite attack. Linguistics is only just starting to take notice of interpersonal and illocutionary aspects of language and of texts. And criticism operates with the weakest possible notion of text structure, a simple geometry formed out of patterns of surface-structure syntax. Generally speaking, modern dogma in literary theory frowns on interpersonal, expressive, sociological, and kinetic aspects of literature (not to mention referential) and preaches an emasculated 'objectivity'. A disciplined study of text-modality ought to benefit both of these academic subjects. In literary criticism 'point of view' is only one of a range of questions, previously regarded as esthetic, which need to be illuminated by reinterpretation within a general theory of discourse; and 'generic sentences' are only one example chosen from several constructions which need intensive descriptive study as determinants of discoursal structure. In my view, the approach to fiction which would best accommodate this sort of work is not the Jamesian esthetic system, but a dialogic approach such as Bakhtin's which is founded on the idea of a typology of discourses. Here, text is viewed as an act of utterance by a speaker with a determinate and esthetically relevant ideological background. Such an approach has the advantage of not being in principle restricted to 'literary' discourses, and it allows literary critics to break down a false distinction and study the rhetoric of fiction in the context of a theory of discourse structure in any texts. Linguistics, of course, cannot proceed in this kind of work unless it assumes the possibility of including all textual modes within a unified modal/illocutionary theory. (I assume that linguistic-stylistic theories of the arch-formalist Jakobsonian kind, which attempt to set off literature as a special non-referential, non-interpersonal, and non-metalinguistic mode of writing, are nothing but naive contributions to the bouregeois conspiracy to make literature inaccessible to ideological analysis and thus inaccessible to readers outside the traditional cultural elite, and must therefore be rejected. But that is the subject for another paper.)

Notes

1. Roland Barthes, *S/Z* (Paris: Seuil, 1970). English translation by Richard Miller (London: Jonathan Cape, 1975).

2. Elsewhere Barthes denies the validity of traditional notions of style, and specifically disavows interest in stylistic analysis as far as *S/Z* is concerned. See 'Style and its Image,' in Seymour Chatman, ed., *Literary Style, A Symposium* (New York and London: Oxford Univ. Press, 1971), p.5.

3. See 'Deuxième entretien avec Roland Barthes,' in Raymond Bellour, ed., *Le livre des autres* (Paris: Seuil, 1973), pp.247-48. See also Frank Kermode, 'The Use of the Codes,' in Seymour Chatman, ed., *Approaches to Poetics, Selected Papers from the English Institute, 1972* (New York and London: Columbia Univ. Press, 1973), pp.54-55; 'Novel and Narrative,' in John Halperin, ed., *The Theory of the Novel: New Essays* (New York and London: Oxford Univ. Press, 1974), pp.169-70.

4. This procedure is common in contemporary text-grammar, e.g. Teun A. van Dijk, *Some Aspects of Text Grammars* (The Hague: Mouton, 1972), and in French semiology. For a literal and detailed appeal to the analogy of linguistic structure for semiological structure outside language, see Christian Metz, trans. Donna Jean Umiker-Sebeok, *Language and Cinema* (The Hague: Mouton, 1974).

5. 'Constituent' here is not meant to suggest that 'sentence' is a regular rank in an immediate-constituent hierarchy for texts. There is no evidence for this. Cf. W.O. Hendricks, 'On the Notion "Beyond the Sentence",' *Linguistics*, 37 (1968), 12-51.

6. *Communications*, 8 (1966), 'L'analyse structurale du récit,' contains articles by Barthes, Greimas, Bremond, Todorov, and others; Greimas, *Sémantique structurale* (Paris: Larousse, 1966). The source for this approach is Vladimir Propp, *Morphology of the Folktale*, first publ. 1928, trans. Laurence Scott, 2nd ed. (Austin, Texas: Univ. of Texas Press, 1968). For a critique of this tradition of analysis, see Seymour Chatman, 'On the Formalist-Structuralist Theory of Character,' *Journal of Literary Semantics*, 1 (1972), 57-79.

7. C.J. Fillmore, 'The Case for Case,' in Emmon Bach and Robert T. Harms, eds., *Universals in Linguistic Theory* (New York: Holt, Rinehart and Winston, 1968), pp.1-88; cf. Wallace L. Chafe, *Meaning and the Structure of Language* (Chicago: Univ. of Chicago Press, 1970).

8. For componential analysis in semantics, see John Lyons, *Introduction to Theoretical Linguistics* (London: Cambridge Univ. Press, 1968), Ch. 10; Fowler, *Understanding Language* (London: Routledge and Kegan Paul, 1974), Ch. 3.

9. For example, Alexander Zholkovsky and Yuri Scheglov. See L.M. O'Toole, 'Analytic and Synthetic Approaches to Narrative Structure,' in Roger Fowler, ed., *Style and*

Structure in Literature: Essays in the New Stylistics (Oxford: Basil Blackwell, 1975), Ch. 5.

10. Jonathan Culler, *Structuralist Poetics: Structuralism, Linguistics and the Study of Literature* (London: Routledge and Kegan Paul, 1975), pp.141-45.

11. A few suggest a quite different function, e.g. the 'code chronologique' noted in lexies 14 and 20, establishing the temporal frame for the sequence of actions in the proairetic code.

12. Cf. Wayne C. Booth, *The Rhetoric of Fiction* (Chicago: Univ. of Chicago Press, 1961).

13. The former is the classic tense of the actional code, the latter associated with the semic. On past-tense generalizations in English, see pp.121-25.

14. Cf. Erich Auerbach, *Mimesis*, trans. Willard R. Trask (Princeton: Princeton Univ. Press, 1971 rpt.), pp.474-76.

15. M.A.K. Halliday, 'Language Structure and Language Function,' in John Lyons, ed., *New Horizons in Linguistics* (Harmondsworth: Penguin Books, 1970), p.143; Roman Jakobson, 'Linguistics and Poetics,' in T.A. Sebeok, ed., *Style in Language* (Cambridge, Mass.: The M.I.T. Press, 1960), p.355.

16. For performatives and speech act theory see John L. Austin, *How to Do Things with Words* (Oxford: Clarendon Press, 1962); John R. Searle, *Speech Acts* (London: Cambridge Univ. Press, 1969). Richard Ohmann has begun to consider the application of speech act theory in stylistics: see 'Speech, Action and Style,' in Chatman, ed., *Literary Style*, pp.241-54; 'Instrumental Style: Notes on the Theory of Speech as Action,' in Braj B. Kachru and Herbert F.W. Stahlke, *Current Trends in Stylistics* (Edmonton, Alberta: Linguistic Research, Inc., 1972), pp.115-41; 'Literature as Act,' in Chatman, ed., *Approaches to Poetics*, pp.81-107.

17. See Van Dijk; P.A.M., Seuren, *Operators and Nucleus* (London: Cambridge Univ. Press, 1969).

18. See Booth; Henry James, *The Art of the Novel: Critical Prefaces by Henry James*, ed. R.P. Blackmur (New York, 1934); Percy Lubbock, *The Craft of Fiction* (London: Jonathan Cape, 1921, rpt. New York: Viking Press, 1957); Robert Scholes and Robert Kellogg, *The Nature of Narrative* (New York and London: Oxford Univ. Press, 1966), Ch. 7; Mikhail Bakhtin, trans. R.W. Rotsel, *Problems of Dostoevsky's Poetics* (Ann Arbor: Ardis, 1973); V.N. Vološinov, *Marxism and the Philosophy of Language*, trans. Ladislaw Matejka and I.R. Titunik (New York and London: Seminar Press, 1973); Boris Uspensky, *A Poetics of Composition*, trans. Valentina Zavarin and Susan Wittig (Berkeley and Los Angeles: Univ. of California Press, 1973).

19. Benedetto Croce, *History as the Story of Liberty* (London: Allen and Unwin, 1941); R.G. Collingwood, *The Idea of History* (Oxford: Clarendon Press, 1946); Herbert Butterfield, *The Whig Interpretation of History* (London: Bell, 1931); E.H. Carr, *What is History?* (Harmondsworth: Penguin Books, 1964).

20. Cf. Vološinov, Part II, Ch.3 on the fallacy of 'individualistic subjectivism.'

21. Sir Walter Scott, 'Tobias Smollett,' *Lives of the Novelists* (1827), rpt. in Miriam Allott, ed., *Novelists on the Novel* (London: Routledge and Kegan Paul, 1959), pp.269-70.

22. Flaubert, letters of December 1866 and February 1857, rpt. in Allott, p.271.

23. See Harry Levin, ed., *The Essential James Joyce* (London: Jonathan Cape, 1948), p.337.

24. Cf. Scholes and Kellogg, p.270.

25. A much neglected and poorly understood subject in linguistics. Two suggestive recent articles by John M. Lawler are 'Generic to a Fault' and 'Tracking the Generic Toad' in Chicago Linguistic Society, *Papers from the Eighth/Ninth Regional Meeting* (1972/1973), pp.247-58, 320-31. But Lawler's use of 'generic' is different from mine in that he does not impose my quantificatory condition (p.114 above), and concentrates on examples with definite subjects like 'Delmer walks to school,' which I would call 'habitual.'

26. These 'generics' do not form a recognized class in logic; they include all forms (A, E, I, and O) of categorical proposition, and also some relational statements. Cf. P.F. Strawson, *Introduction to Logical Theory* (London: Methuen, 1952, rpt. 1967), pp.152 ff., 202 ff. Only some are, or can be treated as, analytic sentences. Their entailment privileges are different. The two quantifiers provided by the predicate calculus are insufficient to capture sub-types within the set of generics. The correlations between quantification, mood, and tense which distinguish generics from non-generics have not been studied. This is one of those tantalizing areas of argument where the apparatus of logic is quite obviously of great relevance to linguistics but because of its extreme power (a true proposition is materially implied by *any* proposition) cannot cope with discriminations required by the semantics of natural language. Some illuminations are guaranteed by the evident overlap of the interests of linguistics and logic; but these are not systematic.

27. Strawson, pp.150-51.

28. Emmon Bach, 'Nouns and Noun Phrases,' in Bach and Harms, pp.91-122; Zeno Vendler, *Linguistics in Philosophy* (Ithaca: Cornell Univ. Press, 1967). On aspect and 'relevance' to present time, see Roger Fowler, *An Introduction to Transformational Syntax* (London: Routledge and Kegan Paul, 1971), p.68.

29. On quantifiers, determiners, and universalization, see Roger Fowler, 'The Design of Rules for DET,' *Archivum Linguisticum* (1971), pp.129-45. For a general discussion of the syntax of determiners, see Robert P. Stockwell, Paul Schachter, and Barbara Hall Partee, *The Major Syntactic Structures of English* (New York: Holt, Rinehart and Winston, 1973), Ch.3.

30. Anyone who uses the term 'subject' in this way, after the introduction of case-grammar (in which 'subject' is a superficial syntactic category), ought to confess that he does so loosely. I am not clear about the *NP*-predicate-*NP* relationships in such pairs of generics as 'Vandals break windows'/'Windows are broken by vandals,' but one can think of reasons why a speaker should express himself one way rather than the other in a given *textual* context. To propose that notions like 'subject' are superficial in relation to the kinds of meaning accounted for in the Fillmorean classification of nouns and verbs is not inevitably to deny that such structural notions have significance with respect to some other aspect or level of meaning: e.g., in Halliday's 'textual function' — see Halliday, 'Language Structure,' and 'Linguistic Function and Literary Style' in Chatman, ed., *Literary Style*, pp.330-65. The importance of the concept 'subject' is witnessed by persistent discussion by linguists and philosophers; cf. Lyons, *Introduction to Theoretical Linguistics*, pp.334 ff.; Strawson, *Individuals* (London: Methuen, 1959, rpt. 1969), Part II. The problem needs much further study; but I do not think that the present argument is materially threatened by this uncertainty.

31. Strawson, *Introduction to Logical Theory*, pp.195-202.

32. See Käte Hamburger, *Die Logik der Dichtung* (Stuttgart: Klett, 1957, 2nd ed., 1968); Harald Weinrich, *Tempus: besprochene und erzählte Welt* (Stuttgart: Kohlhammer, 1964); W.J.M. Bronzwaer, *Tense in the Novel* (Groningen: Wolters-Noordhoff Publishing, 1970).

33. The quotation is from *Barchester Towers* (1857), rpt. Allott, p.270; Henry James's fatuous horrified response to Trollope's 'terrible crime' of directing asides to the reader is reproduced in Allott, p.272.

34. On the persona of the *histor*, see Scholes and Kellogg, pp.265 ff.

35. W.J. Harvey, *The Art of George Eliot* (London: Chatto and Windus, 1961), p.81; Allott, p.224 ('The modern reader flinches as the ominous phrases appear . . . .').

36. Barbara Hardy, *The Novels of George Eliot* (London: The Athlone Press, 1959), pp.161 ff. A specific study of this particular question is Isobel Armstrong, '"Middlemarch": A Note on George Eliot's "Wisdom",' in Barbara Hardy, ed., *Critical Essays on George Eliot* (London: Routledge and Kegan Paul, 1970), pp.116-32.

37. Francis Bacon, *The Advancement of Learning* (1605), Bk. Two, XVII, 4. Bacon writes about aphorisms in the following paragraphs. The whole discussion, implicitly concerning syntax and thought in argument, is interesting. See the World's Classics edition, rpt. 1956, pp.161-64.

38. Nor is there space for study of the forms and the content of Fielding's generics. The overall tone is mock-serious, but there are many generalizations (e.g., in the dialogically slanted sarcasms directed at 'critics' and 'philosophers') through which Fielding's personal concerns show. It would be interesting to look at, for example, Fielding's many metalinguistic generalizations, assertions of the proper definitions of words, and ironic improper definitions, in the light of his views on the misuse and debasement of language. Relevant context would include his ('Modern Glossary' in the *Covent Garden Journal*, January 14, 1752 (rpt. in Ioan Williams, ed., *The Criticism of Henry Fielding* (London: Routledge and Kegan Paul, 1970), pp.91-93); see also Glenn W. Hatfield, *Henry Fielding and the Language of Irony* (Chicago and London: Univ. of Chicago Press, 1968). I would like to assume that what was suggested about Balzac (p.104 above) is generally the case: that the particular syntax used by an author in universalization is likely to be an indicator of some aspect of his *Weltanschauung*. This is, of course, a particular instance of the general Spitzer thesis of the significance of language structure for author's world-view; but in agreement with Vološinov's critique of Spitzer and 'the Vosslerites,' I maintain that the author's world-view is largely a product of his place in a historically definite semiological and ideological matrix.

39. Note the facility with which present-tense universalizations can be accommodated within this style (second and last sentences), contributing to the establishment and maintenance of a 'modern' philosophizing authorial voice. Also worth careful study is the predominance of definite determiners — 'the spinning-wheels,' 'the shepherd,' etc. Within a single sentence, it is difficult to see why one article rather than another (*a*, *the*, Ø) should be used in a generic *NP*, since they all apparently mean the same, with generics. Here the definite article seems to be used to create a definite, but referentially opaque, context, a setting peopled by individual ideal figures designed to be instantiated shortly by the cast-list of the novel: the inhabitants of Raveloe, Silas Marner, etc.

40. Noreen Branson and Margot Heinemann, *Britain in the Nineteen Thirties* (London: Weidenfeld and Nicolson, 1971, rpt. Panther Books, 1973), pp.261-62.

'The reader' — a linguistic view

In this paper I will make some suggestions about (a) the *qualifications* of readers of literature, and (b) the *activity* of reading. My discussion of (a) touches on questions which have previously been discussed under such headings as 'literary competence,' 'ideal reader,' 'archilecteur,' 'average reader,' 'intersubjectivity' and 'code'. My topic (b) relates to 'affective stylistics': in particular, to the effect on the reader's responses of syntagmatic *sequence* in textual structure, and also to the reader's reconstruction of the behaviour of a *persona* in a poem. I shall suggest that, ultimately, the answers to the problems under (a) and (b) are interlinked, dependent on one overall perspective on the conventionality of the medium through which literature works; that progress in understanding problems in these areas has so far been inhibited by formalist tendencies in literary theory and criticism, but that progress can be facilitated by reference to a sufficiently rich linguistic theory — one with a functional and sociological orientation.

I cannot offer a full theoretical discussion in a brief paper, but will argue on the basis of an exemplary critical analysis.[1] Conveniently, many of the issues with which I am concerned are explored in the well-known writings of Michael Riffaterre.[2] A recent essay in *New Literary History*, 'Interpretation and Descriptive Poetry,' discusses Wordsworth's poem 'Yew-Trees' which I shall take as my text. Riffaterre's ideas about this poem, and his famous reply to Jakobson and Lévi-Strauss's analysis of Baudelaire's 'Les Chats,' provide a valuable and relevant starting-point.

The severity of Riffaterre's attack on Jakobson and Lévi-Strauss should not obscure the fact that Riffaterre accepts Jakobson's basic 'poetic principle'. The poetic function of language involves a 'focus on the message for its own sake' — focus on lexis, surface syntax and phonology — thus 'promoting the palpability of signs,' attenuating the importance of referential or cognitive content.[3] This stress on perceptibility of language structure derives of course from Russian formalist aesthetics, in particular the ideas of Viktor Shklovsky.[4] One of Riffaterre's main complaints against Jakobson and Lévi-Strauss is that their analysis offers constituents 'that cannot possibly be perceived by the reader' and which are therefore not, or not proven to be, 'part of the poetic structure' ('Describing Poetic Structures,' pp. 195, 197). That is to say, Riffaterre accuses the two analysts of, not error of principle, but only misapplication in practice.

There seems to be one substantive difference between Jakobson and Riffaterre which will become a significant issue later in this paper. Jakobsonian analysis takes as its input a complete (short) poem and transforms the whole text into a set of coexistent formal patterns coterminous with the complete poem. For Jakobson, the whole text is stylistically marked, whereas Riffaterre has always assumed that stylistic marking is localized. At certain points in the text there occurs a heightening or thickening of linguistic texture, so that, in accordance with the Shklovskian theory, perception is made difficult and the reader is alerted to the need to search for significance — not by mapping words onto reality but by working out the significance of the relationships of words to words. Examples from Riffaterre's work include the sentence from *Moby Dick* in which unusual patterns at several levels 'converge' to produce a striking stylistic effect: 'And heaved and heaved, still unrestingly heaved the black sea, as if its tides were a conscience'.[5] and lines 16-18 of Wordsworth's 'Yew-Trees' which I will discuss shortly. This theory of poetic structure as a network of stylistically (thus perceptually) salient loci is made explicit in 'Describing Poetic Structures': 'Each point of the text that holds up the superreader is tentatively considered a component of the poetic structure' (p. 204).

'Point' and 'holds up' acknowledge what we might call the 'local' and the 'progressive' aspects of the reader's experience/activity, aspects which are lacking in the Jakobsonian account. The reader's attention moves sequentially, and stops at significant points.[6] I will shortly suggest some other aspects of 'reader's activity' but now wish to consider the other topic, 'reader's qualifications'.

In his 1959 paper, Riffaterre introduces the term 'average reader'; in the 1966 reply to Jakobson and Lévi-Strauss this has been replaced by 'superreader'; the 1971 French translation of the 1959 article substitutes 'archilecteur' to avoid the connotations of mediocrity in 'average' or 'moyen'. In fact, all of these terms are metaphorical. Riffaterre is not modelling any actual or potential reader, but offering a 'tool of analysis' (1966: 203). For any given poem, the average reader or superreader is a collation of recorded responses culled from commentaries, dictionaries, translations, etc.: an index to the sites in the text which have struck the attention of various readers. It is not a lowest common denominator, nor, at the other extreme, a hyper-acute Coleridge or Empson of critics. Riffaterre's reader is 'super' in the same sense as Chomsky's speaker-hearer is 'ideal': an analytic abstraction compressing a collective response into a fictional single language-user. Although, from Chomsky's or Riffaterre's point of view, this may be to materialize the concept excessively, I think it is reasonable to ask: for any given plausible reading for a poem, what knowledge does the reader draw upon in arriving at that reading?

A fashionable answer, but in my opinion an unhelpful one, is that a proper reading depends on the reader's possessing 'literary competence' — the attainment of which is said to be the goal of literary education.[7] The idea of literary competence emerges from a reformulation of. notions of essential 'literariness' in terms borrowed from generative grammar. Jakobson and Todorov have promoted the notion that literary texts are characterized by a specific quality of 'literariness' or 'poeticality'; that the objective of poetics is to define this quality; and that, in pursuing this end, the poetician will study texts not as individual pieces for commentary and interpretation, but only as manifestations of the said 'literariness'.[8] This idealizing, platonic, argument parallels Chomsky's claim that the sentence is of interest only as exhibiting the properties of its language, the language only as being a manifestation of linguistic universals. It will be recalled that Chomsky goes on to maintain that the subject of linguistics is not linguistic structures, but the ability of speakers which makes linguistic communication possible: 'linguistic competence'.[9] Exploiting the analogy offered by this argument, the poeticians claim that their subject-matter is a parallel ability to read literary texts in a special 'literary' way, in response to certain crucial arrangements of language structure.

Jakobson's 'Linguistics and Poetics' is a brilliant attempt to specify these structures and their effects on communication. In his theory, 'The poetic function projects the principle of equivalence from the axis of selection into the axis of combination' (p.358). Language is shaped into sequences packed with parallelisms and antitheses. Phonology and syntax become obtrusive, and the semantic level, heavily stocked with tautologies and contradictions, assumes a counter-rational and counter-referential role. The Jakobsonian reader is discouraged from peering through the linguistic surface at any reality beyond, and discouraged from interesting himself in any historical, sociological or interactional implications of a text. He displays his literary competence by dissociating himself from contextual meaning and looking for intra-linguistic significances. As Riffaterre points out, descriptive poetry offers a strong challenge to this kind of reading since it appears to be founded on reference to pre-existent objects outside language. But 'this postulate is a fallacy . . . [T]he representation of reality is a verbal construct in which meaning is achieved by reference from words to words, not to things' ('Interpretation and Descriptive Poetry,' p.230). Though Wordsworth's poem 'Yew-Trees' refers to some actual trees, and to some historical battles, the reader does not interpret the poem by checking the pictorial accuracy of the descriptions of the trees, nor does he respond to the reference 'Azincour' on the basis of what he knows about the battle of Agincourt. A reading of the poem is based solely on linguistic competence in the Chomskian sense, and the ability to find poetic patterns in the structures the writer constructs out of the materials provided by their shared competence. It does not involve non-linguistic knowledge.

Riffaterre's analysis of lines 16-18 illustrates his approach very clearly. Here, however, is the complete text of the poem:

There is a Yew-tree, pride of Lorton Vale,
Which to this day stands single, in the midst
Of its own darkness, as it stood of yore:
Not loth to furnish weapons for the bands
Of Umfraville or Percy ere they marched   5
To Scotland's heaths; or those that crossed the sea
And drew their sounding bows at Azincour,
Perhaps at earlier Crecy, or Poictiers.

Chapter Seven

Of vast circumference and gloom profound
This solitary Tree! a living thing   10
Produced too slowly ever to decay;
Of form and aspect too magnificent
To be destroyed. But worthier still of note
Are those fraternal Four of Borrowdale,
Joined in one solemn and capacious grove;   15
Huge trunks! and each particular trunk a growth
Of intertwisted fibres serpentine
Up-coiling, and inveterately convolved;
Not uninformed with Phantasy, and looks
That threaten the profane; — a pillared shade,   20
Upon whose grassless floor of red-brown hue,
By sheddings from the pining umbrage tinged
Perennially — beneath whose sable roof
Of boughs, as if for festal purpose, decked
With unrejoicing berries — ghostly Shapes   25
May meet at noontide; Fear and trembling Hope,
Silence and Foresight; Death the Skeleton
And Time the Shadow; — there to celebrate,
As in a natural temple scattered o'er
With altars undisturbed of mossy stone,   30
United worship; or in mute repose
To lie, and listen to the mountain flood
Murmuring from Glaramara's inmost caves.

Lines 16-18 constitute, on the face of it, a depiction of the texture of the bark of the trees. For Riffaterre, however, the main feature is not visual precision but linguistic pleonasm:

> But what actually happens in this sentence is that adjectives and participles all spring from one word. They do seem to progress, as a description should, from feature to feature of the trunk. But being synonyms, they actually repeat the same meaning through modulation from code to code. First we have a wood code, or living-matter code, represented by 'intertwisted fibres' (17). 'Intertwisted' not so much adds to 'fibre' as it activates and singles out the most important feature in the semantic complex of 'fibre'. That is to say, 'fibre' as part of an organic, living fabric, 'fibre' as a component incapable of independent existence (except under autopsy), tied to other fibres by something that is not mere contiguity or mere mechanical function, for that would be mineral or metallic or artificial. 'Fibre' as bound to other fibres by links complex enough, and labyrinthine enough, to become a kind of image within an image of the complexity of life. Hence 'intertwisted.' But then 'serpentine' takes up 'intertwisted' by a variation or transformation into 'snake code.' All the more effective because many stereotypes do describe vegetable life in terms of slow, crawling progress, like vines creeping up tree

trunks or walls — that is, reptilian terms. 'Up-coiling' (18) confirms the snake code, but brings it back to the verticality characteristic of vegetable life; and this confirms also the image of the tree as a striving upwards through centuries. 'Inveterately convolved' summarizes what precedes.

Now, all these details are but a grammatical expansion of the meaning of the word 'growth' (16), which is in itself only a generalization of 'trunk' . . . . (234-5)

Synonymous selections from a few lexical sets are spread out along the horizontal syntagm, producing through tautology a hyperbolic assertion of the symbolic value which Wordsworth requires us to attach to the language. For Riffaterre's interpretation of this significance, see p. 237: 'a hymn to . . . Vegetable Life,' etc. I am not concerned to question the substance of this particular interpretation, only to point out what the *method* excludes.

Riffaterre assumes that the poetically competent reader comes to the poem equipped with two, possibly three, aids. First, his basic linguistic competence with the restrictions placed upon that by the formal grammarian: specifically, linguistic competence is regarded as syntax, lexis and phonology to the exclusion of all such dimensions of linguistic variation as are junked by Chomsky into the limbo of 'linguistic performance'. A further restriction is that, within linguistic structure strictly defined, Riffaterre is interested only in lexical paradigms. The second piece of knowledge the reader possesses is not strictly linguistic, but strictly poetic. Following Jakobson, he knows that lexical reduplication indexes sites in a poem which demand scrutiny for symbolism, and inattention to reference. Thus, the lexical part of the reader's native linguistic competence allows him to recognise formal patterns in the text; his literary competence — knowledge of the Jakobsonian poetic principle — sorts out those patterns which are potentially significant. The third piece of equipment which Riffaterre's superreader possesses, I suspect, is an inventory of *topoi*: a dictionary of conventional significances to attach to the hyperbolized places in the text.

This model of the reader seems to me to be excessively and unrealistically limited. I could explain the limitations from two angles. The first would be historical. It is obvious that even a polymath like Jakobson, exceptionally qualified to generalize on the specific qualities of literature, has in fact been socialized into a particular literary culture. His specification for literariness is less likely to be a universal than an account of the formal properties which the literary norms of our culture have trained him/us to expect and value. (Riffaterre's Wordsworth resembles Baudelaire, Jakobson's Baudelaire is like Apollinaire.) The second limitation is theoretical. Riffaterre's adaptation of Jakobson's poetics is suspect because it draws on only a small part of the resources provided by linguistic structure. Riffaterre insists that his reading of 'Yew-Trees' is based solely on ordinary knowledge of the lexical structure of English. That is to say, what Chomsky would call 'performance factors' are excluded. A serious omission is the capacity for stylistic recognition: recognition that a linguistic sequence like lines 16-18 is not only a site of lexical foregrounding (as it is) but also belongs to a certain stylistic register. These lines are plainly 'high Miltonic'. They belong to a register of stylistic loftiness which is indicated by a convergence of structures precisely reminiscent of the language of *Paradise Lost*: the blank verse; the polysyllabic words; the latinate character of the diction; the over-running syntax at line-divisions ('growth/Of', 'fibres serpentine/Up-coiling'[10]); the heavy use of post-modification in NPs; use of numerous participles; the exactly Miltonic metrical elisions in 'particular' and 'inveterately'. Miltonisms are found elsewhere in the poem, but here they cluster spectacularly; Commenting on a possible specific allusion to *Paradise Lost* in lines 20-23, Riffaterre minimizes the importance of recognition. He implies that the reader might not notice the reference, and states that 'even if the reader were aware that Wordsworth's phrasing was inspired by Milton, the Miltonian flavor certain words might seem to take on would at most contribute to their literariness (for instance, would set them at the lexical level characteristic of a lofty genre like the ode). Their relationships within the context would not be modified' (p. 242). In rejecting the significance of an allusion to a particular text, Riffaterre under-rates the importance of an allusion to an institutionalized style. His dismissive 'at most' is regrettable, for if the text does signal a generalized Miltonic loftiness, that is certainly something of note, given Wordsworth's place in the post-Milton tradition of serious blank verse. Moreover, this stylistic allusion cannot come to the consciousness of someone who is equipped only with ordinary lexical competence. It is available only to a reader who has experienced the register in question; who has, to use Chomsky's term, 'internalized' the stylistic history of *Paradise Lost* and its progeny. So in this case literary response would depend on experience of an empirical literary tradition, a fact of society and history, and not just on knowledge of lexical structure and of a poetic absolute.

To acknowledge the relevance of conventional, intersubjective, registers or codes is to place the reader and the poet in a sociolinguistic community. A related process of contextualization is to identify them as participants in a communicative act. (Strictly speaking, of course, the participants are fictionalized as persona and implied reader.) This analysis requires attention to deictic and interpersonal[11] features of language, and to the sequential aspects of language considered as directing the reader's temporal experience. Both of these dimensions of language have been, regrettably, very much neglected in linguistics as well as in Jakobsonian poetics.

In the space remaining, my analysis must be brief and informal. By focussing on sequence, the interplay of registers, and signs of the implicit linguistic activity of persona and reader, I will try to show that 'Yew-Trees' is not only descriptive (referential) and symbolic (metalinguistic) but also dramatic ('emotive' and 'conative' in Jakobson's rather unsatisfactory terms). My starting-point is the observation that disposed along the syntagmatic axis of the poem is an interplay between two registers: a particular, localized, mundane style of statement on the one hand, and on the other, a general, essential, numinous type (of which 'lofty Miltonic' is a sub-variety). These registers have different expressive values for the persona, and define for him a shifting state of mind in which the reader also is involved.

The presence of place-names is the most obvious warrant for the poem's observance of local realism: Lorton Vale, Borrowdale, Glaramara. It is important that an ordinary locational term occurs in the first line: the reader can anchor his perceptions to an innocent topographical fact; then Borrowdale, roughly half-way through the poem, reiterates the geographical basis, and finally Glaramara at the end. This place-name level of geographical actuality is complemented by a deictic apparatus which sets the scene for the verbal transaction between the participants, bringing the reader into the context as someone who listens to a speaker indicating the existence and values of something not far distanced from the two of them. The poem is in present tense, so that the speaker, his addressee and the trees all seem to occupy the same time-sphere. It is assumed that the trees are accessible to the addressee. The opening of the poem, with the phrases 'there is,' 'which . . . stands' and 'in the midst,' suggests a set of directions on how to get to the Lorton Vale tree. The explicitly deictic 'those' in line 14 is an ostensive gesture, pointing to trees which are not within the context of utterance but nevertheless locatable in relation to that point of reference. 'Worthier still of note' (13) again assumes verbal interaction. The nominalized verb 'note,' implicitly imperative, presupposes the presence of someone who is to do the noting, and someone who tells him to do so. Next follows what looks superficially like a description which will allow us to recognise the fraternal Four, and finally we are led to a perspective on the 'mountain flood' and 'inmost caves' of Glaramara. The ostensive speech-act frame, and the topographical register, prevent the reader totally de-particularizing the experience which is to be mediated by the trees. This experience is to be given in heavy symbolism, but the actuality of landscape experience, and of direct speaker-hearer intercourse, is maintained. Another function of the 'directive' language is to engage the reader as a participant, someone who submits to having things pointed out to him, and at the same time the register keeps alive the presence of a guide, an exclaimer, a director of associations and of mythologizings. Since the participants are so manifest, we can fairly regard the poem as 'dramatic' in a more-or-less non-figurative sense.

The dramatic intercourse is sustained by various shifts of register as the persona leads the reader through the poem. The first, and spectacular, shift occurs at the transition of lines 2-3. In the topographical register, the phrase 'in the midst' arouses a strong expectation of locational information: we wait for the direction to be completed by something like 'of a dense forest,' 'of a broad meadow'. The topographical register *versified* allows this expectation to be mimed: the suspension at line-end is significant. When we come to 'of its own darkness' we have to abruptly change our expectation of register. Since the phrase makes little sense as a locative, we have to figure it out as serving some other function. In terms of the poem's drama, it seems to be the starter for a code of symbolic generality, as expressed in the lexical set 'darkness,' 'gloom,' 'shade,' 'umbrage,' 'sable,' 'shadow.' Of course, this vocabulary of darkness and shade conventionally connotes portent, threat, solemnity, melancholy. These associations permeate the poem. Several other lexical sets underscore these connotations: 'solitary,' 'solemn,' 'Death,' and so on. Notice also the many negatives: 'not loth,' 'unrejoicing,' 'nor uninformed,' 'grassless,' 'undisturbed.' This level of portentous generalization is also helped by some of the hyperbolic words and phrases denoting ostensibly purely descriptive aspects of the trees: 'vast,' 'magnificent,' 'capacious,' 'huge,' 'of yore,' 'earlier,' 'slowly,' 'inveterately,' 'perennially.' (Riffaterre's analysis is illuminating on hyperbolic aspects of the language.)

The local, topographical, code and the symbolic, transcendant, code are spread pretty evenly along the length of the poem. The two registers present two concurrent threads of experience, the referential treatment of the landscape and the connotational symbolization of the thoughts it promotes in the mind of a persona who is dramatized as a poet-figure. But if the analysis were to stop at merely identifying the dominant registers, it would fail to do justice to the linear structure of the poem, to the movement and development of the reader's experience. There is a well-marked narrative sectionalization, a dynamic rhetorical development, and a remarkable collage effect of miscellaneous syntactic/metrical materials. The complications of linear reading, and their aesthetic functions, can also be revealed in terms of registers or varieties of language. I mentioned earlier that I regarded the poem as dramatic. The *dramatis personae* can be derived from the exposition of registers, for a register is a code, a language, and code implies speech-community, a set of participants who can use speech as action. The members of the community pertinent to the present text are the poet-persona and the literary tourist whom he leads through a rhetorical journey, part pretend-guided-tour and part exploration of the style appropriate to an emotional 'landscape.'

The poem starts out not simply in guide's language but in guide's language versified. The stylistic transition at lines 2-3 draws attention to this fact. So we should put ourselves on watch for further adjustments of voice which the persona indulges. The style of lines 1-13 is fragmented, indecisive. Lines 1-8 are stylistically, but not referentially, flat and somewhat prosaic contrasted with what is to come. Concessions to the register of traditional serious verse are few: the archaisms 'of yore,' 'ere'; the syntactic portmanteau 'stands single' which is a typically poetic condensation of three separate deep structures ('NP stands,' 'a single NP' and 'NP is Adj'; the rhetorical negative 'not loth'; the compression 'sounding bows', a word-order which in prose would suggest the nonsensical 'sounding-bows', compare 'spinning-tops'; a similar compression in 'earlier Crecy' which in prose would mean, not 'earlier than Agincourt' but 'the earlier of two Crecys'.[12] In narrative, this sparing use of stylistic ornament suits the factual introduction of the tree in advance of full exposition of the tree's symbolic associations. Here, the dignity of the tree is connoted by historical allusions rather than heightened style. Lines 9-13, however, go to town on stylistic heightening. There is no finite verb in these lines; they consist chiefly of complex noun phrases depending on the exclamation 'This solitary tree!' Lines 9 and 10 are inverted phrases with their implied copula not expressed in surface structure; 9 contains an embedded inversion 'gloom profound' and a syntactic chiasmus:

(Adj (vast) + N (circumference)): (N (gloom) + Adj (profound))

Lines 11-13 are based on a syntactic parallelism, 12 contains an inversion and a near-tautology in 'of form and aspect'.

Beneath the stylistic intensity of 9-13 there is a certain logical inconsequentiality:

```
 9 of great size;      casts profound shadow;
10 solitary          organic . . .
11 . . . slow-developing      therefore non-decaying;
12 magnificent in appearance . . .
13 . . . therefore should be protected.
```

This jumble of propositions and inferences, hardly matching the syntactic symmetry, looks more like a gesture than a statement or a description. One is led to ask, not what lines 1-13 say, but what they *do*. I suggest that they act primarily to draw attention to the presence and to the dilemma of the poet-persona. He exclaims (addressing not the tree, as in apostrophe, but the reader); he tries a flat style dignified by historical allusions; then he tries an elevated syntax; he makes some disconnected general assertions about the Lorton Vale tree. The language invites the reader to construct the figure of a poet laboriously searching for adequate expression (as often in Wordsworth). The first tree is not a satisfactory objective correlative. So he abandons this particular tree and starts again. Actually, this is a sleight-of-hand, since the tree *has* served a rhetorical purpose — as we saw above, the two basic registers of particular description and generalized emotion are announced in the presentation of the Lorton Vale tree. So the poet is able to say that the fraternal Four are 'worthier still of note' which implies that the first tree was not simply worthy of note but *rather*, or *quite*, or even *very* worthy of note.

The narrative division at line 13, the introduction of the fraternal Four, is attended by rhetorical escalation. The persona has pretended to dismiss the first tree in favour of the fraternal Four, but since he used the Lorton Vale tree to establish the criteria according to which the Borrowdale trees are preferred, the Borrowdale trees don't actually replace the first tree, but rather take its imperfectly actualized symbolic values a stage further. At this point of transition, even trivial details like the move from *one* tree to *four* signal this climbing effect. As far as the poetic register is concerned, the language becomes more Miltonic, and consistently Miltonic; and as the style grows more intense, the symbolic level of connotation leaves behind the deictic level of landscape specification. For the reader who possesses not simply a generalized 'literary competence' but a specific sensitivity to the values of the principal verse styles in the history of English poetry, the allusion to Milton has a particular significance since the challenge of Milton's language was peculiarly problematic for poets of Wordsworth's generation (*Hyperion, The Prelude*). At the level of description, a new synthesis is suggested in the fusion of the four trees into one mighty and unanalyzable whole. The image of the yew-trees nobly bodies forth the mood of solemnity, humility, temerity, mysticism, grandeur. My point is that the style at this point is dramatically, as well as thematically, significant: the persona of a poet celebrates his achievement (as well as achieving it) by a triumphant stylistic display. I intend the word 'display' literally: the persona has an audience, and he puts on show his new mode of discourse. The interactional level of ostensive speech has been maintained: the phrase 'worthier still of note' is a comment on what the poet is doing (preparing to draw attention to the four trees and to the new high style) and an instruction to the reader. The involvement of both the addressee and the speaker of this poetic register is maintained. The exclamation 'huge trunks' serves a similar purpose. So does the marked deictic 'those' where the unmarked 'the' would have served the semantic context but would have been, interpersonally, much weaker. 'Those' syntactically connotes physical ostension, immediacy of material context. Culturally, it connotes 'those well-known,' as it does today in the register of advertising: 'those wash-day blues,' 'that professional decorator touch.' The sustension of the poet-reader-trees interaction in the second part of the poem serves two functions: making the reader attend to the style as dramatic action, as well as statement; keeping both parties *within* the world of the poem, in preparation for the final lines.

The high-style celebratory lines 16-18, which I discussed above, are not only a stylistic display; they also communicate a description of the four trees, and a highly specified description: we are presented with a picture of the union of the four trees into one whole, the size of the trunks, the composition and texture of the trunks, the shadow cast by the foliage, broken by the pillar-like trunks, the carpet of needles, the berries, the moss-covered stones beneath the trees. But the function of 'description' is not the most important of the roles of this passage. It is rather a linguistic creation of a baroque object, a natural object conceived in such a way as to justify the baroque style. As for the physical details, they are important primarily in preparation for the metamorphosis of the yew-tree grove into a supernatural temple-of-the-woods. We are asked to experience this passage only initially as a detailed picture of the trees, more permanently as a stylistic celebration of the emotions which the poet makes the whole spectacle serve.

The solemnity of the created scene leads conventionally to the spectres which meet at this natural temple. They are not 'real' spectres, since they cannily take advantage of the trees' deep shade to come together at noon rather than midnight. As their names confirm, they are in fact externalizations of the feelings of someone (here, the poet and his addressee) who visits the place — sombre feelings about one's destiny. In terms of the ongoing register at this point, the personification-allegory to which we are treated fits the archaic high style the poet has achieved. I do not think that the characters in this allegory are meant to be taken seriously at the level of narrative. Their behaviour at lines 25-31 is only vaguely delineated — they are not doing anything specific such as dancing or forming a circle, but simply 'celebrating,' 'worshipping.' They gather together, signifying the way such feelings as those named in the 'shapes' flock to a person who may visit such a spot. The notion of 'visit' has been there from the beginning, and Wordsworth has been careful to keep the human participants — his persona and his implied reader — active within the poem. These participants, having been afflicted with the emotions which the yew-trees engender narrationally or objectify symbolically, can rest and be soothed by the natural experience of the sound of water flowing from the mountains. To imagine the Shapes lying listening to the waters would be somewhat comic, and the implied participants in the act of discourse constituted by the poem's language are more plausible candidates.

I am absolutely in agreement with Professor Riffaterre that it is inadequate to regard this merely as a descriptive poem. So to regard it would be to commit the referential fallacy; to offend against the principle, central to philosophy since Frege and to linguistics since Saussure, that meaning is *sense* (a product of coding) and not referent or reference; to regard the poem as strictly a descriptive use of language would also be to ignore the distinction made by Richards, and more subtly by Jakobson, between poetic and referential functions of language. There is a point to be made that 'Yew-Trees' is a structure of language rather than an assemblage of objects in the mimesis of which language is only a transparent medium. This point has immediate procedural implications: if we agree that 'Yew-Trees' is an artifact of linguistic form, we are obligated to pay an exacting respect to the structure of language in the text. Once again, Riffaterre's stringent attention to the linguistic determinants of literary form is wholly admirable. Yet beyond this point I must part company with Riffaterre. His analyses assume only one linguistic code, the one inscribed in the linguistic competence of a Chomskian grammar. But the study of language in use — discourse analysis or sociolinguistics — readily demonstrates that texts display conventional patterning on a number of different levels, answering to the complexity of the speech-community within which verbal interaction takes place. It is a commonplace that discourse is stylistically specialized to its communicative functions and to the relationship between the participants in speech acts. There is no reason in linguistic theory to expect 'literary' texts not to manifest this kind of sociologically and historically sensitive stylistic patterning; indeed, our experience as students and teachers of literature confirms this fact. A universalist linguistic poetics, such as Jakobson's, minimizes stylistic differentiation and its functions. I hope I have shown that an analysis which attends more directly to 'registers' and their historical significances at least produces readings of poems which do more than just say 'this is literary': readings which begin to answer questions about the place of a text in the history of literary forms and of cultural contexts.

A word about the process of literary education in the light of 'literary competence'. In the societies with which I am familiar, literary education is inherently normative. It is a technique of socialization, through saturation in received corpora of texts, through reading of commentaries and through classroom discussions within a determined syllabus, socialization towards the values which, for whatever purpose, a given culture upholds. The trouble with the Jakobsonian model of literary competence is that, by emptying linguistic structure of its socio-historical functions, it denies students a means of insight into the relativity of the values which they are encouraged to support. This is an even more culpable defect of the theory than its basic descriptive failing, namely, denial of the fact that any reading of a text brings to that text knowledge of specific historical structures (usually multiple) coded in the patterns of the language. By emphasizing the importance of these sociolinguistic patterns, I hope I have suggested the beginnings of a descriptive technique which permits critics and students to place texts within historical contexts, and therefore to explore the arbitrariness of current literary ideals.

I am conscious that my remarks about the *activity* of reading have been rather perfunctory, but I have wanted to indicate the importance of two aspects of this activity that are seldom given their due in modern literary criticism. One is the sequential dimension of reading, the reader's experience of a text as a linear progression through which he moves in time. Stanley Fish has examined the relationship between unfolding linguistic surface structure and the reader's responses as they develop through time (see note 6), and this is one aspect of the syntagmatics of reading which merits more formal study. In the present paper I have looked at the effect of rhetorical progression and shift of register on the reader's serial creation of the world of 'Yew-Trees'. The second factor is the reader's engagement with the poem as *speech act*. Modern criticism, dogmatically anti-intentionalist and anti-affective, too readily assumes that a poem is a static artifact, an object for contemplation rather than a process for participation. Linguistic poetics of the Jakobsonian variety colludes with this attitude by its exclusive concentration on purely formal aspects of linguistic patterning. But every well-formed piece of language is not simply a pattern of words, but an interaction between speech participants, with parts of the utterance (or written text) indicating the indented act of the speaker (illocution),[13] his attitude to the propositions he utters (modality) and the orientation of the utterance in space and time (deixis). An essential part of decoding, for the addressee in face-to-face interaction and for the reader in written, is the identification of these features of discourse. The reader must recreate the writer's implicit position, and his own as 'implied reader', from the interpersonal level of discourse. Naturally, in literature the participants are more or less fictionalized: we must be cautious about identifying the speaker in 'Yew-Trees' with the real William Wordsworth. However, it is an inescapable fact that the poem's language offers to create two interacting personae, the implicit speaker and the implicit addressee. The reader imagines himself in the second role, and reconstructs an image of the first. The interplay of the two is a fact of the poem's structure — and a fact of social and historical structure, since the interpersonal level of language encodes conventional, socially validated, patterns of relationship. I regard it as a top priority of linguistics to develop more sophisticated analyses of these aspects of language and to impress its findings upon students of literature.

Notes

1. For further discussion and illustration, see this volume, Chapter five; also 'Language and the Reader,' in Fowler, ed., *Style and Structure in Literature* (Oxford: Basil Blackwell, and Ithaca: Cornell University Press, 1975), pp.79-122.

2. Especially 'Criteria for Style Analysis,' *Word*, 15 (1959), 154-74, reprinted in S. Chatman and S. Levin, eds., *Essays on the Language of Literature* (Boston: Houghton-Mifflin, 1967), pp.412-30; 'Describing Poetic Structures,' *Yale French Studies*, 36-37 (1966), the volume reprinted as *Structuralism* ed. Jacques Ehrmann (New York: Anchor Books, 1970), pp.188-230; 'Interpretation and Descriptive Poetry,' *New Literary History*, 4 (Winter, 1973), 229-56. See also his *Essais de stylistique structurale*, ed. and trans. Daniel Delas (Paris: Flammarion, 1971), containing translations of Riffaterre's earlier English works, with interesting after-thoughts added.

3. See Roman Jakobson, 'Closing Statement: Linguistics and Poetics,' in T.A. Sebeok, ed., *Style in Language* (Cambridge, Mass.: MIT Press, 1960), p.356.

4. Shklovsky, 'Art as Technique,' in Lee T. Lemon and Marion J. Reis, ed. and trans., *Russian Formalist Criticism* (Lincoln: University of Nebraska Press, 1965), pp.5-24; 'L'art comme procédé,' in T. Todorov, ed. and trans., *Théorie de la littérature* (Paris: Seuil, 1965), pp.76-97.

5. 'Criteria for Style Analysis,' p.172.

6. See my 'Cohesive, Progressive and Localizing Aspects of Text Structure,' this volume, Chapter four. Stanley E. Fish is interesting if impressionistic, on what I have called 'progressive' structure: see his 'Literature in the Reader: Affective Stylistics,' *New Literary History*, 2 (Autumn, 1970). 123-62.

7. See Jonathan Culler, *Structural Poetics* (London: Routledge and Kegan Paul, 1975), Ch. 6; Manfred Bierwisch, trans. Peter H. Salus, 'Poetics and Linguistics,' in Donald C. Freeman, ed., *Linguistics and Literary Style* (New York: Holt, Rinehart and Winston, 1970), pp.96-115.

8. Jakobson, 'Poetry of Grammar and Grammar of Poetry,' *Lingua*, 21 (1968), 597-609; Todorov, 'Poétique,' in F. Wahl, ed., *Qu'est-ce que le structuralisme?* (Paris: Seuil, 1968), pp.99-166.

9. Noam Chomsky, *Current Issues in Linguistic Theory* (The Hague: Mouton, 1964); *Aspects of the Theory of Syntax* (Cambridge, Mass.: MIT Press, 1965).

10. The constituent-structure here could be either ((fibres serpentine) up-coiling) or (fibres (serpentine up-coiling)). In both cases we have post-modification extending over the line-division.

11. For the place of the interpersonal function of language within linguistic theory, see M.A.K. Halliday, 'Language Structure and Language Function,' in J. Lyons, ed., *New Horizons in Linguistics* (Harmondsworth: Penguin, 1970), pp.140-65.

12. These 'compressions' are based on a shorthand structure commonly found in English verse, a non-restrictive adjective preceding the noun it modifies.

13. Richard Ohmann has begun the study of illocutionary aspects of literature, following the theory of Austin and Searle, in several papers, most recently 'Literature as Act,' in S. Chatman, ed., *Approaches to Poetics* (New York: Columbia University Press, 1973), pp.81-107.

Anti-language in fiction

In this paper[1] I introduce part of a larger study in which I am exploring the relevance of Mikhail Bakhtin's concept of 'dialogic' or 'polyphonic' structure[2] to some English novels.

The innovation I am making is to interpret Bakhtin in the light of sociolinguistics, or to be more exact, linguistics with a sociological semantic base. I claim that Bakhtin's theory can be restated as a very rich theory of discourse — rich because it is not restricted to literature but captures some fundamental facts about the situation of all language in culture and ideology. Bakhtin withholds the (for him) honorific labels of 'dialogic', 'polyphonic' and 'carnivalesque' from all texts but early, Rabelaisian, literature, and Dostoevsky in the modern period: this restriction is surely wrong. I believe that the dialogic principle can illuminate a wide range of types of prose fiction.

The present paper can deal only with a very special category, novels about extreme social deviance which give their heroes highly abnormal speech-styles. I discuss these novels because they use very visible and extreme styles of oppositional languages associated with explicitly antagonistic sociocultural meanings. I treat these linguistic styles as 'anti-languages', following but modifying Halliday.[3] Anti-language are the special argots of thieves, prison inmates and other sub-cultures which exist in an antagonistic relationship with the norm society. My literary examples are Anthony Burgess, *A Clockwork Orange* (1962) and William S. Burroughs, *Naked Lunch* (1959).[4] These novels exemplify Halliday's ideas in a particularly clear and convenient way, but I must stress that my argument is not just about very deviant social dialects or special vocabulary. The essence of the case is the dialectical thinking which underlies anti-language, and its basis in social ideologies. This is the link with Bakhtin, and my aim is to explicate Bakhtin in those terms and to generalize the principles to novels which on the surface are not at all outrageous or antagonistic in expression.

Bakhtin claims that Dostoevsky was the inventor of a new genre of writing which he (Bakhtin) calls the 'polyphonic' novel. The essence of this genre is the liberation of the hero to the position of a *subject* with his own independent viewpoint; a liberation refused by fiction writers after the decline of carnivalistic writing, and of its social ideology of inversion, negation and levelling, in the Renaissance. Other novelists treat the hero as an *object*, objectify him: except in Dostoevsky, the hero's consciousness is totally limited and definitively evaluated from the point of view of the author: 'Dostoevsky, like Goethe's Prometheus, creates not voiceless slaves (as does Zeus), but rather *free* people who are capable of standing *beside* their creator, of disagreeing with him, and even of rebelling against him' (*Dostoevsky*, p. 4; Bakhtin's emphases, whenever quoted). The distinction of Dostoevsky is that the characters are allowed independent view-points capable of challenging the author's ideology. Raskolnikov in *Crime and Punishment* enjoys the integrity of a morally abhorrent position. Many other cases of deviant world-views respectfully created by very proper authors — not only Dostoevsky — can be recalled. Fictional presentations of criminals, perverts, junkies, political extremists, idiots, children, deities, and other figures beyond the range of accepted experience of the bourgeoisie are potential illustrations of Bakhtin's theory. However, the hero as subject with his own effective voice need not by any means be a deviant; all that is necessary is that s/he should articulate a world-view which is different from the implied author's and which is perceptible as in principle valid, which is not just depicted and dismissed by the author: which is *alien* but *possible*. Bakhtin explains:

> The plurality of independent and unmerged voices and consciousnesses and the genuine polyphony of full-valued voices are in fact characteristics of Dostoevsky's novels. It is not a multitude of characters and fates within a unified objective world, illuminated by the author's unified consciousness that unfolds in his works, but precisely the plurality of equal consciousnesses and their worlds, which are combined here into the unity of a given event, while at the same time retaining their unmergedness. In the author's creative plan, Dostoevsky's principal heroes are indeed not only objects of the author's word, but subjects of their own directly significant word as well. The hero's consciousness is given as a separate, a foreign consciousness, but at the same time it is not objectified, it does not become closed off, it is not made the simple object of the author's consciousness.

The relationship between hero and author (and it can be extended to relationships between character and character) is called by Bakhtin not only 'polyphonic' but also 'dialogic'. If 'polyphonic' refers to compositional structure in an aesthetic and perceptual sense (compare the simultaneous presence of multiple independent voices in the fugue), 'dialogic' refers to the ideological inter-relations between the unmerged voices. 'Dialogic' seems to contain two distinct but compatible meanings. First, it means consciousness of the actual or potential response of an interlocutor, orientation toward a second act of speech. This double-voicedness has been extensively discussed by Bakhtin (*Dostoevsky*, Ch. V), developing Eichenbaum's treatment of the special Russian style of dramatic narrative known as *skaz*.[5] The phenomenon is not, however, just a literary style but a property of all discourse. All language usage shapes itself toward an image of the other to whom it is addressed. As I write this paper, I am aware of the character of my sources and of my probable readership, I anticipate counter-response, challenge, and I adjust my style accordingly. Because I have written many articles for academic journals, my tactics of anticipation, my embrace of the other, are not very conscious or laboured; and our pre-response to the other in spoken face-to-face discourse is usually automatic. Such interpersonal response is recognized in sociolinguistics by such basic concepts as 'tenor' (Halliday) or 'participants' (Hymes).[6] Its effects on the structure of texts are easily demonstrated in practical analysis.[7] I am not slighting Bakhtin by pointing this out, but suggesting that his 'double-voicedness' is, through its fundamental role in discourse, exceptionally important, his attack on 'monologic stylistics' exceptionally just. His second meaning of 'dialogic' takes his argument a stage further by directing our attention to a special angle in this interpersonal rhetoric.

The second meaning which Bakhtin has in mind for 'dialogic' seems to be 'dialectical'. The dialogic relationship confronts unresolved contrary ideologies, opposing voices in which conflicting world-views resist submersion or cancellation. The dialectical nature of Bakhtin's aesthetic can best be seen in his discussion of *carnival*, briefly in *Dostoevsky* and extensively in *Rabelais*. Carnival with its boy kings and other multifarious travesties mediates opposites, associates them while preserving their autonomous identities. It rejoices in negation, inversion, paradoxes, extremes and subversion. In class terms — and class terms will be immediately relevant to my sociolinguistic treatment of 'polyphony' — the carnivalistic dialectic is the tension between mutually supportive but antithetical partners such as ruler and subject, employer and worker, teacher and pupil, husband and wife. The formal and theatrical expressions of this class dialectic, as well as its logical structure, are described in Bakhtin. Its linguistic realizations include negation and contradiction among the poetic figures (cf. Kress, footnote 1); other linguistic expressions have these logical and poetic properties, plus an explicit class basis, and it is these which I hope to illuminate by relating the processes of anti-language to fiction.

Although Bakhtin refers liberally to 'voices' and 'the word' as components of polyphony, he is very reluctant to provide precise *linguistic* descriptions for the voices in dialogue. This caution is strategic. He concedes that Dostoevsky is stylistically flat, that his heroes have little stylistic differentiation. He must show that his thesis works even in such a linguistically subtle case. Bakhtin also observes, surely correctly, that marked linguistic individuation of fictional characters may lead to an impression of closure, a feeling that the author has definitively analyzed a character and placed a boundary around its imaginative or moral potential: 'characters' linguistic differentiation and clear-cut "characteristics of speech" have the greatest significance precisely for the creation of objectivized, finalized images of people'. In my view this is an unnecessarily strong dismissal of linguistic differentiation, but one can see why Bakhtin had to say this. He does immediately qualify the judgement: 'the point is not the mere presence of specific styles, social dialects, ect., . . . the point is the dialogical *angle* at which they . . . are juxtaposed or counterposed in the work'; finally he concedes that 'dialogical relationships are possible among linguistic styles, social dialects, etc., if those phenomena are perceived as semantic positions, as a sort of linguistic *Weltanschauung*'.[8]

Part of the reluctance to allow stylistic or dialectal varieties as components in polyphonic design is Bakhtin's and Vološinov's lack of faith in the ability of the conventional linguistics of their time to describe adequately the relevant linguistic factors. The negativism of Bakhtin toward linguistics and stylistics comes out strongly in the passage from the beginning of Ch. V of *Dostoevsky* from which I have just quoted, and the dual critique of 'individualistic subjectivism' and 'abstract objectivism' is made at length and trenchantly in Vološinov, *Marxism and the Philosophy of Language*. Vološinov's analysis of reported speech and of the infiltration of the 'alien word' into authorial voice is an important advance in the development of a concept of language as utterance, as speech acts in an interactional setting: this concept is likely to be sympathetically received in the climate of linguistics of the 70s and 80s, with its rediscovery of pragmatics and of discourse. Vološinov's condemnation of the abstract objectivism of the Saussurean linguistics of the 20s seems, from today's viewpoint, equally applicable to the system-building and idealizing tendencies of structuralist and transformationalist linguistics 1930-1970. But that is a question with which I am only indirectly concerned here. Nor do I wish in this paper to develop Bakhtin's and Vološinov's specific (and admirable) ideas on dialogue and reported speech, but to add another area of 'linguistic styles' which can be perceived as 'semantic positions': 'social dialects', and anti-languages within the category of social dialects.

It is impossible in one paper to justify or even to expound fully the unconventional theoretical linguistic premises on which my analysis depends. I am just going to state them as working hypotheses and add some comments on how they appear in their sources — especially the 'systemic-functional' linguistics of M.A.K. Halliday.[9]

1. *The semantic resources of a language are in large part the product of the social/cultural/economic/technological structure within which the language's speakers live and are constituted.*

This seems to be heresy as far as the received Chomskyan orthodoxy is concerned, but by my qualification 'in large part' I do allow for the contribution of natural cognitive categories to what *must* or is *very likely* to be coded in any language (agency, process, location, colour and shape categories, binary oppositions, etc.).[10] But note that the very important research of Berlin and Kay and of Rosch tells us not that there are semantic universals but that there are certain concepts, presumably natural, which tend to be coded in many languages, which tend to receive short, simple signs, of native origin, which are learned easily if they are not already encoded.[11] Not all languages have all of Berlin and Kay's basic colour terms, and it could well be that which ones are present in a language — particularly, which of the colours 'low down' in the hierarchy of eleven — depends on cultural and technological factors. The socio-cultural importance of certain phenomena (culture-relative) is the most reasonable explanation for the examples of special lexical differentiations which are customarily mentioned in discussions of the 'Sapir-Whorf hypothesis' (Eskimo words for snow, etc.). Anyone who takes semiotics seriously (as I do) is likely to believe that all meanings which are worth discussing arise as a result of the knowledges, preoccupations and hegemonic necessities of specific societies and kinds of societies. Halliday's *Learning How to Mean* is a study of one child's development of a lexico-grammatical coding system for the concepts which his socializing mediators (family and wider forces; the family as microcosm of the wider forces of control) impress on him as the culture's legitimated responses to his needs.

2. *Linguistic varieties in the sociolinguistic sense* — styles, registers, dialects, codes, even distinct languages in diglossia — *encode different semantic potentials.* They are not merely automatic reflexes of, or indices of, different social circumstances; and they are not just variable realization rules of the same meanings within one hypergrammar. One says different things in different varieties, for they have diverse semantic potentials. They mean differently, and the sources of these meanings are social differences, principally class divisions and social categorizations of the occasions of speaking. Bernstein offers a version of this hypothesis in his differentiation of 'universalistic' and 'particularistic' meanings allegedly associated with 'elaborated' and 'restricted' codes respectively.[12] Halliday in his more recent writings defines 'register' not just as a situationally determined variety of language, but 'a range of meaning potential . . . the semantic configuration that is typically associated with the situation type in question.'[13] Almost all the empirical work which might bear out this hypothesis is still to be done; it is an idea which has been totally neglected in correlation sociolinguistics. Such description as has been carried out with this idea in mind — Halliday's own work, and the studies in our *Language and Control* (see note 7) — suggests to me that it is a good hypothesis.

Hypotheses 1 and 2 equip me to respond to the challenge offered by Bakhtin at the beginning of his chapter on 'The Word in Dostoevsky'. Insofar as his dialogic relationships are semantic relationships, they are linguistically coded relationships between social ideologies (hypothesis 1). Writers have available a great range of ways of realizing them in texts. Sometimes, as allegedly with Dostoevsky, stylistic differentiation will be barely visible; sometimes, as in the cases I am going to examine, these dialogic relationships are manifested as overtly marked, salient and classifiable, social styles and dialects. These social varieties encode semantic differentials (hypothesis 2) and so count as styles with (to quote Bakhtin again) 'semantic positions, . . . a sort of linguistic *Weltanschauung*'.

The term 'anti-language' was coined by Halliday to refer to the special jargons or canting slang, or secret languages, spoken by the members of what he calls 'anti-societies'. For Halliday, anti-language is the extreme case of social dialect. Its speakers are not simply special groups contained *within* a society (like teachers or advertisers) but sub-communities in an *antagonistic* relationship to the dominant culture: people categorized as 'deviant' or 'criminal' or 'deficient' — thieves, junkies, sexual perverts, convicts, political terrorists, street vandals, etc. Because they are antithetical to the norm society, Halliday argues, their language structure will involve systematic inversion and negation of the structures and semantics of the norm languages. Halliday illustrates this sociolinguistic antithesis from Elizabethan rogues' cant, and the special languages of the underworld of Calcutta and of the inmates of Polish prisons. The interest of such special languages is not only their practical functions such as secrecy, solidarity and verbal play; their most important value is that they facilitate an alternative social and conceptual reality for their speakers. There is a Whorfian argument here: the anti-language creates an anti-world-view.

As far as structure is concerned, lexical transformations are the most visible and easiest to study (though phonological, syntactic and semantic processes are almost always involved, too):

> The simplest form taken by an anti-language is that of new words for old; it is a language relexicalized ... Typically this relexicalization is partial, not total: not all words in the language have their equivalents in the anti-language .... The principle is that of same grammar, different vocabulary: but different vocabulary only in certain areas, typically those that are central to the activities of the subculture and that set it off most sharply from the established society. So we expect to find new words for types of criminal act, and classes of criminal and victim; for the tools of the trade; for police and other representatives of the law enforcement structure of the society; for penalties, penal institutions, and the like.[14]

In fact, Halliday refers to *two* lexical processes, which he calls 'relexicalization' and 'overlexicalization'. 'Relexicalization' is the provision of a new vocabulary item for a new concept peculiar to the deviant group, or adaptation of an existing item in such a way as to make it clear that a shift or an inversion of values has occurred. 'Overlexicalization' is the provision of a large number of alternatives for the important concepts of the counter-culture, either synonyms or finely differentiated variants. Both processes are illustrated in Halliday's sixteenth-century English examples:

> The Elizabethan chroniclers of the pelting speech list upwards of twenty terms for the main classes of members of the fraternity of vagabonds, such as *upright man, rogue, wild rogue, prigger of prancers* (= horse thief) *counterfeit crank, jarkman, bawdy basket, walking mort, kinchin mort, doxy,* and *dell*; numerous terms for specific roles in their often highly elaborate villainies, and names for the strategies themselves, which are known collectively as *laws* — for example *lifting law* (stealing packages), which involves a *lift, a marker and a santer* (the one who steals the package, the one to whom it is handed, and the one who waits outside to carry it off); names for the tools, e.g. *wresters* (for picking locks), and for the spoils, e.g. *snappings,* or *garbage*; and names for various penalties that may be suffered, such as *clying the jerk* (being whipped) or *trining on the chats* (getting hanged).[15]

Overlexicalization is logically dependent on relexicalization, but I will comment on it first because its significance is very straightforward. Its importance for the literary critic, the sociologist, or anyone from the norm culture inspecting the counter-culture is that this hyperbolic proliferation of terms identifies the dominant values of the counter-culture, the obsessive semantic fields within which the deviant group thinks and works. The glossary in Burgess's *A Clockwork Orange* is dominated by multiple terms for acts of violence and other criminal activities, for women, sex, parts of the body, money: it gives a sharp picture of the values of the group of teenage thugs from whose point of view the novel is narrated.

Relexicalization is provision of special terms for specific activities and objects of the counter-culture, and is basically a technical necessity, like a specialized scientific terminology. Many of Halliday's examples are very precise and functional. From the Calcutta underworld: *logam* 'theft in a moving goods train', *nicu-cakka* 'pick pockets by standing on footboard of train or bus'. But specialist terminology is not just functional. Used in context, it carries social meanings too: the metalanguage in a scientific article doesn't merely facilitate handling concepts, it also, rhetorically, suggests the authority of the writer. Sociolinguistically, one may switch into an occupational code in a non-professional context to signify status, distance from the ongoing conversational trivia, possession of uncommon privilege, etc. The point is that jargon has inherent dialogic potential because it has a specialized social origin. The jargon of anti-language originates in an unofficial opposition, so its dialogic angle is, specifically, antithetical — which is the precise dialogic angle which is at the heart of Bakhtin's enquiries.

We need to study relexicalization from two points of view, or on two levels: expression (phonology, morphology, etymology); and semantics. The relexicalizations of anti-language often signal their resistance to the norm language by expressive peculiarities. Many of Halliday's examples from Calcutta involve phonological transformations of standard Bengali words: *dhok > ghot, ulat > ulti*, etc. Others are marked by morphological transformations such as suffixation, compounding, back-formation, etc. — morphological changes are very common and pretty regular in slangs and argots from different cultures.[16] Note that phonological and morphological alternations of existing standard terms (where completely new words might have been invented) signify an explicit relationship with the norm society, and a transactive relationship: the claimed privilege of deforming the standard. Moving to etymology: foreign loan words, and domesticated words with obviously foreign elements in their derivation, play their part in anti-language and in the anti-norm usage of professional jargons. As an example of the first of these processes, consider the status of Yiddish words in Jewish English, or European-derived 'cultural' terms like *Weltanschauung, Angst, élan, afficionado* in the affected speech of intellectuals and (one has to relexicalize them) connoisseurs. (Note that, contrary to the impression given by Halliday's paper, anti-language can be a code of the over-privileged just as well as of the under-privileged.) The second of these foreign borrowing processes is in fact an attenuation of the first: it may be illustrated by the use of 'learned' words of classical origin (*attenuation, heliotrope, spectrogram, hegemony*). Bakhtin and Vološinov, and their follower Boris Uspensky, are well aware of this literal use of the 'alien word' in literature.[17] The theory of anti-language adds to their observations the possibility that a foreign lexis may be used systematically and with a consistent semantic import, rather than as an occasional foregrounded intervention in the surface texture of a work. The criminal anti-heroes of *A Clockwork Orange* use an invented anti-language derived from Russian words (*baboochka, slovo, govoreet*, etc.), and the oppositional significance of this, particularly in a book published just after the erection of the Berlin Wall, is obvious. Burroughs lards *Naked Lunch* with medical, anatomical and chemical terms (*peristalsis, dihydro-oxy-codeine, lymphogranulomas*) which are just as much of an affront to the reader seeking the stability of a 'normal' discourse as the book's native obscenities and slang terms.

'Oppositional significance' brings us to the second (and basic) aspect of anti-language, its dialectical semantics.[18] Anti-language doesn't depend on overt deformations of the material sign any more than polyphony, on Bakhtin's account, depends on overt presentation of social and stylistic varieties. (*But*, pace *Bakhtin, the latter situation is possible*.) Transformations such as inversion (*scob = box, yennep = penny*) are highly appropriate, but optional, expressions of the basic characteristic of anti-language, *dialectical semantics*. Among Halliday's examples there are the relexicalizations *law* = 'crime' and *upright man* = 'leader of a band of criminals or beggars'.[19] Reversing the normal meanings of the words, the users of anti-language address the norm society dialectically. The rogues' *law* only works, semantically, if the original meaning is not completely erased; that which is refused legitimation by your society is precisely that which receives honour and legitimation in ours. There are similar modern slang usages, e.g. *bad* = 'eminently appropriate or suitable; excellent, wonderful'.[20] Such words become the sites of dialogue between society and anti-society. I will illustrate this process of dialogue between antithetical ideologies with a contemporary example which uses quite ordinary words. The London *Observer* newspaper of Sunday, March 26 1978 contains two items about the kidnapping of the former Italian Prime Minister, Aldo Moro. On the front page there is a brief item headed 'MORO "ON TRIAL"'. It reads:

> The kidnappers of the former Italian Prime Minister, Signor Aldo Moro, have begun proceedings against him in a 'people's trial', according to an announcement by the Red Brigades urban guerilla group.

Inside the paper is a report of the trial in Turin of fifteen members of the Red Brigade, who

> take it in turns, three at a time in alphabetical order, to be present purely as 'observers', of their trial, since they do not recognise the court ... They show little apparent interest in the proceedings, spending the time chatting to each other and smoking, never standing with everyone else when the court president enters or leaves. From time to time, they stroll across their cage to get a light through the bars from one of the line of armed policemen.

The paper goes on:

> Yesterday's announcement by the Red Brigades that they have put Signor Moro on trial in a 'people's court' has increased the tension. The guerillas said they had begun interrogating the former Prime Minister and added: 'He will be brought to justice'.

149

The coordinated behaviour of the two groups of Red Brigades aims at an attack on legal institutions and concepts not only through violence but through a parodic logic of inversion. One group rejects the role of 'accused', relexicalizing themselves as 'observers'. They refuse to acknowledge the court, and behave carnivalistically, degrading it with physical disrespect. The other group parodies the Turin trial by staging a 'people's trial' of Moro, transforming him into a criminal, a 'political godfather' accused of 'crimes against the proletariat'. Established values are negated and replaced by subversive antitheses. And language, as well as the court-room, becomes the locus within which the norm society and the deviant group confront and negotiate. The Red Brigades relexicalize, offering words and phrases for concepts which are travesties of established concepts. The norm society rejects these new classifications; the newspaper, a mouthpiece of the establishment, signals *its* rejection by putting the relexicalizations in dissociating quotation marks. Language here is working dialogically, each participant using language ironically and with acute consciousness of the alien character of the other.[21]

Before turning to the novels, I want to make explicit an important modification of Halliday's concept of anti-language. The title of his paper has the noun in the plural, 'anti-languages'; elsewhere he speaks of 'an anti-language'. For Halliday an anti-language is primarily a variety, like a dialect or a register. While I accept the varietal status of anti-language, I also want to say that anti-language is a *process* as well as a *variety*. Emphasizing the 'secret language' aspect of anti-language, one might regard it as an isolated variety, cut off from the norm just as its speakers are segregated from the mass of the population. But our examples show that anti-language is essentially connected to standard language. It is not a static mirror-image, but a medium of negotiation between two communities, a transaction through which conflicts of ideology and identity are actively waged. Similiarly, it is not satisfactory to regard anti-language as creating a completely autonomous alternative reality (which might be *any* ideology); the alternative is most fruitfully seen as provoked by, and a creative critique of, the norm. It is in this sense of dialogue between ideologies, reflected in linguistic transformations, that I am going to apply the concept of anti-language to literature.

In passing it is worth noting that this modified notion of anti-language as a process is more compatible with current sociological theory of deviance than is Halliday's. As Stanley Cohen puts it, 'Deviance is not a quality inherent in any behaviour or person but rests on society's reaction to certain types of rule-breaking . . . One must understand deviance as the product of some sort of transaction that takes place between the rule-breaker and the rest of society.'[22] Deviance is not an objective phenomenon, it is an image, a negotiated perception. Anti-language is one of the mechanisms by which negotiations are conducted, and one of the media in which ideological interactions are most clearly visible.

I have offered a view of anti-language as relational, contextualized: language sensitive to and working on its relationship with some norm of 'official', 'institutional' language. This dialogic awareness may be only implicit in the real speech of a junkie or a teenage gang member or a confidence trickster, but it is explicit when such language is found in a printed fiction, since the novel form brings with it a precise framework of readers' expectations. The novel is consumed largely by a literate middle-class readership, so the novelist who chooses to depict a deviant hero or minor characters knows that their voices, and the world-views which they project, are going to be perceived as alien, as objects for inspection rather than subjects for sympathy. The act of putting the speech of Huck Finn or Holden Caulfield into printed prose jerks them into an unnatural context, a context which more easily receives the speech of Edmund Bertram or Lambert Strether. From my interpretation of Bakhtin, I would predict that a novelist representing a social dialect remote from that of printed narrative prose — such as, for example, the speech characteristic of a youth culture — would have great difficulty avoiding the 'objectivization' that Bakhtin deplores. Characters would tend towards 'characters': lovable rogues, comic grotesques, harmless eccentrics incapable of embodying a mind-style[23] which could be experienced as valid; or they would be irredeemably unsympathetic 'villains'. This problem of expression and response is likely to be compounded when protagonists can be neatly slotted into scandalous categories which our norm society has lexicalized and agreed are the object of natural abhorrence: 'murderer', 'rapist', 'drug addict', 'vandal', 'terrorist' and the like. How can sociolinguistic varieties which evoke such responses be used in an inescapably hostile context (novel genre) to constitute an experience of the other as subject? The answer predicted by the theory of the semantics of anti-language must be that the language of the novel must construct the complete dialectic between the ideologies at issue without totally subjugating one to the categories of the other. As yet, I understand very little of the linguistic techniques by which this might be done or fail to be done, and the following brief explorations of the two novels examine some linguistic features of social varieties in a provisional way. And since I am by no means an 'expert' on Burgess or Burroughs, my judgements may appear to others to be wrong.

A Clockwork Orange is a first-person narrative by the leader of a teenage gang, Alex, set in urban England some time in a terrifying *1984*-type future. His gang, like others which roam the streets, is devoted to a life of theft, violence and rape. The extract to which I shall refer (p.27, 'So off we went . . .' to p.30, '. . . on their own floor.') comes at the end of an account of a typical evening's work, in which the boys have robbed a cigarette shop, beating up its owners, mugged a teacher and a drunk, stolen a car and driven it into the country where they invade a cottage and assault and gang-rape its occupants. Subsequently, Alex is caught by the police and subjected to an aversion therapy called 'Ludovico's Technique'. He is 'cured' of violence, but loses his free will in the process, is manipulated for political reasons, and finally, with treatment reversed, he is 'cured' again, this time restored to his former ethos of violence. The violence is, throughout, connected with a love of classical music. It is implicitly argued that his experience, though antagonistic to the norms of the society, has its own aesthetic validity.

The social situation of Alex and his associates is a paradigm case for the formation of an anti-language. They constantly assert their opposition and con- tempt for all that is, in their own words, bourgeois, middle-aged, middle-class.

They attack the representatives of these values by violent assaults on property and people. Since their actions are illegal, they are also at war with the state and its law enforcement agencies. Their speech is an invented argot (invented by Burgess) very much on the principles of classic criminal slang, and contrasted with the speech of members of the norm society. (See, for example, the representations of the language of Dr. Brodsky and Dr. Branom, pp. 84 ff, and of Alex's parents, pp. 107–109). The main feature of the teenage gang speech is a special vocabulary, mostly Russian in origin, with some rhyming slang — 'hound and horny', 'twenty-to-one' — the latter presumably designed to connect the anti-language with that of the modern London underworld. Burgess provides a glossary of around 250 words, which the reader has to consult for quite a time on first reading. Here's a brief and typical sample:

> So off we went our several ways, me belching arrrgh on the cold coke I'd peeted. I had my cut-throat britva handy in case any of Billyboy's droogs should be around near the flat-block waiting, or for that matter any of the other bandas or gruppas or shaikas that from time to time were at war with one.

Here we have both relexicalization and overlexicalization. *Peet, britva*, and *droog* are simply arbitrary relexicalizations, for 'drink', 'razor' and 'friend'. Other relexicalizations display the semantic inversions noted elsewhere. The best example is the word *horrorshow*, meaning 'good', derived from the Russian word *xorosho* which means 'good'. Alex consistently applies it to acts of violence, that is, acts which are positive in his system of values but negative for the culture generally. The double-valued semantic of the word is signalled in its English spelling: the English transliteration produces a word which is overtly bad in meaning for, for example, Alex's parents, but implicitly good in meaning for Alex: horror plus show.

Overlexicalization is illustrated by 'bandas or gruppas or shaikas': three words all referring to marauding teenage gangs. It is not clear whether these words have three distinct meanings — which is possible if they reflect a diversified, special knowledge in the sub-culture — or all mean the same, in which case the phrase is an hyperbole. Interestingly, the same problem is presented by other anti-languages: in Elizabethan rogues' slang, for instance, there are numerous words for 'woman' and it is not possible to tell whether they have different meanings. Perhaps, on the analogy of the well-known Eskimo overlexicalization for 'snow', the sub-culture possesses a highly differentiated sexual world-view; on the other hand, they may be boastfully playing with words.

The element of verbal play links anti-language with the special rhymes and sayings of children's culture (cf. the Opies' work) and with the ritual insults and flytings which have been much studied in BEV and in other societies.[24] Alex's language is permeated with puns and phonetic games, to a large extent but not exclusively playing on the invented lexicon: 'The stripy shest', 'the old cold moloko. Hohoho, the old moloko', 'slooshying the sluice'. Or his friend Dim: 'Bedways is rightways now, so best we go homeways. Right?'. Or a pun, very self-conscious: 'the fuel needle had like collapsed, like our own hahaha needles had'. Alliteration, onomatopoeia, rhyme, chiasmus, hyperbole, parallelism — all are plentiful in the speech of Alex and his friends. Presumably, these devices are meant to signify energy, confidence, creativity: to emphasise their freedom from the patterns of the language and so their freedom from the norms of the society.

Alex's stance towards his implied readers suggests intimacy: 'O my brothers'; When he speaks contemptuously of the bourgeoisie, the middle-aged, it is as if they are alien to the reader as well as to himself. Yet, Alex's implicit addressee *is* the book-reading class, assumed to be mature, curious and sympathetic. The narrative is certainly not addressed to his peer-group. The special words are often glossed: 'a rooker (a hand, that is)', 'litso (face, that is)', 'nagoy (bare, that is)' or the anti-language word is added as an after-thought to the normal word: 'very big built up shoulders ("pletchoes" we called them)'. A helpful, mediating, rather than resistant strategy. As we shall see, the glosses in *Naked Lunch* have a very different effect.

Overall, the impression is given that speech antitheses can be mediated: the implicit dialogue is cooperative rather than antagonistic. In fact, beneath the provocative surface of the vocabulary, Alex's own language is thoroughly middle-class. Burgess gives Alex none of the conventional signs of non-standard speech: no regional dialect, no ungrammaticality, no restricted code in Bernstein's sense (Alex once produces a comic illiteracy: see p.21). In this Alex is distinguished from his aptly named friend 'Dim', who is linguistically coded as socially and mentally deficient. Alex's language characterizes him as an anti-social deviant, a violent thug, but one who possesses the faculties of discrimination and evaluation usually assumed to be the prerogative of the middle-class intelligentsia. From this point of view, pp. 27-31 are revealing. Returning from a night of violence and murder, Alex masturbates to the accompaniment of some *recherché* contemporary serious music, after which he settles down to Mozart and Bach. An equation of two experiences is being implied. Burgess wants us to see Alex's delinquency as producing experiences which are, for him, as aesthetically satisfying as the Jupiter and the Brandenburgs are for us. This is crude; and it prepares for the later judgement, that the aversion conditioning was immoral because, although it 'cured' Alex of his destructive anti-social behaviour, it deprived him of the power to express himself in his own way.

The rapprochement of norm and deviation is done in the language of the extract. Alex's speech, always elaborate in syntax, is especially so here. The sentence structure is varied; sometimes elaborately hypotactic, sometimes appropriately paratactic, as in the mimetic last sentence of the penultimate paragraph taking the narrative to a climax. There is parallelism, repetition with variation ('embellished and decorated'), syntactic chiasmus ('the trombones crunched redgold under my bed, and behind my gulliver trumpets three-wise silverflamed'). Most nouns are subject to complex pre-modification and post-modification. There are nominalizations and thematizations. Phonetic devices such as alliteration mount to Jakobsonian density. Metaphor is endemic and extravagant. The invented words are absorbed in a context which transforms them from deviations to poeticisms: the context is no longer that of urban delinquency and violence, but one of high literariness, with strong associations of Hopkins and Joyce. If Burgess is trying to argue the authenticity of the values of the anti-society, he does so by assimilating the anti-language to an extreme form of the high language, the language of literary modernism. The verbal play, which I suggested above might signify freedom and creativity, in effect signifies the reverse: socialization into the aesthetic norms of the (for the reader) dominant society. Burgess has closed the dialogic gap, neutralized the antithesis. Instead of allowing us to experience Alex's world-view as that of an alien but authentic subject, he translates that world-view into mediating terms which draw on our own, habitualized, norm-ideology.

Before discussing *Naked Lunch*, I must point out that, not being an American nor a student of American underworlds or their media representations, I am well aware that some of my comments may be misinformed or injudicious. The point is the illustration of the theory through this novel, not the adequacy of my critical interpretation of the book.

Naked Lunch contrasts with *A Clockwork Orange* first in drawing on real language rather than a constructed variety. I am not sure whether it is the style of a specific social group: whether the jargon and slang characterize the total speech of a junkie group. The language is dense, and incorporates a very wide range of jargons. However, the elements are real. I checked as much as I could in Wentworth and Flexner, *Dictionary of American Slang*, published in 1960, a year after the first American edition of *Naked Lunch*. The majority of the words for which I needed a more exact definition are in the *Dictionary*, but the dictionary shows no evidence of having used the novel as a source: for instance, the relevant sense of the phrase 'hot shot' (p.2) is not included, though you can see how it could be generated from Sense 5, 'the electric chair'.[25] The language of *Naked Lunch* is based in an American slang tradition which has a wider and much older hinterland then the drug culture of the fifties and sixties. Its general characteristic, signalled in the attack on the fruit in the first pages,[26] is cool or anti-square: much of the vocabulary tilts against naiveté, gullibility, pretence, against incompetence in *any* sub-culture requiring specialized knowledge, and beyond that against the pretension to understand such sub-cultures without possessing that knowledge. The book cannot be understood without decoding such classifications as 'the heat', 'doll', 'stool pigeon', 'shake', 'wig'. And the very density of the terms makes heavier demands than can be coped with through casual exposure to similar vocabulary in gangster movies and other legitimated mediators of the underworld. The novel opens with a reference to 'the heat' which demands an antagonistic perspective; almost immediately, then consistently, words like 'fruit', 'dick' and 'fag' force you to see the people designated by these terms with the contempt with which the narrator sees them. The language does not allow you to categorize people in the terms of the norm society, but inexorably works through substitutes which connote disrespect, resistance.

The first sentence also initiates one of the book's many antithetical oppositions between linguistic registers:

I can feel the heat closing in, feel them out there making their moves,
setting up their devil doll stool pigeons, crooning over my spoon and dropper
I throw away at Washington Square Station, vault a turnstile and two flights
down the iron stairs, catch an uptown A train.

The phrases to note are 'closing in', 'making their moves' and 'setting up'. These
are phrases from the colloquial register (and/or its novelistic and cinematic
representations) of the police and private investigators. The effect is not obvious
immediately, from the first sentence, though it becomes so fairly quickly: within
the discourse of junkie, thief, con-man, hip, gay, pornographer, are quoted fragments of the language of various groups from the 'straight' world — *quoted* dis-
sociatingly, as the *Observer* and *New York Times* quote the utterances of the Red
Brigades. This is one of the techniques by which, in this book, the discourses of
the norm society are always contained, always put in a context which balances
them against the perspective of whatever anti-social dialect prevails at that point.

Dialogue with the straight world is indicated, as in *A Clockwork Orange*, by a
technique of glossing: '(Note: Grass is English thief slang for inform)'. But,
because the language of the glosses is so different from that of the surrounding
text, its effect is different: it draws attention to the limitations of readers'
knowledge; suggests that the narrator knows that the reader's knowledge is
limited, that the reader is an outsider. Usually the glosses are plain and exagger-
atedly simple, giving semantic information in terms which the non-addict can
understand. They travesty the norm language, diluting it and keeping it
contained wihtin parentheses. Sometimes they mockingly define a slang word in
terms of other slang words, excluding the naive reader while pretending to assist
him: '(Note: Make in the sense of dig or size up.)'.

A further mark of anti-language's resistance to the norm is the use of non-
standard syntactic and morphological constructions. By 'non-standard' I refer to
features like the zero-suffix (no-*s*) in third person singular present tense verbs: in
the first few pages, 'call', 'hit', 'smoke', 'say', 'begin'. Also lack of a copula in continuous present: 'Eager Beaver wooing him much too fast.' These features occur
sporadically and inconsistently in the text, but frequently enough to make an
impact. These are standard features of some varieties of working class speech,
including BEV. Others give a general impression of casualness or illiteracy: 'We is
working', 'So I says'. The point about these usages is that they have definite
connotations of low socio-economic class — but *without* any suggestion of
criminality or deviancy. These usages broaden the base of resistance to the norm
world, and diversity it. In the case of the anti-social jargon of deviancy, the
straight is being attacked for limitation of experience; the working class syntax
additionally attacks the middle class reader for being middle class — that is, it
asserts an economic as well as an experiential antithesis.

Finally, passages of middle class language occur frequently later in the novel, in
the mouths of, and in the descriptions of, figures such as politicians, doctors,
bureaucrats. These passages are always parodic, and the speakers are always dis-
integrating into some other, less prestigious and usually debasing mode of speech.

There is a great deal more to say about *Naked Lunch*. So far, all I have claimed is that in this novel the anti-linguistic relationship between norm and deviant speech, with the deviant speech strongly attacking and subverting the norm, is real and powerful. In *A Clockwork Orange* the anti-linguistic process is phoney and naturalized, not so much because of the invented lexis, and because the narrator Alex's syntax is elaborated and his world-play bourgeois poetic.

But *Naked Lunch* is very much more complex than this account, or the first few pages which I asked you to read, suggests. There is one principle of consistency, which is antagonism to officialdom and commercialism in post-war American society. The slang anti-language of the counterculture carries part of the attack, and the narrative content and structure make their anarchic contribution. The narrator and his/our society are projected into a futuristic, insanely rationalistic state, the 'Freeland Republic', reminiscent of *1984* and *Brave New World*. The corruption and ineffectiveness of the professional and administrative institutions allows the state to be destroyed, or liberated, by the carnivalistic and orgiastic activities of its citizens. Riots of debasing sex level the oppositions of sane: insane; normal: deviant; governing: governed. On another level, the violence and diversity of the carnivals, riots, orgies, disintegrations mime the narrator's own heightened and kaleidoscoping hallucinatory consciousness as he moves through and out of a variety of drugs. Both content and style become Rabelaisian. At the level of content the model of Rabelais is present almost anywhere one takes a sample (but for one hilarious passage which compresses the essence of Rabelaisian comic anarchy into one paragraph I recommend 'Rock and Roll adolescent hoodlums . . .', p.44).

The Rabelaisian or carnivalistic principle in *style* is the presence of multiple, conflicting, unresolved voices. It is not simply two opposed class languages, anti-thetically related, but anti-language developed to a polyphony of voices and ideological positions all with their separate identities, deriving from distinct and irreconcilable parts of social structure. *Naked Lunch* provides one of the best English examples I know of carnivalistic polyphony. There is no space to illustrate the separate styles; politicians, technicians, doctors, bureaucrats, American Housewives all have their say. Some of the most memorable passages include the rustic old-timer monologue of the County Clerk; the British Colonials; the take-off of written porn in the section 'A.J.'s Annual Party'; the various voices through which Dr. Benway ranges; the disintegrated speech of the reflective junkie contrasting with the controlled irony of the narrator's opening pages and elsewhere. Towards the end, the book describes its own multiple-voiced technique:

The Word is divided into units which be all in one piece and should be so taken, but the pieces can be had in any order being tied up back and forth, in and out fore and aft like an inarresting sex arrangement. This book spill off the page in all directions, kaleidoscope of vistas, medley of tunes and street noises, farts and riot yipes and the slamming steel shutters of commerce, screams of pain and pathos and screams plain pathic, copulating cats and out-raged squawk of the displaced bull head, prophetic mutterings

of brujo in nutmeg trances, snapping necks and screaming mandrakes, sigh
of orgasm, heroin silent as dawn in the thirsty cells, Radio Cairo screaming
like a berserk tobacco auction, and flutes of Ramadan fanning the sick
junky like a gentle lush worker in the grey subway dawn feeling with delicate
fingers for the green folding crackle . . . (p.229)

Before leaving *Naked Lunch* with my suggestion that its multiple-voicedness is
polyphonic in a way which would satisfy Bakhtin, I should add a qualification
which I am sure Bakhtin would make. If *Naked Lunch* is successfully polyphonic,
it is not so merely because it includes a large number of distinct social voices.[27] It is
so because each of these voices embodies a significant ideological position (is
motivated, in formalist terminology) and because these ideologies relate to one
another, and to an implicit norm ideology, dialectically. I am fully aware that I
have not demonstrated this, but I believe that I could do so.

I'd like to end with some general comments and questions about anti-language
in fiction. Can any general aesthetic function be proposed for it? On first sight, if
we consider anti-languages as class codes or social dialects, then anti-language as
a technique in fiction seems to be a technique of representation. If you have
speakers from deviant groups in your novels, then you get their speech code right.
However, I have argued that anti-language is a process rather than a code. In
social reality, the process is a negotiation of status, identity and ideology between
an official establishment and a group which diverges from its norms. In fiction,
the negotiation becomes one between the groups of protagonists within the
fiction: between the author, his characters, and the reader. From a compositional
point of view, the process comes under the heading of techniques of defamiliarization. Technically, it impedes perception in just the way that Shklovsky's theory
requires. It allows the writer to thicken the texture of his prose, not only by the
Jakobsonian phonetics of rhyming slang and the like, but also by the lexical and
semantic devices which I have illustrated. There are also, very frequently,
syntactic indicators of the class affiliations of speakers. These peculiarities —
peculiarities, that is the say, from the point of view of the bourgeois reader — are
not *just* poetic in the Jakobsonian sense, i.e. unmotivated verbal play. Nor do
these linguistic processes simply identify a social group. Their motivation is to
reveal to the bourgeois reader the life-experience, or world-view, of the deviant
group, to give access to an alternative reality. The revelation of an alien mode of
experience from an outside world and an underworld is valuable enough within a
literary genre which assumes *possession* of language as an object, in the form of
novels possessed as books on the shelf; which assumes that language is closed and
monolithic; and which assumes privatization, enclosure, of experience and ideas.
At the very least, the reading of a novel of deviancy does something to enlarge the
experience of middle class readers by *showing* alternative life-styles and modes of
speech. And it does much more if these are presented as a troubling challenge to
the norms encoded in middle class language.

But the justification of anti-language in relation to fiction is not just that it
allows the middle class reader a vicarious experience of an illegitimate life-style. It

is the *logic*, not the *content*, of anti-language which offers to be interesting for the study of fiction. Neither the violence and criminality of the cases I have discussed, nor the manifest unconventionality of their language, defines the essence of anti-language. The essential feature is the antithetical logic of the relationship between an official and an unofficial voice: an unresolved, unmediated, antithesis which preserves a critical, dialogic openness in the novel's examination of its central ethical or social or psychological (or whatever) concerns. My fictional examples were chosen to be compatible with Halliday's presentation of the social content of anti-language, and to illustrate the concept with some linguistically striking examples. In fact, the dialectical logic can be found in texts which are less extreme linguistically and sociologically. Halliday himself says that anti-language is only the limiting case of social dialect, suggesting that the same processes are present in sociolinguistic varieties where there is less of a gulf between norm and variant.

The studies on which I have reported in this paper are only part of a larger project which includes also studies of antilinguistic and dialogic processes in less ostentatiously defamiliarizing fictions. For the moment I am staying with novels in which the opposed voices have some historical/sociological substance similar to Halliday's cases but less extreme. I have been looking at the relationship between authorial discourse and working-class speech in some English social-problem novels of the 1840s and 1950s — particularly Dickens' *Hard Times* and Mrs. Gaskell's *Mary Barton* and *North and South*. The questions I ask about these novels do not concern *mimetic* issues such as fidelity of representation of working-class speech. The language attributed to Stephen Blackpool, the Bartons, etc., and the relationship between that language and author's discourse, is analysed for the social theory or ideology which it embodies. The question is whether the author is prepared to allow his working class characters any kind of free identity, freedom to challenge or even invert the middle class norms, or whether their values are submerged, neutralized by a middle class ideology. Finally, I believe that these questions can be asked about much more delicate oppositions of world-view examined in conventional novels with minimum stylistic differentiation. I am looking at George Eliot from this point of view. Here the concept of anti-language merges explicitly with Bakhtin's 'dialogic structure', and helps explain the device he is proposing. The major difference between my approach and Bakhtin's is that I am able to investigate these questions with the support of a detailed linguistic and sociolinguistic analysis, even in cases where he would see only stylistic flatness.

Notes

1. I am grateful to my colleagues and students at the University of East Anglia, Norwich, for many helpful discussions on the issues in linguistics and poetics raised in this paper; particularly to Tony Gash for help with 'polyphony' and to Gunther Kress for 'anti-language'. See Kress's paper 'Poetry as Anti-language: A Reconsideration of Donne's "Nocturnall Upon S. Lucies Day,"' *PTL*, 3 (1978), 327-44. Earlier versions of the present article were given as lectures at the University of Michigan, Loyola University of Chicago, the University of Connecticut, Regensburg University, W. Germany, and Seville University, Spain, and I have been much helped by the responses of my hosts and audiences at these universities.

2. See M. Bakhtin, trans. R.W. Rotsel *Problem of Dostoevsky's Poetics* (Ann Arbor: Ardis, 1973); Bakhtin, trans. H. Iswolsky, *Rabelais and his World* (Cambridge, Mass.: MIT Press, 1968). *Dostoevsky* was first published in 1929; *Rabelais* was written in 1940 and first published in 1965. The important Ch. V of *Dostoevsky*, 'The Word in Dostoevsky,' appears in a different translation as 'Discourse Typology in Prose' in L. Matejka and K. Pomorska, eds., *Readings in Russian Poetics* (Cambridge, Mass.: MIT Press, 1971). Also highly relevant to Bakhtin's work (and possibly written by him) is V.N. Vološinov, trans. L. Matejka and I.R. Titunik, *Marxism and the Philosophy of Language* ([1930] New York: Seminar Press, 1973); see also B. Uspensky, trans. V. Zavarin and S. Wittig, *A Poetics of Composition* (Berkeley: University of California Press, 1973).

3. M.À.K. Halliday, 'Anti-languages', *Language as Social Semiotic* (London: Edward Arnold, 1978), pp. 164-82. There is a longer version in *American Anthropologist*, 78 (1976) and in *UEA Papers in Linguistics*, 1 (1976), 15-45.

4. The editions which I have used and from which I quote are Anthony Burgess, *A Clockwork Orange* (Harmondsworth: Penguin, 1974); William Burroughs, *Naked Lunch* (New York: Grove Press, 1966).

5. B. Eichenbaum, trans. T. Todorov, 'Comment est fait "le Manteau" de Gogol,' in Todorov, ed., *Théorie de la littérature* (Paris: Seuil, 1965), pp. 212-33; trans. B. Paul and M. Nesbitt, 'The Structure of Gogol's "The Overcoat",' *Russian Review*, 22 (1963), 377-99.

6. M.A.K. Halliday, *Language as Social Semiotic* (London: Edward Arnold, 1978), p. 33; D. Hymes, 'Models of the Interaction of Language and Social Life' in J.J. Gumperz and D. Hymes, eds., *Directions in Sociolinguistics* (New York: Holt, Rinehart and Winston, 1972), pp. 60-61.

7. E.g. R. Fowler, R. Hodge, G. Kress and T. Trew, *Language and Control* (London: Routledge and Kegan Paul, 1979), Ch. 4, 'Interviews'.

8. All three quotations from *Dostoevsky*, p. 150.

9. The most relevant of Halliday's publications are *Learning How to Mean* (London: Edward Arnold, 1975); *System and Function in Language*, ed. G. Kress (London: OUP, 1976); *Language as Social Semiotic* (London: Edward Arnold, 1978). In a forthcoming review article for *Comparative Criticism* (1981) I will be evaluating the significance of Halliday's linguistics for linguistic criticism. See also the first three chapters of my book *Linguistic Criticism* (Oxford: OUP, forthcoming) for an elementary account of the 'sociological semantics' or 'linguistics of ideology' which the present paper presupposes. Other work by my colleagues which develops this model includes R. Hodge and G. Kress, *Language as Ideology* (London: Routledge and Kegan Paul, 1979) and Fowler *et*

al., Language and Control (note 7 above). Less direct sources for my own position include Althusser, Barthes, B. Bernstein, Eco, E. Leach, Macherey, Saussure, Whorf — but it would be misleading to give exact references without the opportunity for extensive commentary and qualification.

10. See H.H. Clark and E.V. Clark, *Psychology and Language* (New York: Harcourt, Brace, Jovanovich, 1977), Ch. 14 and references. Fillmore's suggestions about the universality of the semantic categories underlying cases would be relevant: 'The Case for Case,' in E. Bach and R.T. Harms, eds., *Universals in Linguistic Theory* (New York: Holt, Rinehart and Winston, 1968), pp. 1-88, see esp. pp. 24 ff.; also R. Brown's revaluation of the early Harvard studies of language acquisition to suggest that 'the meanings of the constructions of Stage I derive from sensorimotor intelligence, in Piaget's sense.' *A First Language* (London: George Allen and Unwin Ltd., 1973), pp. 189-201.

11. This work is summarized in Clark and Clark, *op. cit.*

12. B. Bernstein, 'Social Class, Language and Socialization,' in P.P. Giglioli, ed., *Language and Social Context* 'Harmondsworth: Penguin, 1972), pp. 157-78.

13. *Language as Social Semiotic*, p. 133; cf. pp. 34, 111.

14. 'Anti-languages,' *Language as Social Semiotic*, p. 165.

15. Ibid.

16. Some of these modifications are usefully classified and illustrated in appendices to H. Wentworth and S.B. Flexner, eds., *Dictionary of American Slang* (New York: Harrap. 1960), pp. 610-50.

17. See references, note 2 above. Here my discussion connects with standard discussions of the use of related types of 'alien words' in literature, e.g. archaism; cf. Jan Mukařovský, 'Standard Language and Poetic Language,' in P.L. Garvin, ed., *A Prague School Reader on Esthetics, Literary Structure, and Style* (Washington, D.C.: Georgetown University Press, 1964), pp. 17-30.

18. Kress's article cited in note 1 is particularly helpful on negation and contradiction as aspects of anti-language in poetry.

19. Halliday's sixteenth-century English examples are taken from Thomas Harman, *A Caveat or Warening for Commen Cursetores vulgarely called Vagabones* (1567), for which see G. Salgado, ed., *Cony-Catchers and Bawdy Baskets* (Harmondsworth: Penguin, 1972). For other early English materials see E. Partridge, *A Dictionary of Historical Slang* (Harmondsworth: Penguin, 1972) (from which I have taken the definition of *upright man*) and F. Grose, ed., E. Partridge, *A Classical Dictionary of the Vulgar Tongue* ([1785] London: Routledge and Kegan Paul, 1963).

20. Definition from Wentworth and Flexner, *op. cit.* There is a wittily dialectical use of *bad* in one of the narratives of the ingenious street gang leader Larry H. quoted by W. Labov in *Language in the Inner City* (Philadelphia: University of Pennsylvania Press, 1972), p. 357.

21. Exactly the same processes of inversion and dissociation were found in other newspaper reports of the capture, 'trial' and death of Moro; cf. the *New York Times*, Sunday, April 16, 1978: '"proceedings"', '"trial"', '"death verdict"', '"accomplice"', '"spy"', etc.

22. Stanley Cohen, ed., *Images of Deviance* (Harmondsworth: Penguin, 1971), p. 14.

23. See my *Linguistics and the Novel* (London: Methuen, 1977), pp. 103-13. I would now prefer a less fanciful term such as 'theory' or 'ideology'.

24. I. and P. Opie, *The Lore and Language of School Children* ([1959] Frogmore, St. Albans: Paladin, 1977); T. Kochman, ed., *Rappin' and Stylin' Out* (Urbana: University of Illinois Press, 1972); A. Dundes, J.W. Leach and Bora Özkök, 'The Strategy of Turkish Boys' Verbal Dueling Rhymes,' in Gumperz and Hymes, *op. cit.*, pp. 130-60.

25. The point of this check is that the dictionaries of older slang are often unhelpful because their sources are exactly the texts whose meanings one wants to look up.

26. I shall take my examples mainly from the first four pages of the Grove Press paperback edition, and the reader is advised to study them carefully.

27. One of the conclusions which might be drawn from a recent research dissertation by Brian McHale (*Stylistic Registers and Free Indirect Discourse in John Dos Passos' 'U.S.A.'*, D. Phil., Oxford, 1978) is that Dos Passos' *U.S.A.* trilogy, though structured on a multiplicity of sociolinguistic varieties, fails to achieve Bakhtinian polyphony.

CHAPTER NINE

Linguistics and, and versus, poetics

1. POETICS AND LINGUISTICS IN AN INTERDISCIPLINARY PERSPECTIVE

Throughout this century, various branches of the human sciences have striven to establish themselves as autonomous disciplines. New candidates emerge all the time, and at least get prompt, if temporary, recognition in the lexicon: ethnomethodology, urban anthropology, ethnomusicology, stylistics, hermeneutics. Some subjects are transient, fashionable, sports from established major fields. Others make plausible claims for distinctive identity on the grounds of distinctiveness of subject-matter, of conceptual framework, of methodology. The ambitions of linguists towards the establishment of their own subject as a separate science, from Saussure and Bloomfield down to Chomsky, are well documented. Poetics or science of literature, more recently, cherishes similar ambitions, as the flow of new journals, and of programmatic articles, indicates.[1]

There is a paradox about the quasi-autonomous 'linguistics' and 'poetics'. One brand of poetics, at least, is primarily concerned to sever itself from other branches of literary studies such as criticism and interpretation (Todorov, 1968; Hrushovski, 1976), while granting an affinity with linguistics — linguistics provides a theoretical model, linguistics deals with materials which are also materials for poetics, even if the two have their sights on different goals. Thus one school of poetics (I am going to simplify it as 'Jakobsonian poetics') relies for its own definition of itself on an image of linguistics, and also takes for granted the relevance and competence of linguistics, which seem to be automatically justified insofar as poetics concerns itself with *verbal* art. I think that this reliance is naive and uncritical. The insistence on separateness which characterises the self-presentation of 'new disciplines' in the humanities has caused the poeticians to misinterpret their situation, to see themselves as standing in a *bi-disciplinary* relationship to linguistics: two separate, parallel, disciplines, one contributing a conceptual model for the other. In preference, the relationship may be seen as *inter-disciplinary*. I think the two subjects ought to be experienced as in dialogue, in a state of mutual critique. Disciplines which rely on one another are in a privileged position to question one another's constitutions and assumptions; rather than accept one another passively, each can help to reform the other. In the case of linguistics and poetics, the reform comes close to disestablishment of both. I shall argue that, if one tries to make sense of the proposal to found a generative poetics on the analogy of generative linguistics, one discovers large 'holes' in both disciplines, prejudicial to each and disabling for the bi-disciplinary

162

project. Establishment linguistics is crippled in its capacity to deal with language communication by its refusal to face up to linguistic variation, and to intentional, pragmatic and interactional aspects of discourse (cf. Hymes, 1964, 1974; Fowler, 1970; Searle, 1976). Relatedly, poetics as conceived by those who invoke the linguistic analogy can only maintain its claimed status by accepting the same idealization strategies that so impoverish linguistics. In effect, when 'Jakobsonian' linguistic poetics is subjected to the perspective of a realistic linguistic theory, it is forced to transform itself into a quite different approach to literature which can no longer be called 'poetics'.[2] This is the kind of dynamic consequence that one expects to issue from genuinely questioning inter-disciplinary studies.

To refer briefly to the positive results of this dismantling of theoretical models, I think one is left with a tremendously rich potential for descriptive work on the forms of the languages of literature, and the interpretation of individual texts, with a linguistics which is alert sociologically, culturally, as well as merely responsive to formal patterns at the levels of phonology and syntax. At this point we make contact with the linguistics-and-criticism controversy (as opposed to the linguistics-and-poetics conjunction), and although I do not intend to re-enter the polemics of this wretched confrontation, I hope to be able to contribute a new perspective to the linguistic side of the case. I shall conclude this paper with a programmatic list of specific aspects of linguistic description relevant to literature which my critique of linguistics and of poetics will have shown to be culpably neglected. In stressing these aspects of literary form (interactional, pragmatic, etc.) I make an explicit critique of the dominant ideology of 'objective' literary criticism.

2. CLAIMS AND LIMITATIONS OF 'JAKOBSONIAN' OR 'GENERATIVE' POETICS

By 'Jakobsonian poetics' I mean not only Jakobson's major theoretical statements (e.g. 1960; 1968) and the notorious analyses of poems by Baudelaire and Shakespeare (Jakobson and Lévi-Strauss, 1962; Jakobson and Jones, 1970) but also the theoretical proposals of linguistic structuralists who have accepted his general ideas as axioms and, in some cases, explicated and developed them in terms of generative linguistics (e.g. Todorov, 1968; Bierwisch, 1970; Culler, 1975 ch. 6). Readers will be familiar with the arguments, but I just want to recall the fact that there are two quite independent proposals: one setting out the goals of poetics, the other asserting a specific structural universal as the substance of what poeticians study. Reconstructing the first proposal as it appears in Jakobson and in Todorov, the starting-point is a hypothesis of a property of literariness or poeticality presumed to characterise literary discourse — and therefore all texts constructed in that discourse. This literariness being the proper subject-matter of the literary scientist or poetician, he will interest himself in particular texts *only* as manifestations of literariness; thus poetics or literary science is to be distinguished from all branches of literary studies which engage with the text for its individuality or for a relationship with some entity beyond itself and other than 'literary discourse' (society, author's psychology, etc.). Literature-associated activities such as evaluative criticism, interpretation, biographical study, sociology and history of literature, are not the concern of the literary scientist, whose sole objective is to discover and to describe the nature of literary discourse.

This austere programme may be and has been readily transposed into the framework of generative linguistics. The poetician is interested in individual texts merely as realizations of literariness, in the same way that the linguist looks beyond a corpus of attested sentences, or even a whole natural language, to abstract linguistic universals, defining properties of all language. Once this procedural analogy has been recognised, poetics can be thought of as 'generative', and further apparatus from generative linguistics can be invoked. It is a short step to 'literary competence' and 'ideal reader' (cf. 'linguistic competence' and 'ideal speaker-hearer' of Chomsky, 1965): literariness is re-located as 'idea of literariness', the ability which has been acquired by those few readers who can manage the special kind of reading and commentary which, it is claimed, literary discourse demands. At a certain level, this approach is very plausible. There is a marked difference between the (verbalized, anyway) responses to literary texts of educated, practised, readers who have gone through a literary training, read lots of criticism, etc., and those who have had little exposure to literature; and training in literary appreciation in schools and universities is a lengthy, rather formal, specialized process (cf. Culler, 1975: Ch. 6). Someone who has passed through a literary education has certainly 'internalized' (in Chomsky's jargon) some knowledge of literature which many other language-users have not acquired: this radical difference can be experienced every time we 'literarily competent' folk have conversations about books with people untrained in literature.

But what does this experience, and its rationalization through the generative linguistic analogy, prove? There is a strong suggestion (intensified by Chomsky's commitment to the search for language universals) that 'literary competence' is knowledge of some inherent property of all and any literature (Sophocles, Tolstoy, Yeats, skaldic poetry, haiku, ijala): the argument starts, in Jakobson, with 'literariness', a claimed universal. But it is not clear that any 'universal' (with its connotation of naturalness and therefore innateness) is at all necessary or pertinent to the generative study of literary styles. More likely, 'literary competence' is an uncommon manner or strategy of reading certain culturally selected texts, a 'competence' not based on innate ideas and unfolding in infancy, like Chomsky's 'linguistic competence', but a specialized skill of a *sociolinguistic* kind acquired in secondary socialization: an ability to handle some varieties of English (etc.) which are clearly related to English in general but which occur in special social contexts.

Let us hypothesize that the production and reception of literary texts is to a large extent a rule-governed activity (*to a large extent, but, crucially, not wholly*[3]); and that literary texts belong to linguistic varieties located in history. The linguistic analogy would avoid over-reaching if it were re-cast as follows. A generative grammar of a specific natural language accounts for a set of conventions (knowledge) for communication (behaviour) through language; these conventions are located in a history and a society, so that on two counts the same grammar will not describe French in 1700 and English in 1900. Giving this concept of grammar more socio-historical specificity still, we may say that such a grammar should, *pace* Chomsky, account for rule-governed linguistic variation and for plans of communicative behaviour within a community (Fowler, 1970; Halliday, 1973; Hymes, 1974). So, for instance, it should provide an account of differences of degree of communicative competence; of specialized, e.g. occupational, varieties or registers; of class-based variation; of the rules of discourse, including pragmatics, implicatures, cohesion or well-formedness of different conversational genres, etc. Varieties of discourse in literary texts may receive analogous generative descriptions, so that, for instance, the conventions of Miltonic blank verse are dealt with in one compartment of the description of English literary languages, the varieties of internal monologue in another, the narrative syntax of different story-telling genres elsewhere, and so on. Such a programme would more realistically reflect the empirical diversity of literary forms (which must not be reductively idealized) and the manifest variation in even professional critics' and teachers' competent-reading repertoires. In fact, this approach matches the practice of those modern scholars who have explicitly or implicitly worked on literary texts using 'generative' principles: Propp (1928), Todorov (1967, 1971), Scheglov and Zholkovsky (1971 and cf. O'Toole, 1975) and particularly Zumthor (1971). They propose underlying rules for a 'code' from which instances of texts in a genre can be generated, sometimes referring these codes to sets of socio-semiological regularities embracing and influencing the literary corpus (cf. Barthes, 1970; Chapter 5 above). Todorov's work, despite his gestures towards a general poetics, comprises a set of studies of conventions underlying specific and diverse genres (fantastic, epistolary, detective); in this respect his work follows the pioneer generic study of Propp. Zumthor (who uses linguistic terms like 'deep structure', albeit metaphorically) finds stylistic regularities in the thirteenth century *grand chant courtois* which he attributes to codes — cultural conventions — existing abstractly 'at a hierarchically different level' from the individual poems, indicating an 'ideological schema' which was accessible to the contemporary audience through perception of style: an ideology of love which of course ultimately derives from the structure of the society.

In the method which can be extrapolated from these writers, poetic interpretation becomes a kind of generative sociolinguistics (or 'sociological semantics' as the Firth-Halliday linguistic school might label it). Returning our attention to readers and their 'literary competence', I propose a sociolinguistic alternative to the 'competence' spoken of in the Jakobsonian school of poetics. The suggestion of this school that there is a unique and absolute literary competence possessed by 'the' ideal reader and operative for any literary text is challenged by the diversity of literary forms and by the historical relativity of readings (Culler's report of an interpretation of Blake's 'Sunflower', 1975, pp. 115-6 is indeed interestingly different from any conceivable response to 'practical language', but the reading is itself surely the product of a historically specific literary culture). Instead I propose that a reader is 'competent' with respect to his repertoire of the forms of writing he can cope with, and with respect to the cultural functions which his society requires of him (as critic, reviewer, consumer, etc.) at a certain point of time. I use the term 'repertoire' in the way that it is used in sociolinguistics: a set of language-using skills which vary systematically according to the circumstances of linguistic performance (resulting in different context-appropriate levels of formality, registers, modes of response, etc.); a set which varies in extent and in content from individual to individual; which is acquired by the individual through socialization and which is thus a function of group-membership rather than individuality. We learn to read Shakespeare if we pass through a certain kind of school system, in exactly the same way that we come to write journalese if we work on a newspaper, or understand the conventions of official memos if we work in a bureaucratic department, or speak deferentially if our house, job and food prices are controlled by others. To present the facts this way is not to injure the greatness of Shakespeare, but it is clear that the sociolinguistic approach diverges substantially from a 'poetics' which claims to explain that greatness in terms of some universal property of 'literariness'.

I do, then, believe that it is possible to support and explicate a notion of 'literary competence' — equivalently, to show the distinctive qualities of different forms of writing — through linguistic theory and description. Whereas Jakobsonian poetics appeals to linguistic theory as a model or metaphor or analogy (a standard, and by no means reprehensible, manoeuvre in semiology: see Barthes, 1964), I suggest that a linguistic theory of the right kind can profitably be focussed *directly* on literary texts and institutions. Of course, the result is not 'poetics' in the sense required by Jakobson, but in view of the shifting forms in the history of literature, such an absolute concept of poetic discourse is most probably a wild goose chase. Readers become competent in varieties which count as literature; not competent *in literature*. Linguistic poetics is the description of these varieties; linguistic criticism, their interpretation and evaluation.

Let us now briefly examine the more specific part of Jakobson's proposal, that is, his idea of what in Chomskyan terms would be called a substantive universal of poetic structure. I shall not expound the details of his proposal at any length, since it is readily accessible in 'Linguistics and Poetics' (1960), and anyway very familiar. The mechanism of the 'poetic function of language' is that it 'projects the principle of equivalence from the axis of selection into the axis of combination'; the effect of this is to 'promote the palpability of signs' or 'focus on the message for its own sake', thus 'deepening the fundamental dichotomy of signs and objects' (and so making the poetic text an autonomous construct, released from reference to material things, experience and history). Although Jakobson illustrates the principle most copiously from the levels of sound-texture and metre, he makes it clear that it operates at other levels of structure as well: e.g. parallelism in syntax, contradiction and tautology in semantics; also, inter-level connexions are significant, e.g. 'rhyme necessarily involves the semantic relationship between rhyming units' (1960: 367).

I am not qualified to judge the applicability of this formula to the full range of examples which Jakobson offers. One is impressed, however, with how well it works for that part of Jakobson's materials with which one is familiar: lyric poetry, including oral folk poetry and some dramatic speech, in the major European literatures. 'Working well' here means offering satisfying structural explanations, very abstract and apparently powerful explanations, for a wide range of figures of speech and of thought expressed in verse. But 'working well' also means something more limited if (a) one considers the *critical* limitations of his practical analyses; (b) one tries to stand outside the literary traditions which make the centre of Jakobson's materials.

(a) Jakobson's 'exhaustive' analyses of Baudelaire and Shakespeare are notoriously shallow, formalistic, dominated by mechanical and perhaps spurious patterns in phonology and syntax, absolutely uninformative when the analyst comes to interpretation or to placing in history. That is, 'working well' applies to intensity and ingenuity at a certain level of rhetorical description.

(b) However much critics may object (rightly, I think) to the mechanistic character of Jakobson's analyses, the fact is that both the approach and the materials to which it is applied are actually extremely consonant with the methods and favoured texts of literary scholars up to recently. Jakobson's 'poetic principle' is essentially an extremely abstract analysis of the basis of many of the stock figures in the European rhetorical tradition (as is evidenced by the appearance of an old-fashioned rhetorical terminology in Jakobson's descriptive writings). This rhetorical background is in turn a link between Jakobson and the English and American 'New Critics' of the thirties and forties; and there are specific connexions in such mutual interests as, say, paradox, metaphor and the whole area of the irrational and symbolic in language.[4] It is not surprising that Jakobson and the New Critics work largely with a rather homogeneous set of verse corpora: the English lyric tradition from the late sixteenth century, omitting some poets and promoting others, and the major poets of symbolism and modernism in the nineteenth-early twentieth-century Europe. Jakobson's early affiliations with Russian formalism explain his predilection for phonetic and other surface-structure patterning. Now there is no doubt that all this adds up to an enormous temporal and cultural range, but, on the other hand, this body of literature can be seen as having a somewhat specialized role within European-American culture; as excluding a vast amount which counts as literature within that culture (much drama, and all discursive and narrative prose except the oratorical and aphoristic fragments enclosed within it[5]); and as excluding, potentially, an even greater mass of speakings and writings which may count as literature within societies unknown to western literary scholars.

3. THE LINGUISTICS OF 'JAKOBSONIAN POETICS' AND OF 'OBJECTIVE CRITICISM'

I have examined the notion that there can be a generative poetics *like* generative linguistics, and suggested that such a proposal would make sense only if what was generated was a set of literary languages related to varying cultural structures and 'internalised' variously depending on the different socialized qualifications of readers.

Now Jakobson makes a stronger claim than that poetics is *like* linguistics: he insists that it is *part* of linguistics (1960: 350, 352) except when 'the field of linguistics appears to be illicitly restricted'. His initial definition of the field of linguistics is inclusive indeed. Whereas modern linguistics generally assumes (or used until very recently to assume) a mere two-level model, meaning expressed through sound, Jakobson enumerates six 'constitutive factors in any speech event' (353): addresser, addressee, context, code, message, contact. He recognises the complexity of the situation and the process of communication, or to put it another way, the *situatedness* of linguistic communication. Next Jakobson sketches a set of linguistic 'functions', each one distinguished by a special degree of importance accorded to one of the constitutive factors. The functions are said to be not exclusive, but relative, so that, for instance, tinges of the poetic use of language may be found in non-poetic discourse, e.g. slogans. According to this theory, then, it seems that the structure of language in use responds to the circumstances, motives, etc., of its use. Jakobson does not commit himself to a full functional theory, however; he would not maintain, with Halliday, that all parts of language structure have their origins in functional adaptation, only that different aspects of language structure are foregrounded in different situations of usage; so that, e.g., vocatives and imperatives become important in the language of persuasion.

As functional theories go, Jakobson's is crucially different from Halliday's in one respect. Halliday's three functions are conceived of as *simultaneously* operative, Jakobson's six — despite the concession of partial overlap — as *alternative*. If a text is poetic it is not referential, and so on; whereas, in Halliday, every text, whatever its specific purpose, has dimensions of linguistic structure fulfilling all three of what he calls the 'ideational', 'textual' and 'interpersonal' functions (see Halliday, 1970, 1973). Obviously the cateogories of these two functional theories cannot be mapped onto one another, because they have very different logical statuses: we must not equate, say, 'ideational' with 'referential'. The theories are interestingly comparable in two respects, though. First, they dispose their proponents to take different lines on the general question of classifying texts into communicative types. In Jakobson, or I.A. Richards, the coupling of language and function is so tight that a text must be either one thing or another — language seems to be a different phenomenon in each one of its small finite taxonomy of types.[6] On the other hand, Hallidayan or Firthian or sociolinguistic functionalism allows a much more complex and fluid relationship between texts and their contexts of use. Though still committed to accounting for structural choices in terms of contextual/sociological function, it assumes that any particular text or discourse is usually doing more than one thing at once: this is a natural consequence of the fact that (as Jakobson's diagram goes some way towards showing) language in use connects with life at a variety of different points. So, for instance, a speaker's syntactic choices may 'mean' one thing for him (e.g. formality) or more than one thing (e.g. formality plus solidarity with a polite group) and something else for his interlocutor (e.g. authoritarianism, snobbishness). Or, a writer's status in relation to his readership may be complex and ambiguous, as, for instance, a writer working for a popular newspaper, much more highly educated than his readership, but much less powerful than the newspaper's proprietors or the firms that advertise in the paper: his language has to satisfy a range of highly differentiated interested parties. Or, consider the situation of an advertiser who must simultaneously inform (at the referential level, in relation to the availability of the product) and deceive (at the perlocutionary level, in relation to the consumer).[7] A functional theory of language must be flexible enough to allow for the multi-functional status of texts, the complexity of which emerges strikingly when we begin to consider texts within their pragmatic contexts.

In the case of literary texts, the specific dangers of too-rigid typology are the exclusion of referential and interpersonal qualities. Anglo-American literary theory has in fact since the 1920's argued strongly for refining these qualities out of literary texts. I.A. Richards tried to draw a line between 'scientific' and 'emotive' uses of language, placing poetry in the latter category and denying that it has any responsibility for the truth or referentiality of the 'statements' it makes; in these terms he defended *The Waste Land* against allegations of incoherence (1926: Ch. 34 and Appendix B). Archibald MacLeish's 'A poem should not mean/But be' became widely quoted as a poet's confirmation that poetry has no business making statements about the real world. In literary theory which is based principally on the model of verse, and specifically, of lyric poetry, this 'objectivity' and 'non-referentiality' has hardened into a dogma: the critic is not concerned with the poem's relationships with or statements about the world, but with what it uniquely says 'in and of itself'. For typical formulations, see Abrams, 1953 (the first chapter of which is highly compatible with Jakobson, 1960), and Wellek and Warren, 1963.

In discussions of narrative, and in the practice of narrative writing, the absoluteness and arbitrariness of fiction has come to be more and more insisted upon: reference to, or reflection of, the real world gives way to the absolute shaping power of the novelist (Kermode, 1967; Fowles, 1969). But, in fact, to claim that the imaginative writer creates through language a new world distinct from the real world referred to by history-books, newspapers, etc., is not to justify separating imaginative writing absolutely from 'referential' discourse. A series of propositions about non-existent people or events has, for the reader, the same status as a series of propositions about real historical circumstances of which the reader was previously unaware. In both cases, the reader has to make sense of the content by reconstructing it as a world which is plausible in terms of the world he knows. (Or, in the case of the fantastic, related to 'our' world by systematic transformations.) In both cases, the writer's arrangements of words and sentences impose an artificial order upon the events real or non-real referred to, so that historical narrative is ordered, edited, by language, in the way that 'pure fiction' is. And in both cases — indeed, in all examples of linguistic performance — the writer's choice of words and sentences may be explained in terms of the social and historical circumstances in which the writer and his readers communicate; so that words which refer to fictional entities may be interpreted in the light of real material and social situations. (This, it seems to me, is a type of historical explanation that the proponents of fictionality particularly want to preclude.)

As reference has been denied literature in modern literary theory, so also have personal origin and personal response. Wimsatt and Beardsley pronounced against the 'intentional fallacy' and the 'affective fallacy' in 1946 and 1949 (in Wimsatt, 1954). Although repeatedly discredited by aestheticians and critics, these fallacious fallacies are still rehearsed in the dominant text-books used in England and America. They are fallacious because all discourse emanates from a person,[8] and any discourse received by a person has some effect on that individual's behaviour or state. All languages are provided with 'interpersonal' structures which effect these particular links between text and life. To deny these links seems to me to dehumanize the very texts which the critics claim have a special significance for humanity.

'Fictionality' and 'impersonality' are central doctrines in the tradition of 'intrinsic' or 'objective' criticism which, though rejected by most serious contemporary scholars in literary theory, still dominates literary education in schools and universities. Students are presented with clichés like 'autonomous whole', 'organic unity', 'stasis', 'inner coherence' as ways of thinking about the alleged self-sufficiency and uniqueness of structural pattern of the individual literary text. They are exhorted to consider poetry 'primarily as poetry and not another thing' (T.S. Eliot) — e.g. not as social document, not as personal expression. Literary language is different from ordinary language, and, furthermore, each individual text is inclined to invent its own unique 'language' which the critic has to decode like a cryptographer. Noticeably, poems become extremely complex, difficult and equivocal (how daunting Empson's *Seven Types of Ambiguity* is for students, how satisfying for the initiated!). The general difficulty for the student is that the 'objective' critical school, in pleading the special formal character of literature, deliberately removes it from the world of ordinary experience, and compounds the difficulty at the linguistic level by disconnecting 'literary language' from everyday usage — in effect insisting that the student's well-developed 'practical language' is a poor qualification for reading literature.

An analysis of the historical context of this ideology of 'criticism', its relationships to literature and to education, would I think reveal something fairly sinister. Whatever the conscious motives of these critics and theoreticians might be, despite whatever protestations they might make, the purposes and effects of their programme are divisive and elitist. Literary education in the 'new critical' or 'practical criticism' tradition presents its object as mysterious, and its methods and analytic terms are vague and imprecise. This critical theory and metalanguage is guaranteed to make literature inaccessible to all but a small fraction of the educated population. Accessibility is made even more difficult by the isolation and 'professionalism' of literature teaching, reviewing and criticism (see Ohmann, 1976). It is now extremely difficult to get a job teaching English or modern languages/literatures in a university: in addition to the severe hurdles placed in the way of the aspirant in the PhD programme, both initial entry and tenure are becoming less and less achievable as the numbers of students majoring in the humanities diminish and as staff-student ratios are deteriorated. This situation is advantageous to those already established in the teaching and criticism industry, since it makes their own positions more prestigious and gives them greater control over the dissemination of knowledge about literature. Similarly, young critics find it difficult to get their books and papers published, and everyone's work is subject to long delays (around three years). Bright radical ideas do not appear or, through delay, lose their force. In the case of reviews of academic books, a delay of three years means that good books go unnoticed and bad books sell steadily without radical critique. Literature teachers of my acquaintance are scathing about the prompt weekly reviews, rejecting their quick judgements by contrast with the 'mature thought' of the 'scholarly review'.

We have, then, an intricate paradox in the institution of literature and literature teaching. Though literature is held to possess revelatory powers, it is not allowed to say very much, or to speak to many people. 'Objective' critical theory mystifies literary texts; 'poetics' similarly, by stressing remoteness from 'practical' communication. Though literature teachers and literary critics are (very largely) public employees with obligations to make available their special knowledge, the ethos of their profession forbids them to make pronouncements about the world (cf. Ohmann, 1976, on the MLA and the Vietnam War). The situation of academic publishing ensures that, though a vast quantity of trivial and self-indulgent rubbish is issued each year under the name of literary criticism or history or scholarship, intelligent criticism intended to *let literature speak* is rejected, delayed or at the least buried under other people's dull and routine 'scholarship'.

The above is my view of the context of academic criticism and poetics, and an indication of my motives for desiring reform. It is not my business in this paper to outline general reforms for the profession, but to suggest some methodological reorientations in linguistic poetics and linguistic criticism which would at least counter mystificatory practices and doctrines for criticism. It is time now to return to linguistic methodology and theory.

I mentioned that there are two principal drawbacks to a 'alternative-functions' model of communication (like Richards's or Jakobson's). One, already elaborated, is its dogmatic determination to see a text 'primarily as X and not another thing' — against the commonsense view that actual language (including literature) is usually doing more than one thing at once. The second criticism of this model concerns the aspects of linguistic structure which the analyst is disposed to notice. Once he has taken a decision that a text is of a certain communicative type (referential, or emotive, or poetic, or whatever), the linguist may decide that only certain parts of linguistic structure merit his attention. In some respects, this selectivity is a reasonable plan; exhaustiveness is impossible anyway, and one often does know in advance that certain features are going to be relevant: for instance, in language which is very much directed to the addressee, such as advertising, it is natural to look closely at personal pronouns, imperatives, evaluative adjectives, and modals. It is not reasonable, however, to *exclude* some area of structure from analysis on the strength of a prior decision about the type of text we are dealing with, e.g. to fail to look at interpersonal structures in a text which we have decided is scientific and therefore impersonal. The danger in literary studies is that, when the apologists for poetry decide to ignore the interpersonal and referential dimensions of literary texts, they remove attention from real and potentially significant parts of the language of poems and plays and novels. In particular, erasure of 'context' or 'universe' diminishes attention to the linguistic constructions which express what Halliday has called the 'ideational' function of language: lexicalization and the classification of referents, syntax as conceptual process (e.g. transitivity), etc. Erasure of 'artist' and 'audience' or 'addresser' and 'addressee' encourages neglect of 'interpersonal' structures: modality, personal pronouns, forms of address, illocution, etc., and their sociological extensions such as solidarity, anti-language. (See section 4 below for more details.) It is undeniable that all such constructions *do* appear in literary texts, and that they *have* been ignored in formalist criticism. My positive technical proposal is that criticism should be deliberately and systematically attentive to such forms and to their significances. This strategy would return the study of literary languages into contact with the study of 'ordinary language'; would help to re-connect the student's experience of literary languages with his practical language experience; and would encourage literary scholars to restore the historical, sociological and pragmatic dimensions which have, prejudicially, been withdrawn from the study of the institution of literature — thereby helping to de-mythologize it and to combat the expropriation which it has suffered in the modern period.

4. LINGUISTICS AND THE DESCRIPTION OF LITERARY LANGUAGES

I have argued against linguistics being invoked to support 'poetics' partly on empirical grounds (Jakobson's substantive universal is quite implausible for a great range of literary texts), partly on ideological (the texts which do illustrate his poetic principle have a determinate, and in some lights objectionable, role in Western society), partly on theoretical grounds. The theoretical objection is that using linguistics in the manner of this particular Jakobsonian conjunction does, *pace* Jakobson, restrict linguistics illicitly. Jakobsonian poetics demands of linguistics nothing more than a metalanguage for describing syntactic and phonological recurrences, and perhaps componential strucuture in semantics. Conveniently, and notoriously, exactly those aspects of language structure were the central preoccupations and limitations of the dominant schools of linguistics down to the late 1960s — a correspondence which is perfectly comprehensible if we think of linguistics from the time of Saussure and developing within the same historical and intellectual climate as poetics from the time of Shklovsky (which is the same time).

My complaint against poetic theory's use of linguistic theory is that the recipient discipline (poetics) did not sufficiently challenge the donor discipline (linguistics), did not press linguistics to develop its now evidently inadequate power and comprehensiveness. I suggested at the beginning of this paper that one important measure of success in interdisciplinary studies is the effect of the conjunction on scholars' conceptions of their separate unidisciplinary assumptions. In a trivial metaphor, unusual exercise ought to remind us that we have muscles which we haven't been using, and encourage us to develop these. Linguistics and poetics haven't tested one another's capabilities and limitations at all radically enough.

An instructive contrast to the conservatism of linguistic poetics is the rapidly innovative development of psycholinguistics. The Chomsky-Skinner dispute symbolizes, if in extreme form, the gulf between psychology and linguistics twenty years ago. But Chomsky's new grammar, and the mentalistic claims made for it, opened up to psychologists the prospect that they might 'construct an experimental mentalism' (Fodor, Bever and Garrett, 1974:xi). The attraction for linguists was no less than that for psychologists: it was exciting that psycholinguistic research might show that their grammars really did offer something more humanly significant than a mere formal account of sentence structures. Early experiments seemed to confirm the psychological validity of transformational rules, to suggest that they were 'really' operative in influencing ease of sentence comprehension and recall, that they took up space in memory, etc. It was very quickly realised that transformational complexity neither correlated with nor explained ease or difficulty of sentence processing. Far more influential were semantic and pragmatic factors such as negation, truth-value, roles of nouns, relation to linguistic and non-linguistic context. Thus, pressure was put upon linguistics to extend its horizons to account for such factors: psycholinguistics, in a precipitously rapid series of research findings, provoked linguistics to seek a richer theory of communication than Chomsky's grammar provided. The story of excitement, disillusion, then radicalizing progress is told in recent textbooks, e.g. Aitchison, 1976; Cairns and Cairns, 1976; Greene, 1972. The same progress from syntactic to much richer semantic and pragmatic explanations, making increasing demands on linguistics to extend its capacities, is found in studies of first language acquisition: see Brown, 1973; Dale,[2] 1976.

No such dynamic can be found in the progress of linguistic poetics. During the same twenty years that psycholinguistics and sociolinguistics have developed so radically and demanded so much change within linguistics, poetics has done little more than keep up with a few independently motivated developments in linguistics, e.g. taking cognisance of the deep/surface distinction, selection restrictions, case grammar, etc. and utilizing such concepts in particular descriptive studies. Poeticians (and stylisticians) have remained extremely complacent about the adequacies of the two disciplines they conjoin; poetics has done little to question the paradigm it offers or the paradigm it invokes. Both paradigms, I have suggested, are suspect, and their weaknesses seem to be similar and cognate. The prevailing literary-theoretical paradigm suppresses interpersonal, sociological and referential dimensions of literary texts; the dominant linguistic model is also highly formalistic, and is increasingly under pressure (but, on the whole, not from the poeticians) to reform itself towards recognition *in the grammar* of sociolinguistic variation, contextual appropriateness, pragmatics, discourse well-formedness, presupposition. I am suggesting that the grounds for questioning the two paradigms are closely linked; and that attention to the relatedness of the problems would benefit both literary theory and linguistic theory. Benefits would accrue to literary and linguistic scholars separately, whether or not they were directly interested in the other discipline. But my specific interest, of course, is in a reformulation of the linguistics/poetics/criticism interdiscipline which would require linguistics to contribute on a large scale, and radically, to literary theory, literary history, and literary education.

My main object in this paper has been to outline a problem and its dimensions, not to detail a response to the problem. However, my own proposal for a way forward has been — I hope — clearly implied throughout, and I shall be brief and programmatic on the positive outcome.

The first move is a shift from absolutism to pluralism: to see the field study not as 'theory of literary language' but as 'theory of literary languages' (cf. Fowler, 1971, especially Ch. 7; Posner, 1976). The theory is then properly linguistic, or sociolinguistic (not just metaphorically linguistic): basically it is a theory of varieties, of correlations between distinctive linguistic choices and particular socio-cultural circumstances. The individual text can be described and interpreted in relation to the stylistic conventions which generate it and the historical and sociological situation which brought it into existence (cf. Zumthor, 1971, referred to above). Authors and readers — hypothesized 'ideal readers' — can be characterized in relation to whatever literary communities are relevant: often, since critics are frequently dealing with 'our' relationship to works of the past, the interplay between two communities, or among multiple communities, and between their differing semiological conventions, will be at issue.

So far, my proposal amounts to no more than a suggestion that the primary task of linguistic poetics is the description of literary styles in their synchronic and diachronic variety; placing these styles in their cultural contexts; and carrying out this programme without any prejudice as to what might constitute 'literary language'. What counts as literature (or poetry or whatever equivalent term) in a given period or milieu is a sociocultural fact about the specific community and time, and is not predictable in advance; in any case, *genre* terms are more important than very general concepts like 'literature', in this sociolinguistic theory. If we were to leave the proposal at this, however, we would, happily, banish the ghost of 'literariness' but, regrettably, retain a programme for merely formalist accounts of the history of styles. We need to go a stage further and specify the design of our sociolinguistic stylistics in more detail. It should regard linguistic structures as *functionally motivated*; and among linguistic structures, it should focus with special concentration on those that function *interpersonally* — the ones which allow texts and discourses to work as interactional behaviour between the members of a language community. I intend these two concepts to have the meaning given in M.A.K. Halliday's recent writings (1970; 1973; 1976); rather than defining them here, I will mention some sociolinguistic examples which will illustrate their force. Labov's classic research in sociolinguistics is nonfunctional. Wanting to show that variation in language form correlates systematically with social stratification, he observes a number of phonological indices such as post-vocalic /r/ and finds that the incidence of such phonemes does indeed vary informatively with social class (1966; 1972). The demonstration is absolutely convincing, but no-one could conceivably claim that it is the *function* of /r/ to mark class differences. /r/ is an arbitrary, fortuitous, index in this sociological context;

its meaning and status within the English language are not motivated by its imposed role as an observed variable in a study of the social stratification of English in New York City. By contrast, the 'pronouns of power and solidarity' described by Brown and Gilman (1960) take their systemic structure and their meanings directly from the class structures of the societies which the authors studied: they are functionally motivated. Many other examples of functional vs. non-functional explanations of structure come to mind: e.g. the TG account of passives which treats them as synonyms of actives, versus the various functional explanations of passives as having specific roles in communicative contexts: as being motivated by a particular distribution of given and new information, by non-availability of agent, etc.

The extreme position in functionalism, probably untenable, is that *all* aspects of linguistic structure are to be explained as motivated by function in context; I am advocating a more modest position, namely that any constructions which seem to be sociologically or stylistically interesting should be treated as subjects not just for notice but for strong functional explanation. (In classic stylistics, Spitzer's most brilliant commentaries rest on extremely daring functional explanations of linguistic recurrences: see Spitzer, 1948). In this way, stylistic features cease to be 'merely stylistic' or 'merely formal', and attain real cultural substance.

My insistence on the importance of studying interpersonal features of language — which is obviously not meant to be exclusive — stems from the principle that texts should be considered in relation to their communicative contexts: context comprising not only the broad cultural situation but also the narrower context of interpersonal relationships mediated by a text or discourse. These relationships are, of course, not literal as they are in the face-to-face mode when A says to B 'Please pass me the salt'. But the doctrine of fictionality in modern literary theory has obscured the fact that literary texts *do* imply speakers and addressees in inter-action, and that both author and reader have the task of orienting themselves on whatever network of interacting voices is constructed by the interpersonal parts of the text. In general terms, recognising these facts has the effect of restoring the components of the communicative event which Jakobson first placed on the periphery of his diagram and then erased; and also has the effect of challenging the 'objective fallacy', the erroneous belief that a text can be represented as an autonomous verbal artefact dissociated from its interpersonal and cultural co-ordinates. I have offered some informal analyses, illustrating the kinds of features which should be noticed, elsewhere (Fowler, 1977a, Ch. 4; this volume Chapters five and seven). A list of crucially noteworthy linguistic features would include the following. Most have received sporadic attention in stylistics, some are immediately relevant to exciting developments in literary studies (e.g. dialogic structure, Bakhtin 1973; *Rezeptionsaesthetik*, Iser 1974; narrative modality, Doleżel 1976); all are problematic in linguistics, in the good sense that they are still poorly understood and cry out for thought, empirical research and articulation.[9]

Personal pronouns, forms of address, and names connect discourse with its participants and protagonists; first and second person are especially significant in creating fictional speakers and addressees in relation to whom the reader can orient himself and his image of the author; names are stylistically significant, particularly variation of naming (Uspensky, 1973).

Illocutionary force and *speech act* are controversial in linguistics (Searle, 1969; Sadock, 1974; Cole and Morgan, 1975.; Verschueren, 1976) and in literary theory (Levin, 1976; Ohmann, 1973 and earlier papers; Searle, 1975; van Dijk, 1976; Pratt, 1977). Even if one grants that speakers have intentions, and that participants in discourse have beliefs about the world and make assumptions about one another's beliefs, it is clear from the current literature that the problem of formalizing the semantics of these matters is immense; similarly, it is not at all easy to imagine developing realization rules which will derive the great variety of surface structures which are associated with speech acts (once one goes beyond the speech act locutions marked by lexicalized performative verbs like 'promise'). For literature, there are additional problems. The question has usually been posed: what kind of speech act is performed by a literary text? or, who performs the speech act? Given the usual assumptions about the impersonality of literature (fictionality, withdrawal of the real author, stative character of aesthetic response), it is tempting to say that speech act theory does not apply in a literal way: that literary texts are used to perform pretend speech acts, or the normal felicity conditions are suspended or broken. This is rather an extreme departure: I would prefer to see the illocutionary problems of literary texts considered not as problems of a poetic discourse diametrically opposite from 'ordinary language', but as problems of indirectness of contact between addresser and addressee which affect written texts generally.[10] In any event, one can very profitably study the significance of speech acts *within* literary texts: as contributing to characterization, to the construction of personas, narrators, implied authors and readers; to the creation of interaction between fictional consciousnesses (cf. Bakhtin, 1973; Fowler, 1977a, Ch. 4).

At the more 'superficial' end of linguistics, illocutionary or pragmatic theory leads to us study explicitly *manipulative* constructions such as imperatives, interrogatives, responses, vocatives, threats, etc. At a more abstract level, implicature (Grice, 1975), presupposition (Keenan, 1971) and other assumptions about relevant knowledge which we rely on when making sense of discourse (e.g. Sacks, 1972) are highly promising for literary theory and analysis. Candidate topics for investigation from this angle are irony, ambiguity, ellipsis, metaphor, misunderstanding, dramatic dialogue. Since the study of discourse semantics is only just beginning to be developed, and is one of the most compelling areas of contemporary linguistics, while irony, ambiguity, etc., are established as central preoccupations in literary studies, there is every incentive to make the connections between linguistic and literary studies in this area extremely stimulating and fruitful for both sides.

Another area of linguistic structure which needs and promises rich development, and which is of great importance to the view of literature which I am advocating, is *modality* — the speaker's or writer's commitment to or evaluation of the content of the propositions he utters.[11] The principal linguistic surface structures associated with modality are the modal auxiliaries ('may', etc.), sentence-adverbs ('possibly'), evaluative adjectives ('good'), certain verbal predicates ('seem', 'feel') but in fact modality is pervasive and may be expressed in a very wide range of forms, e.g. nominalization to delete the auxiliary and thus avoid modal marking, or the use in newspapers of quotation marks to indicate dissociation from the values of a quoted word. The most obvious application of modal analysis, for our purposes, is to narrative texts: to the classification of types of narrator (impersonal, intrusive, unreliable, etc., cf. Booth, 1961; Todorov, 1966) and of narrative (historical, fantastic, exemplary, etc.). Doležel (1976) suggests a classification of 'narrative modalities' following the four modal logics but does not cross-check it with either the semantics or syntax/lexis of linguistic modality. Lots of textual description needs to be done, but not in an *ad hoc* way: we need radical hypotheses about the system of meanings subsumed under modality — in fact, a rethinking of the whole set of categories collected under 'Aux' in traditional grammar. Once again, there is a prospect of interdisciplinary dialogue leading to theoretical reorientation on both (in this case three) sides.

In a stimulating paper, Kress (1977) has hypothesized that the tense morphemes in English do not signal just time reference; they (also or really?) communicate a 'modality of non-actuality'. Interestingly, *tense* has been much studied as a marker of narrative distance (Benveniste, 1966; Bronzwaer, 1970; Hamburger, ²1968; Simonin-Grumbach, 1975; Weinrich, 1964). As a deictic feature, orienting the narrative source and the reader in relation to the content of the narrative, it is an interpersonal feature. And since it serves to mark different degrees of intimacy between narrator and material, it is also in a sense modal. For instance, the present tense 'She is sad', or the present tense 'now' of the indirect free style 'She was sad now' affirms the certainty of the speaker's knowledge just as modal forms do: 'She felt sad', 'Certainly, she was sad'. Evidently there is an interrelated set of problems here concerning the linguistic coding of intimacy and distance, authority and diffidence, which needs investigation as a whole set, and probably a revision of theory. Narrative is a provocative part of the *explicanda*.

This list could be considerably extended, but there would be little purpose, and some danger, in doing so. I hope I have made my point about the magnitude of the challenge to both linguistics and literary studies when texts are regarded, untraditionally, as functional interactions. The hazard in extending the list (including, say, information structure, class responses to registers, etc.) is simply that it is unhelpful to structure the problem as an inventory of issues labelled according to the categories of the disciplines as they stand at the moment. What begins as a list of descriptive tasks rapidly transforms into a need for a much more adequate unified theory of texts than we possess. The centre of the need, in my opinion, is an account of pragmatics, or discourse, or interaction or whatever one wishes to call it. Fortunately, linguistics has over the past few years begun to reform itself in that direction (yet without approaching anything like the degree of complexity of the problems which literary critics are accustomed to confront [and confront so amateurishly]). I have tried to present 'poetics' as both a potential advocate of such reform and an actual censor; thus itself a suitable case for reform.

Chapter Nine

Notes

1. An early version of this paper was delivered at the first British Comparative Literature conference at the University of East Anglia in December, 1975. I am indebted to Christine Brooke-Rose and to Gunther Kress for helpful comments on my first draft. Posner (1976) has helped me to clarify some of my own ideas. For related discussion, see Chapters five, six and seven, Ch. 3). Pratt (1977), which I had not read until my final version, provides general support for my argument, and some specific suggestions in the areas mentioned in my last few pages.

2. An alternative procedure to this particular 'transformation', which will appeal to non-linguists but which is quite outside the scope of this paper, would be to begin the project for poetics afresh, starting from some quite different kind of aesehetic hypothesis.

3. The crucial exemption from conventionality is, of course, 'creativity' which I take to be, at the level of imagination, divergent thinking; at the level of experience, defamiliarization; at the level of language, transmutation of the forms available at a particular point in the history of a literary culture. See Posner, 1976, drawing on the Shklovsky tradition; Fowler, 1977a, Ch. 5, for a discussion of convention as a prerequisite to creativity. Creativity deserves better than a footnote, I know; but it is not the main topic of this paper.

4. Jakobson's scheme of functions of language, with (among other oppositions) the 'poetic' contrasting with the 'referential', is surely a development of I.A. Richards's 'two uses of language' (1926: Ch. 34) in which 'emotive' opposes 'scientific'.

5. Deep narrative syntax as analysed by Propp, Todorov, Greimas, Barthes follows schemes of equivalence and opposition, but noone could pretend that the textual substance or the cultural significance of the great European novels is much illuminated by Jakobson's poetic principle,

6. Not surprisingly, the taxonomy is often compressed into a dichotomy, e.g. 'scientific' vs. 'emotive' or 'scientific' vs. 'poetic'.

7. For some examples of the complexities of these processes, see Fowler, Hodge, Kress, and Trew (1979).

8. 'Person' and 'individual' here are not intended to eliminate social existence; far from it. The individual speaks or writes, hears or reads, very much according to his situation in a culture — subject to the qualification mentioned in note 3 above.

9. May I anticipate a rationalist objection? Literary critics who oppose the linguistics-literature coupling expect there to be a set of efficient linguistic 'tools' available, which can be applied to texts in a methodologically transparent way, so that either the procedure can be condemned as mis-conceived or the result condemned as trivial (Bateson, 1967; Smith, 1977). For such people, it is doubtless outrageous to confess at the start that the 'tools' proposed have not yet been fully developed. This objection would miss the dialectical content of my proposal: that intellectual positions are productive not when experienced as settled and complete but when placed under stress by the demands of new materials and approaches.

10. Pratt (1977) argues persuasively that the speech-act contract between narrator and reader in prose fiction is essentially the same as that between story-teller and audience in oral 'natural narrative'.

11. This informal definition focuses on the attitude of the speaker in accordance with my emphasis in this paper on interpersonal factors. Alternative (though not equivalent) formulations would be in terms of the modal logics or of possible-world semantics (see Moravcsik, 1975). It has been plausibly suggested that a possible-world analysis could illuminate our understanding of metaphoric processes. Doležel (1976) has advocated reference to the modal logics for classifying types of fiction.

Preliminaries to a sociolinguistic theory of literary discourse

This paper is a critique of the accepted role of linguistics in structural poetics, and an argument for a revised and enlarged role. I grant that linguistics has been extremely influential and productive as a model for a developing poetic theory. However, the appeal to linguistics as an analogue or metaphoric vehicle has been accompanied by a very restricted use of linguistic *description* in literary studies. I argue for an increased use of linguistic analysis in descriptive poetics, as part of a general programme aiming to encourage more descriptive, specialized, empirical research in poetics.

I also criticize some specific received opinions about language in literature: principally, the view that there is a special 'poetic language' or 'language of literature', and the 'objective' theory that a text is an autonomous verbal structure which has been severed from the processes of communication. To the alleged unitary poetic language I oppose the idea of a plurality of varieties, thus opening the way for sociolinguistic concepts in descriptive poetics. As for the objective theory, I suggest that we avoid and attack that doctrine by substituting a communication model of discourse, emphasizing aspects of language which have pragmatic and interpersonal functions. Since the interpersonal and pragmatic parts of communication have their sources in social structure, my answer to the objective fallacy is integrally linked to my remedy for the poetic language fallacy. The two amount to a unified but multi-part proposal for descriptive studies of language in literature concentrating on socio-cultural extensions of linguistic codes. Though my proposal is, immediately, for empirical studies in the (socio) linguistics of literary texts, this approach is not at all anti-theoretical: in fact, a new sociolinguistic theory of literary discourse is presupposed.

In taking sides on these theoretical premises in structural poetics, I am not simply taking a stance on a purely academic, intellectual question. The issues involved are ultimately socio-academic and, instrumentally, institutional. The idea of a special poetic language remote from common speech suits a society in which only a very small special class of people read the texts in that language. Schools and universities select members of that class from the mass of the population and train only them in 'literary competence'; since schools and universities are geared to reproducing the economic élite and its discriminatory values, only the children of the already privileged learn 'literary competence', and their parents' privilege is reproduced in them: literature is appropriated as an instrument in the reproduction of the dominant class. Similarly, the idea of the objective text without intention or effect functions to exclude participation in the writings of Shakespeare and Stevens by people who certainly participate communicatively in all other language that comes their way. I do not say that we poeticians consciously intend to produce these discriminatory consequences; but I do claim that our received theories of literariness, articulated within the privileged institutions and media through which we work, contribute to these effects. I articulate my alternative approach, using sociolinguistic, pragmatic and interpersonal linguistic tools to explicate language in literature, with the conscious intention of challenging received literary theory and education and hopefully contributing something to social change.

The linguistic model for poetics has proved particularly fruitful, compared with possible competitors such as ethnography, psychology, sociology. Linguistics has long been the most reflexive social science, the one most concerned with its own status and its theoretical basis. Literary structuralism has inherited from linguistics a laudable desire to get the categories right, to make the metalanguage well-defined, to keep the formalism simple and transparent, to systematize, to clarify, to ensure that arguments and procedures are regular and rational. (I am talking about the goals, not the achievements, of linguistics!) Under the influence of linguistics, structural poetics has, in the work of its best exponents, attained a theoretical coherence which is rare in the human sciences and particularly lacking in traditional literary theory and criticism. Second, the descriptive categories of linguistics are directly pertinent to the medium of literature: a seemingly trite point but one worth asserting in view of the numerous counter-arguments of critics that literature is special in some way that makes linguistics irrelevant — as if literature were a form of language not constructed of nouns, verbs, sentences, etc., or in which these units are not important. I do not say that all aspects of language are equally interesting in literary texts: but that structural poetics shows that more of them are than is traditionally granted by literary critics. A thoroughgoing linguistic poetics would enlarge even further the range of language features deemed to be significant.

Structural poetics 'works', and commands a level of general agreement, to the extent that a number of concepts and habits of thought are now general currency and, though they are not unproblematic, provide points of reference and topics for study which give some unity of aim and of procedure to students of poetics. I am thinking of notions like 'code', 'paradigm/syntagm', 'connotation', '*histoire/discours*', '*actant*', 'metaphor/metonymy', 'speech act', 'dialogic structure', etc. Agreement does not extend to most of the specific claims that have been floated in our discipline. For instance, few of us would be prepared to accept as proven the claim that all narratives can be reduced to a small set of action-sequences; or that complete texts can be generated from abstract underlying structures in Chomskyan step-by-step derivations; or that 'characters' in fiction are totally constituted through semes analogous to those of componential analysis; or that the techniques of defamiliarization of *Tristram Shandy* stand for all the techniques of modern fiction. Such proposals are characteristic of structural poetics, and can be debated in the terms provided by this discipline, but are not *findings* of structural poetics.

From the perspective of linguistics I have to find fault with some semi-accepted assumptions about 'poetic language' which are somewhat of the status of the unproven proposals mentioned in the last paragraph.

1. LANGUAGE AS METAPHOR, LINGUISTICS AS MODEL

Under the influence of semiological thought in the Saussure-Barthes tradition, literature tends to be regarded as an object or a system which is structurally LIKE language, rather than as something which IS language. A literary text, or a corpus of literary texts, is seen as a cultural object constituted in a code, a system of signs, which is not the linguistic code itself but which mirrors the structural properties of that code. In this respect literature is, in the theory of the early Barthes (1967), like other cultural signifying systems such as architecture, fashion, cinema. The position is basically the same in the higher-magnification analyses Barthes offers in the late sixties and early seventies — classically, *S/Z* (1970). Here the literary text is not an utterance in a single code but a medium through which a number of codes are spoken. Again the codes are language-like rather than linguistic.

The methodological step which this hypothesis permits is simple and has been extremely productive. Saussure's claim that language is only one of numerous semiological systems is revised by Barthes to the effect that language is the primary semiological system and the one on which others are structurally based. Whether the relation between the 'primary' and 'secondary' systems is one of homology, analogy or influence is in the present context immaterial. Methodologically, the revised Saussurean position allows the semiotician to apply the categories developed for linguistic analysis to the 'secondary' languages. So for instance paradigm and syntagm, 'emic' and 'etic', transformation and so on are applied to dress, architecture, menus. Extreme examples of the transference of linguistic categories to other codes — extreme in their literalness and exhaustiveness — are Christian Metz' analysis of cinematic 'language' (Metz, 1974) and Leonard Bernstein's attempt, in his 1976 Harvard lectures, to construct a Chomskyan generative grammar for western classical music. There have been scores of slighter projects, e.g. for visual arts, Wollheim, 1968.

The results of this methodological transportation in poetics are well known; they have been lucidly discussed by Culler (1975: esp. Ch. 5). In general terms, the effect is to make instantly available a highly developed analytic terminology for investigating aspects of textual, narrative and poetic structure which previously had either no metalanguage available, or only a rudimentary pre-scientific terminology concocted from classical rhetoric and modern 'practical criticism'. Merely to mention some instances: plot-structure (Propp, 1928) has become much more comprehensible since it has been discussed as narrative *syntax*, applying types of sentence syntax ordering to 'deep structure' narrative strings (Todorov, 1966, 1967, etc.), with 'functions' and 'actors' like those of case grammar (Barthes, 1966; Greimas, 1966); point of view has been illuminated by the use of the verbal semantic categories of tense and mood (Todorov, 1966;

Doležel, 1976) and other properties of narrative ordering have been explicated in terms of aspect (Genette, 1972); componential semantic analysis has been suggestive in the discussion of character and setting in fiction (Barthes, 1970; Fowler, 1977a); some poeticians and text-grammarians have even tried to derive whole texts using procedures and notations drawn from generative grammar (Scheglov and Zholkovsky, 1971 — cf. O'Toole, 1975; Brooke-Rose, 1977). All of this work using the model of linguistic concepts for structures that are not strictly linguistic has been necessarily speculative and sometimes dangerously, vulnerably, speculative. Yet this procedure has enabled fairly formal exploration of matters which were virtually undiscussable before.

But — a very large 'but' — the analogic use of linguistics is a speculative and subsidiary use of linguistics, and unfortunately the higher the degree of abstraction in this use of the linguistic metaphor, the less analysis of language *as language* is practised. Some poeticians even make the limitations of linguistic description a matter of principle:

> ... the direct application of techniques for linguistic description may be a useful approach if it begins with literary effects and attempts to account for them, but ... it does not in itself serve as a method of literary analysis. The reason is simply that both author and reader bring to the text more than a knowledge of language and this additional experience — expectations about the forms of literary organization, implicit models of literary structures, practice in forming and testing hypothesis about literary works — is what guides one in the perception and construction of relevant patterns. (Culler, 1975: 95)

This assertion is misleading and disappointing rather than wrong. I have entered debate on the issues raised often enough to prefer not to take the stand again (Fowler, 1966a, 1967, 1968) but my aim here is to make a strong case for literal linguistics in descriptive poetics, so I comment briefly on Culler's representative dismissal. First, the apparently small contribution that is grudgingly allowed in his first sentence is in fact a vast potential for critically valuable linguistic description. Suppose we take his phrase 'literary effects' to refer to some traditionally recognised major categories of literary structure — e.g. metaphor, metre, parallelism, ambiguity, syntactic style, lexis — and literary response — defamiliarization, atmosphere (e.g. gothic), tone (e.g. satiric). Linguistic stylistics practised within traditional literary frameworks such as these (e.g. Leech, 1969; Halle and Keyser, 1971; Cluysenaar, 1976) has surely demonstrated its practical validity and potential. What is so surprising is that this has remained a very small 'industry': there is still enormous potential for this kind of descriptive practice. Hrushovski (1976 xxxi-xxxiii) regrets the lack of specialized studies in descriptive poetics, points out areas of need, and relates the neglect to the current state of the job market in literature. I would add the suggestion that empirical linguistic studies are discouraged in literary studies in universities because such studies are essentially *subversive* and felt (however vaguely) to be a threat. The detailed knowledge produced by empirical description is a very superior form of knowledge, and a powerful challenge to generalists and to establishment 'lettrists' whose grasp of the facts of literary structures is notoriously slight. What is more, empirical linguistic description starting from traditional critical categories is very likely to suggest the need to *change* those categories, so we have a double threat, one to authority and one to received concepts. The real potential of these challenges is, from my point of view, a powerful incentive to empirical work which will activate the challenges.

My second comment on Culler's dismissal of linguistic description concerns his assertion that 'linguistic description' cannot 'serve as a method of literary analysis' because (to paraphrase him) literary communication involves knowledge additional to that of formal structures of the language — in that respect literary analysis exceeds linguistic description. Stylisticians have in fact repeatedly made this disavowal. I conceded this very point in an early paper (1966a), but linguistics, and my conception of the goals of linguistics, have enlarged so much since the early sixties that I am no longer willing to accept that literary description exceeds linguistic description. Is not the situation of all communication like that attributed by Culler to literature? This is to say, all discourse depends on 'additional experience' beyond knowledge of grammatical structures or 'linguistic competence': on the participants' judgements about their relative social statuses, privileges, and the institutional character of the situation; about the illocutionary and perlocutionary possibilities of the particular discourse-in-situation; thus, about its functional genre; about each co-locutor's knowledge of the world immediately relevant and more distant, and about his analysis of the relevant world (his ideology) and of other possible worlds. No case can be made that literary analysis exceeds linguistic description in terms such as Culler uses, unless (to recall Jakobson, 1960:352) 'the field of linguistics appear to be illicitly restricted'. Contemporary linguistics is beginning to accept pragmatic and socio-cultural factors as part of the matter to be described and in this respect literature offers no exceptional *prima facie* difficulties.

2. THE 'POETIC LANGUAGE' FALLACY

I have commented upon this structuralist fallacy at some length (Chapter nine); and an excellent paper by Roland Posner (1976) makes the essential points with remarkable succinctness and power, attacking what he calls 'the linguistic fallacy in poetics' within the framework of a trenchant (if somewhat over-pessimistic) critique of the limitations of modern linguistics.

This fallacy asserts that there is a single unified phenomenon 'literature' marked by a property 'literariness' which in turn is expressed or constituted by a special 'literary' or 'poetic' 'language' or 'discourse'. The proponents of this view venture to specify the linguistic character of literary discourse with varying degrees of exactness, the most extreme detailing being Jakobson's famous (1960) formula. Let us look briefly at the route by which this audacious claim has emerged.

It is well known that the concept of literature in its unitary and honorific sense is a quite recent development, of roughly the last hundred years: see Wellek,

1970: 3-8; Williams, 1976: 150-54; Fowler, 1973: 105-8. Its earlier connotations are of knowledge or literacy. In the nineteenth century it came to mean writings of special (high) cultural or aesthetic importance. Perhaps significantly, this development coincided with the establishment of university departments devoted to the academic study of English and other national literatures: see Palmer, 1965; Tillyard, 1958. Since this academic institutionalization of literature, it has been a natural question whether the study of literature is an integrated science with its own distinctive subject-matter and methods, like physics or calculus, or whether its object is an assortment of plays, poems and novels that 'have simply got into a university course of "great books" (Frye, 1957: 13). It was in response to this problem — the provision of a principled science of literature to legitimate the institution of literary studies — that classic primitive works of literary theory such as I.A. Richards' *Principles of Literary Criticism* (1924) and Wellek and Warren's *Theory of Literature* (1949) were undertaken. It is in almost exactly these terms that the problem is posed in modern structural poetics; for instance, by Todorov:

> In all the universities of the countries I am familiar with, the division of departments reflects [this anomaly]: we have, side by side, linguistics, economics, physics, psychology — and then suddenly heterogeneous names appear, such as 'English literature,' 'French literature,' 'Russian literature,' etc. Sciences on the one hand, fields of inquiry on the other ... ...[T]he structural analysis of literature is nothing other than an attempt to transform literary studies into a scientific discipline. By this term, 'scientific', I ... mean ... a coherent body of concepts and methods aiming at the knowledge of underlying laws. (1973: 153, 154)

This scientific discipline is 'poétique'. It takes as its motto a dictum of Jakobson's: 'Étudier la "littérarité" et non la littérature' (Todorov, 1966: 125). Non-scientific 'description' is the study of *literature* in the sense of the study of individual texts; poetics attempts to set forth the property of *literariness*:

> .... cette science se préoccupe non plus de la littérature réelle, mais de la littérature possible, en d'autres mots: de cette propriété abstraite qui fait la singularité du fait littéraire, *la littérarité* (Todorov, 1968: 102).

In another formulation, poetics is 'l'étude des conditions qui rendent possible l'existence de ces oeuvres' (1967: 8). These 'conditions' or 'laws' are like the rules of a generative grammar which describe the abstract patterns of knowledge which constitute a language and only indirectly the actual sentences performed by speakers of that language. Elsewhere in Todorov, the methodological analogy of generative grammar is explicit: the object of poetics 'n'est pas l'ensemble des oeuvres littéraires existantes, mais le discours littéraire en tant que *principe d'engendrement* d'une infinité de textes' (1972: 106-7; Todorov's emphasis). 'Littérarité is now given as 'le discours littéraire', a designation which crops up elsewhere:

> ... l'object de la poétique n'est pas les oeuvres mais le discours littéraire; et la poétique se rangera à côté des autres sciences du discours qui devront se constituer à partir de chacun des types de discours (1967: 8).

'Literary discourse' is an ambiguous term. It might mean a *form* of language, that is to say a variety or register with specifiable formal characteristics. Or it might mean a mode of communication, a set of conventions agreed among authors and readers, for instance the expectations and hypotheses mentioned in the latter part of the quotation from Culler given on p.183 above and elaborated in his Ch. 6, 'Literary Competence'. The latter sense is the acceptable one, the former is the linguistic fallacy: the misconception that what is distinctive about literature is that it is, or employs, a distinctive language. I do not think that Todorov means this (his own descriptive work is essentially generic/pluralistic); but repeated use of the phrase 'literary discourse' in the context of discussions of the quintessence of literature can only lend weight to the fallacy of a special poetic language.

The existence of this belief hardly needs documenting. Probably the two most frequently cited papers in stylistics are Mukařovský, 'Standard Language and Poetic Language' (1932) and Jakobson, 'Linguistics and Poetics' (1960). Both contain subtle and complex arguments, but they have certainly been interpreted as demonstration that literature, or at any rate verse, does have its own special language systematically different from 'ordinary', 'casual', 'everyday', 'colloquial' language. This alleged distinction was a preoccupation in several papers and discussions at the 1958 Indiana conference. Its validity is presupposed by the foremost linguistic stylisticians of the 1960s, as a glance at the terms used by the contributors to, and the editors of, the major anthologies will reveal: see Chatman and Levin, 1967; Freeman, 1970; Chatman, 1971. The same is true of the non-linguistic tradition of 'practical criticism', e.g. Nowottny, 1962. So deep-rooted is the assumption that there is a special 'poetic language' or 'literary language' that it has been impressed on the very language that we use to write about the issue.

The title of my book *The Languages of Literature* (1971) is often mis-cited as *The Language of Literature*, doubtless as a result of the habit I have just mentioned. The plural is, of course, quite deliberate. From my earliest writings on this subject I have insisted that, though language in literature is of the utmost interest, there is no linguistic constant that will criterially distinguish and unite all literature (e.g. 1966b: 11-13); therefore no constant and predictable focus for linguistic description. Indeed, linguistic heterogeneity in literature seems to be an empirical fact to start with, and in the final section of this paper I shall suggest a programme for the empirical study of language in literature regarded from a pluralistic standpoint.

3. THE OBJECTIVE FALLACY

This is not a fallacy of structural poetics in particular, but of formalist theory and criticism generally. It consists of the assumption that the literary text is a discrete object (physical or abstract) with its own inherent or intrinsic formal properties — 'structural characteristics' which can be and must be explained without reference to any extrinsic factors. This objectivism became a matter of dogma in Anglo-American 'New Criticism' and its relatives: see Abrams, 1953; Wimsatt and Beardsley, 1946 and 1949 (in Wimsatt, 1954); Wellek and Warren, 1949. A literary work was to be discussed 'in its own terms' and not with reference to any 'extrinsic' factors such as author's biography or intentions, the historical background of the work, readers' responses to it, its effect on the society in which it was published, or on later societies. The prevalence of this objective ideology until very recently can be detected in the very linguistic style of criticism itself: as well as objectifying metaphors projected on texts, such as 'monument', 'urn', 'icon', there is a predominance of nominal references to literature — 'work', 'text', 'object', 'thing (to be explained, etc.)', 'artefact' — pronominal substitutes ('it', 'itself') and endemic spatial metaphors such as 'core', 'level', 'structure', 'parts', 'balance', etc.

In two papers (Fowler, 1975; 1979b) I have suggested that the specific structuralist poetic theory developed from Jakobson's 'Linguistics and Poetics' has an unfortunate objectivist tendency. By separating out the six 'constitutive factors in any speech event' and identifying the poetic function as focussing on one of them — MESSAGE i.e. overt linguistic form or surface structure — Jakobson encourages neglect of other factors — pragmatic, referential, metalinguistic. And his own practical analyses work basically to transform lyric poems into spatial formats, calligram-like arrangements. This objectivization is not however an inevitable outcome of Jakobson's poetic theory. The linguistic model on which it is based contains the elements of a communication theory of language, accommodating as it does referential and interpersonal aspects of language use: they are simply given low attention when Jakobson hierarchizes the factors to place MESSAGE at the top for the 'poetic function'. The preference for text, message, surface structure patterning or whatever one calls it reflects exactly the twentieth century ideology of the 'art object' which Abrams describes. But a shift is occurring.

Indicative is the essay from which I have taken my label 'the objective fallacy': Miner (1976) — an attack on the objectivism of Wellek and Warren, and Wimsatt, written by a scholarly and unrevolutionary American critic and historian of literature. His argument does not get very far — concluding with the vague assertion that 'the status of literature is cognitive rather than objective or otherwise hypostatic' (13) — and it proceeds by analogic assertions rather than systematic analysis; but it is vigorous, apparently sincere and makes an attractive case for regarding works of art as physical expressions of a 'complex human activity' (24) involving an activity of participatory reconstruction by the reader or other consumer. Or again, the very counter-Wimsattian work in 'affective stylistics' by Stanley Fish, whose best paper (1970) is called 'Literature in the Reader: Affective Stylistics'. For Fish, a text or a sentence is not 'an object, a thing-in-itself, but an *event*, something that *happens* to, and with the participation of, the reader' (125); and his method is '*an analysis of the developing responses of the reader in relation to the words as they succeed one another in time.*' (126-7; Fish's emphasis in both quotations). Fish's practical criticism is sensitive and lively, and makes reference to several of the desirable coordinates of a communication model of language, but he lacks a systematic theory and is vehemently opposed to linguistics and stylistics so must forego some of the potentially most useful analytic tools. A similar replacement of the objective model by a communication model is found in the work — based on phenomenology more than linguistics — of the 'Constance School' of *Rezeptionsästhetik*, notably Wolfgang Iser (1972; 1974; 1975; 1976): 'if the reader and the literary text are partners in a process of communication . . . our prime concern will no longer be the *meaning* of that text . . . but its *effect*' (1975: 7; Iser's emphasis). Meaning is not *in* the text, but the text is arranged so that the reader produces a meaning from it; since this involves a transformation of the repertoire of meanings the reader possessed before, a communicative transaction has taken place in which the text is not object but instrument. Iser's most recent book, *Der Akt des Lesens*, draws extensively on speech-act theory to support his argument, and in this respect it agrees with a trend in stylistics, the application of the concepts of illocution, perlocution and implicature (Austin, 1962; Searle, 1969; Grice [1967] 1975) to literature: see Ohmann, 1971 1973; Levin, 1976; Pratt, 1977. Although this venture cannot be said to have been very successful yet, it is part of the welcome tendency being discussed, namely the move away from objective to communication models of language in poetics and criticism, and thus from text to discourse (cf. Chapter five).

Sweeping away some misconceptions and misformulations in structural poetic theory leaves the way clear for a new programme of theory and description. Exposing the partiality of the socio-cultural origins of these fallacies provides strong motives for a new programme, though this is something that I can only hint, not prove. In summary, the programme assumes that

a) 'literary' texts are simply those which are designated and used as literature by the relevant society (cf. Frye, above, p.185);
b) they are not linguistically special or linguistically unitary;
c) their stylistic or codal variation is a major fact for synchronic and diachronic exploration;
d) the *significances* of styles and varieties are the object of interpretation and criticism in linguistic poetics.

c) and d) involve a strong definition of sociolinguistics which I shall detail in the latter part of this paper.

e) the idea of text is subordinate to the idea of discourse, that is, texts are the medium of communication for literature-using societies;
f) literary communication (a type of language use) may be a distinctive form of behaviour even though 'literary texts' and 'poetic language' are not distinctive; cf. Posner, 1976. This is not a matter of central concern to the present paper.[1]

In elaborating the programme built on these principles, we need to start with the most general premise, e; then c and d, my own particular interests, can be handled within the framework of a linguistic theory of discourse. That is to say, we need a *linguistic* theory to organise and make sense of the theories of literary discourse which are emerging in poetics. If we consider what is available in current linguistics, we will rapidly come to the conclusion that there is no such linguistic theory at present in existence. The requisite theory would have to integrate formal linguistics, sociolinguistics and cognitive semantics. The only theory which acknowledges the responsibility to cover and integrate these areas of communicative knowledge and behaviour is M.A.K. Halliday's systemic-functional linguistics developed from the British tradition of Firth and Malinowski and from Prague School linguistics (see Halliday, 1976; 1978). I have drawn support and insights from Halliday's work, but unfortunately his theory cannot be offered as an internationally accessible model: its terminological idio-syncrasy and inconsistency necessitate a tough hermeneutic activity, and Halliday's resistance to the insights of other models (e.g. TG, case grammar) makes it difficult to relate his theory to mainstream linguistics. By contrast, TG grammarians maintain that all factors having to do with 'language use' or 'linguistic performance' are outside the scope of grammar. Thus, from the point of view of TG, language variation — dialects, registers, etc. — is consigned to sociolinguistics which is not really linguistics; and pragmatic factors like speakers' intentions, their knowledge of the world, the effects of utterances, cannot be formalized and are not part of the business of linguistics. Admittedly, attitudes to the scope of linguistics are becoming more generous and inclusive, particularly in Europe as work in text-grammar and pragmatics demonstrates the inadequacy of a theory of linguistic communication which limits itself to the formal syntax and semantics of sentences and neglects inter-sentential, interpersonal and epistemic aspects of the relationship between text and context (i.e., in my terms, it is necessary to treat text as discourse). Research progresses steadily in text-grammar (Van Dijk, 1972; Halliday and Hasan, 1976, Van Dijk and Petöfi, 1977; Dressler, 1977); discourse analysis and the sociology of discourse (Coulthard, 1977; Fowler, Hodge, Kress and Trew, 1979); pragmatics (Van Dijk, 1976, 1977); speech acts (Cole and Morgan, 1975); cognitive semantics (stereotypes and natural categories: see Clark and Clark, 1977, Ch. 14 for introduction and references, and NB the work of Rosch); sociolinguistics (Giglioli, 1972; Gumperz and Hymes, 1972; Pride and Holmes, 1972) and particularly, sociolinguistic thought which takes the radically un-Chomskyan view that linguistics in some sense *should be* socio-linguistics, i.e. linguistic forms should be related to motivating social functions, sociological parameters should be recognised in grammatical theory etc. — a view with which I have a great deal of sympathy: see Hymes, 1977; Halliday, 1978; Fowler, Hodge, Kress and Trew, 1979, esp. Ch. 10).

Thus while we do not possess an integrated theory of language as discourse, the climate outside American mainstream formal linguistics is sympathetic to the possibility of such a theory, and some of the tools for the description of discourse structures which would be included in this theory are being actively developed. In Chapters five, seven and nine above I have recommended that empirical research descriptions concentrating on interpersonal, modal, deictic, socio-linguistic, text-cohesive, etc. dimensions of literary texts should proceed in advance of (and as a contribution to) the formation of a general theory of dis-course. This recommendation is compatible with the call (p.183 above) for more empirical studies in descriptive poetics.

One more general point needs to be made about alternative perspectives which might be taken on communication models of discourse and of literary structure. When we think of language as communication, we tend to think about it in terms of individual people talking to one another: person A gives some information to person B, intends a speech act in relation to B, wants to change B's behaviour, etc.; a perlocutionary effect is produced in B, B responds to the text in such and such a way, etc. This individualistic, interactional, model of literary communication is the dominant one in most of the familiar critical/theoretical approaches which make extensive reference to such concepts as author and implied author (Booth, 1961), reader and implied reader (Fish, Iser). It is paralleled in sociolinguistics by one tradition of analysis which concentrates on spoken discourse in face-to-face interaction, either dyadic or small-group (e.g. Laver and Hutcheson, 1972; Argyle, 1973), and which is underpinned by an interactionist brand of social psychological theory in which the crucial theoretical concepts include 'transaction', 'negotiation', 'face', 'presentation', 'planning', 'problem-solving' (e.g. Argyle, 1967; Berger and Luckmann, 1967; Goffman, 1969). This stream of sociology and sociolinguistics fits very well with the bourgeois aesthetic ideology which emphasizes individual creativity, the singularity of the art object, and the private, individual, character of reading (for some critiques and discussions, see Althusser, 1963; Macherey, 1966; Eagleton, 1976; Coward and Ellis, 1977). This person-centred, or subject-centred, approach to literary communication has been the assumed replacement for objectivism for those critics and poeticians who have made that move, and it has increased in plausibility with the eclectic assimilation of linguistics and particularly for the several prominent poeticians who have used speech act theory (e.g. Iser). This interactionist view of communication and of literary activity enshrines a quite specific and partial (and in my view undesirable) social theory. It suggests that the individual constructs himself, the discourse he utters, and the texts he reads, under weak general constraints such as 'appropriateness', 'cues', etc. Thus discourse is regarded as freely chosen, and structured by the speaker or writer according to his assessment of what is suitable for the situation.

Because it embodies this individualistic social theory, the sociolinguistic study of literature within an *ethnographic* framework is less helpful that it might be. Bauman and Sherzer, for instance, define an 'ethnographic approach to verbal art' as 'a focus upon the situated use of verbal art forms conceived of as communicative process' (1974: 311). This wording at first sight appears to promise just the approach I have been calling for, but Bauman and Sherzer's further comments, and the contents of the papers on which they are commenting editorially, make it clear that 'situated' is meant in an unacceptably narrow sense: it refers to the immediate speech situation within which a literary performance occurs. When Regna Darnell states that 'Narrative performance is in essence *social* activity' she does not mean that it has its basis in social structure, but that it is a cooperative product of a gathering of people: 'The feedback between audience and performer may be crucial to the organization of a performance' (1974: 315). Bauman and Sherzer specifically deny the usefulness of a context seen as 'the culture or society as a whole' and thus neglect socio-historical determination.

But we need to insist that no discourse by individuals within a given speech situation is possible, and no semantic and social meanings of such discourse are possible, without the prior determination of the possibilities within the broader context of the whole culture, diachronic as well as synchronic. The same principle of social determination bears upon non-linguistic behaviour. It is wrong to think of a communicative situation as a kind of stage setting within which the actors have freedom to move around and improvise as they will; equally, it is wrong to regard the language as a stock of resources from which a speaker freely selects. The immediate speech situation and what is said and done within it are constituted by, and simultaneously constitute, social macro-structure. This can be understood with reference to a very familiar sociolinguistic example, pronominal and naming conventions in interpersonal address. It is well known that in very many communities and languages, relationships of power and solidarity are coded in the name variants and pronouns which speakers and writers use to address and refer to one another (see Brown and Gilman, 1960; Brown and Ford, 1961; Ervin-Tripp, 1969; Friedrich, 1972; for a recent literary analysis in these terms, see Uspensky, 1973: 20-32). The conventions are highly structured and clear, even though many of the systems are undergoing transformation at the moment. I have been told by German speakers that the distribution rules for *du* and *Sie* are clear and untransgressable — I don't think this is quite true, but it is instructive that native speakers *believe* that their system is inflexible and mandatory. British modern-language students who have stayed with families in France report with virtual unanimity that the passage from *vous* to reciprocal *tu* is a vital and conscious prerequisite to integration in the family and that this is usually managed by explicit dispensation by the host parents. Now these people are undeniably negotiating an interpersonal relationship; but the important point is that it is social macrostructure which demands and provides the resources for resolution to mutual T (or whatever) and that in addition to fixing their own personal affairs the speakers are also mediating a mandatory social code. Even apparent breaches of the conventions imply, not freedom to speak as you choose, but systematic transgression in terms of the potential of the code. An excellent literary example of this is found in Shakespeare's *King Lear*, Act I Sc. i. While Lear is distributing his lands in accordance with his measure of his daughters' love, the usage of *you* and *thou* by all participants is exactly as one would predict from the Brown and Gilman study. It is a situation of extreme power differential. Only Lear uses T, as an expression of his power as king and father; V signals deference or mutual distance. When Kent rebels against Lear's tyrannous and inhuman behaviour, he systematically addresses Lear as T (where he had consistently used V before) and his other terms of address also replace respect by insult. My point is that, though Kent does indeed rebel, his linguistic choice is not free at that point: disrespect and contempt for a superior are already coded in the address system in the form of an inverted transformation of the system.

To return to the general issue: a linguistic theory of discourse (including literary discourse) emphasizing its interactive and communicational dimension must be a sociolinguistic theory, but not within the tradition of interactional or micro-sociolinguistics. Rather, discourse must be seen from a macro-sociolinguistic perspective, as the product and expression of broadly-based facts of social and economic organization. In no way does this concern with the wider social order imply a suppression of the directly interpersonal in language use; on the contrary, it guarantees a richer explanation of the interpersonal. The social theory is of course quite different from the one I characterized above: it is a theory of social determinism in which the actions of the individual, and communicative performances such as specific linguistic texts, are seen as practices enabled and necessitated by social and economic structure.[2] My own preference would be for a sociolinguistic theory of discourse to be expressed in the framework of an explicitly materialist theory of society, but given all the problems which have troubled Marxism in its relationships with linguistics and with structuralism (Coward and Ellis, 1977; Williams, 1977) we will have to wait a while for such a theory. The most relevant sociolinguistics includes the work of Bernstein (1971), Halliday (1975; 1978) and Labov (1972a; 1972b); for criticism and developmental suggestions, see Dittmar (1976) and Fowler, Hodge, Kress and Trew (1979).

My Preliminaries have produced two converging arguments for the application in literary studies of a certain kind of sociolinguistics. First, literary texts should be put on a par with other texts and regarded as socially situated ('enabled and necessitated') discourse. (Concomitantly, 'literariness' should be shifted from texts themselves and re-identified in terms of the various productive and receptive behaviours of people in different literature-using societies.) This programme raises the necessity of a global social theory of discourse. Second, it is a fact that the canon of 'literary texts' with which descriptive poetics is concerned is very diverse stylistically — yet not randomly varied, for stylistic recurrences are easily visible. This stylistic plurality (better, plurality of codes; see below) is a postulate in the global theory of discourse, and it is also the starting-point for descriptive studies. One prominent task of sociolinguistics is the description, interpretation and explanation of language varieties, and that package of analytic activities becomes usable and important in the present theory of literature. Because the construction of the overall theory itself is going to be so difficult — involving as it does major ideological and methodological revolutions in both poetics and linguistics — I think that descriptive studies should proceed right away with the goal of clarifying some parts of the theory as well as of gathering information about some actual varieties of language in literature.

I return to premisses c. and d. (p.188 above):

c. The stylistic or codal variation of literary texts is a major fact for synchronic and diachronic exploration;

d. The *significances* of literary styles and varieties are the object of interpretation and criticism in linguistic poetics.

These premisses have been phrased in terms which relate specifically to literary texts, but each assumes a general linguistic[3] principle. The first (c.) assumes VARIETY: the second (d.) FUNCTION.

Variety is a familiar and basic principle in sociolinguistics;[3] but it is a somewhat difficult concept because its extension is very diverse. It is founded on the simpler, in the sense of more local and 'atomic', notion of *sociolinguistic variable*. A sociolinguistic variable is a paradigmatic alternation of linguistic forms, at any level of linguistic structure, the alternates of which correlate regularly with contextual circumstances which can be referred to socio-economic macrostructure. Well known examples are Labov's postvocalic /r/; /-ɪn/ and /-ɪŋ/; /θ/ and /tʰ/; *lift* and *elevator*; T and V; *that needs washing* and *that needs washed*; /-s/ and /-φ/ on third person singular present tense English verbs, etc. A sociolinguistic *variety* is marked by co-occurrence of consistent options from several variable paradigms (cf. Gumperz & Hymes, 1972: 21). A working-class speaker from Labov's New York population is likely to have a low incidence of postvocalic /r/s *and* /-ɪn/ (or /ən/) rather than /-ɪŋ/, *and* a number of other features that are consistent with one another and indicative of his socioeconomic class. A speaker who uses the word *elevator* will use *sidewalk* not *pavement, fill out* rather than *fill in*, etc. A systematic use of consistent alternatives gives rise to a recognisable mode of discourse which can be characterised as a variety. Some familiar examples of varieties include Ranamål and Bokmål (Blom and Gumperz, 1972); H and L versions in diglossia (Ferguson, 1959); elaborated and restricted codes (Bernstein, 1971); registers and occupational and situational varieties (Halliday, McIntosh and Strevens, 1964: Ch. 4; Crystal and Davy, 1969; Leech, 1966); hierarchical levels of formality (Joos, 1961). The extreme case of alternative sociolinguistic varieties is choice of different language in bilingualism — English and Welsh, English and Spanish, English and Yoruba, etc. This sociolinguistic alternation among different languages shows that a variety is not a sub-division of a given language but any consistent mode of discourse, marked by any formal features whatever, which has some constant function in relation to a given socio-economic community.

Two further qualifications need to be made. First, speakers do not have to consciously recognise the existence of specific varieties, still less have names for them — 'that's "Swiss German"', 'that's "advertising language"'. Recognition can simply be 'reaction to' on the part of the listener, 'describability' or 'consistency' from the viewpoint of the linguist. Second and relatedly, a variety may be something less than a whole autonomous linguistic system such as French in bilingualism, or Norfolk dialect. It may be a very parsimonious but very meaningful sprinkling of linguistic features so long as the principle of consistency is observed. Also, one feature can stand for a whole variety: for instance, I can signal my profession as an academic linguist by using two or three technical terms during an informal conversation in a non-professional situation. This means that one discourse can encompass and interweave several varieties, a most important facility for language in the social complexity of an advanced industrial society and an important consideration for a sociolinguistic theory of modern European and American literature, which notoriously mixes and alludes to different varieties (cf. intertextuality).

Characterization of a mode of discourse as a variety presupposes that there are other varieties which are in complementary distribution with it; the concept of variety is essentially plural. Inseparable from the idea of variety is that of *repertoire*, which is a set of varieties which possesses validity as a set by its relationship with and use within some specific socio-cultural structure or 'speech community' (cf. Gumperz, 1968: 230; Gumperz and Hymes, 1972: 20-21; Edwards, 1976: 54-8). Note that 'speech community' is inconstant in its scope: it has no fixed geographical, political, economic or cultural parameters but is simply whatever population displays significant patterns of sociolinguistic variation, from a small isolated and contained community like Hemnesberget at one extreme to many other types of larger community, often so diffusely distributed that they never gather as a whole population, e.g. 'speakers of English' or 'academics'. Repertoire is therefore similarly variable in scope; the important point is that it relates primarily to a population and only by derivation to the individual members of that population. It makes sense to say that different individuals have repertoires of different sizes, containing different varieties, according to the breadth and variety of their experience, education, etc.;[4] the sociolinguistic or communicative competences (Hymes, 1971) of individuals (better, representative or specific individual socializeds) are of intense interest to, for instance, educationists and people studying authors. But it must be remembered that the communicative attributes of individuals derive from those of the societies within which they communicate. What is more, communication takes place between individuals with different personal repertoires — this is true of the relationship between a literary writer, who may read, research and travel vastly, have a certain (perhaps wide) network of social contacts, and his readers, whose patterns of language production and consumption, and social circumstances, may be very different and from the writer's point of view largely unknowable. Discussion of the form of the text which links them must not assume identity of linguistic competence between the writer and reader but must contextualize the work in a larger repertorire of varieties within which producer and consumer happen to differentially located.

The interest of variety theory for descriptive poetics is enhanced if we add to the notion of variety that of *function*. I intend 'function' in the sense of the Prague School (Vachek, 1966) and Halliday: 'The particular form taken by the grammatical system of language is closely related to the social and personal needs that language is required to serve' (Halliday, 1970:142). This hypothesis that function determines structure (and conversely, from the critic's point of view, that structure indicates function) can be applied at several different levels of generality. At one extreme, it is compatible with traditional explanations for linguistic universals and the terms for natural categories: so many languages lexicalize 'red' because the mechanisms of visual perception make red a focal colour. At the other extreme, some specific construction in a specific language may receive a functional explanation, e.g. passives in English or the constructions associated with indirect speech acts. In functionalist theory, every construction has its motivation in natural or social structure; there may be ambiguity, but no synonymy, for 'alternative ways of saying the same thing' (active versus passive, one lexical option rather than another, etc.) must be motivated alternatives — there must always be a reason. If we extend this hypothesis to sociolinguistics, it is possible to suggest that a consistent selection of sociolinguistic variables, constituting a variety, realizes a consistent set of semantic options. I suggest that linguistic varieties in the sociolinguistic sense — register, dialects, codes, distinct languages in diglossia — encode different semantic potentials.[5] They are not merely automatic reflexes of, or indices of, different social circumstances; and they are not just variable realization rules of the same meanings within one hyper-grammar. One says different things in different varieties, for they have diverse semantic potentials. They mean differently — and the sources of these meanings are social differences, principally class divisions and social categorizations of the occasions of speaking. Bernstein offers a version of this hypothesis in his differentiation of 'universalistic' and 'particularistic' meanings allegedly associated with 'elaborated' and 'restricted' codes respectively (Bernstein, 1971: Ch.9). Halliday in his more recent writings defines 'register' not just as a situationally determined variety of language, but 'a range of meaning potential . . . the semantic configuration that is typically associated with the situation type in question' (1978: 133). Almost all the empirical work which might bear out this hypothesis remains to be done; it is an idea which has been totally neglected in correlation sociolinguistics. Such description as has been carried out with this idea in mind — e.g. Halliday, 1975; Fowler, Hodge, Kress and Trew, 1979 — suggests to me that it is a good hypothesis.

The effect of regarding language varieties as alternative ranges of meaning is to treat them as CODES in the semiological sense (Barthes, 1967; Eco, 1977) of distinct systems of signs with intersubjectively recognised meanings. Semiology itself does not make this move: for semiology, *langue* is one code, architecture another, fashion another, etc.; so 'Birmingham dialect', 'scientific English' would in semiology be treated as merely sub-codes of English. But as we have seen, varieties are *not* divisions of a language but options within a repertoire. Their relationship is not taxonomic. As far as meanings are concerned, each variety is the articulation of a distinct set of meanings, a coding of meanings. To translate this into traditional literary terms, we must insist that stylistic variation is not 'mere' stylistic variation but that styles encode specific and separate meanings.[6]

The implications of this sociolinguistic theory for our conception of (literary) texts, and for practical study, are straightforward if far-reaching. A text is seen as the material realization of a discourse involving a number of codes 'selected' from a repertoire relevant to the function of the communication between source and addressee(s). Since communicative functions are trans-personal (social, economic, political, cultural) in origin, the relevant repertoire is — to abbreviate — social and not personal. The repertoires of the individuals who participate in this communication may be very different. Personal repertoires are not irrelevant: what an author does with the codal resource accessible to him is of great interest to students of formal (thus semantic) innovation, or 'creativity'; and how readers real or ideal build a text-relevant repertoire on the basis of their personal repertoires is a prime concern of reception theory and sociology of reading. However, it is in principle possible to identify and interpret the codes of the text without reference to the personal codes of its source and addressees. For the purposes of preliminary identification, the literary-historical concept of GENRE, and the sets of major and minor genres that have actually been proposed in literary studies, will be useful. Genres are conventional classes of texts, with distinct formal characteristics, that answer to the 'communicative functions' just mentioned. Of course genre is not the same as variety/code, though in some cases a particular code will dominate the constitution of the texts in a genre. Most often, each of the texts in a genre will be formed drawing on a range of varieties coexisting and woven together, or syntagmatically juxtaposed — both types of co-occurrence are illustrated in the instances alluded to below. Note that genre, like all the other terms in this sociolinguistic theory of (literary) discourse, is not an exclusively literary term: there are recognisable genres in non-literary discourse (interview, news bulletin, newspaper advertisement, legal document, etc.) and I believe the concept should be extended and used in sociolinguistics generally.

I would like briefly to refer to some types of code which are likely to be relevant to literary texts, simply to illustrate the *diversity* of the linguistic structures and significances with which we are concerned.

Literary languages, i.e. styles specialized to different fashions or genres or periods of literary production: for instance, eighteenth century pastoral; gothic; Anglo-Saxon heroic; Miltonic epic; skaldic; French heroic; Imagism. These varieties are always structurally complex, in the sense that arrangements of elements at different linguistic levels enter into their construction. So, for instance, the predominant eighteenth century English verse style of which Gray and Collins may be taken as representative examples is not characterised only by a special 'poetic diction' of swains and groves, but also by an interdependent set of metrical and syntactic conventions: an insistently iambic metre; constant premodification of nouns by adjectives with the consequence that adjectives tend to become non-restrictive, redundant, un-critical; a preference for certain syllabic patterns, particularly two-syllable adjectives followed by monosyllabic nouns; routine syntactic inversions, particularly SOV, VS and VSO. A comparable inter-locking of lexis, metre and syntax occurs in Anglo-Saxon verse, 'Miltonic' style as it persists in the eighteenth and early nineteenth centuries, and presumably many other poetic registers.

To give a different kind of example, gothic fiction has its own conventional morbid and sensational vocabulary for settings and events, plus special syntactic and semantic characteristics, e.g.: inanimate objects as the syntactic subjects of clauses, often breaking selection restrictions; a scarcity of human agents as subjects, especially subjects of transitive verbs; many clauses relating human agents to locations, rather than processes. This code has endured from the late eighteenth century to contemporary popular romantic fiction with remarkable linguistic stability.

With changes in the vocabulary but preservation of the syntactic and semantic patterns just described, the gothic code becomes the stylized literary language of cognitive deficiency identified by Halliday (1971) in Golding's *The Inheritors* and used in the presentation of naifs, idiots and children (Benjy in *The Sound and the Fury*, the young Stephen in *A Portrait of the Artist as a Young Man*, some of the childhood sections of Dos Passos' trilogy *U.S.A.*). This example shows how literary codes are not only linguistically complex but also adaptable from genre to genre, suggesting different effects in different contexts with slight linguistic transformation.

Literary texts draw copiously on codes which are not specialized to the institution of literature. Although the verse examples I referred to above are consciously stylized away from ordinary speech (which is *not* to say that they encode no social meanings), in general texts are written with an awareness of the general linguistic resources available to a writer, and to some extent the resources of his implied reader. The development of the novel as our dominant literary mode — with its pretensions to representation of social structure and personal behaviour — has been a great influence on opening up literature to non-literary sociolinguistic codes. (I am not competent to discuss drama, but its influence also must have been considerable.)

Straightforward examples include the representation of social dialects, for example adolescent and in one case working-class speech in *The Catcher in the Rye* and *Huckleberry Finn*; regionally-based class varieties, for instance Mrs. Gaskell's treatment of northern working-class speech in *Mary Barton* and *North and South*, Hardy's or George Eliot's rural dialects, or Dickens' Cockney. Needless to say, these uses of 'extrinsic' varieties are not transcriptions of real speech, but stylizations (cf. Page, 1973). The techniques of editing and notation are of great interest to a sociolinguistically committed literary criticism: novelists have constructed conventional notations which mediate between speech and writing, lower and middle classes, the class of the represented subject and the different and usually higher class of novelistic producer and consumer. In this area there are important ideological transactions which, I would claim, are visible in language.

Related to social dialects are speech styles which may be claimed to encode different social statuses, personal orientations and cognitive possibilities. In Fowler (1977a) I tried to show how Lawrence in *Sons and Lovers* encoded differences of attitude and of personal relationship in styles rather like those postulated by Bernstein in his theory of 'elaborated and restricted codes' (1971). Similar encodings of personal values and relationships, based apparently on implicit socio-cognitive theories, are widely evidenced in fiction, and well before Bernstein and Halliday. For instance, in *Hard Times* Dickens differentiates sharply (but not consistently) the speech of the Coketown workers and that of their employers: not only by presence or absence of dialect features but by syntaxes which imply contrasting modes of utterance. Contrast, for instance, the first conversation of Stephen Blackpool and Rachel (1969: 104-105) with one between Louisa and Harthouse (200-201). In the first, short and syntactically simple clauses seem to reproduce very closely the intonation and information structure of colloquial speech claimed by Halliday to be very distinct from written prose (Halliday, 1967; cf. Kress, 1976). Syntax in the second is hypotactic, elaborately modalized and qualified, with complex pre- and post-modification in NPs. I suggest that there is a sociolinguistic theory of the expression of personal relationships behind this very marked contrast of stylistic variety.

Many other kinds of variety which can be drawn into literary texts could be mentioned: specialist registers and jargons, occupational varieties, etc. (the jargon of the circus people, or that of the demagogue Slackbridge, in *Hard Times*, besides many others in Dickens); anti-languages (Halliday, 1978; Ch.9, and see this volume Chapter eight on anti-languages in *A Clockwork Orange* and *Naked Lunch*); and analogous functional social varieties. There is no point giving further examples. The only further observation I want to make about sociolinguistic varieties is that, although the examples I have given are all very salient and involve continuous structuration of the whole sequence of discourse, we must be alert to codes which affect only a few structures and surface only intermittently in the syntagm. I am thinking of devices such as Barthes' 'referential code' which, as I have shown elsewhere (Chapter six) consists of a distinctive linguistic recurrence encoding a particular ideological consistency: generic sentences under various transformations used to infiltrate the narrative discourse with clichéd prejudices which construct an evaluative frame for the story. Such phenomena may not be whole varieties in themselves (not even Polonius could sustain 'referential code') for they are too local and fragmentary. Their status may be akin to the stylistic regularities observed and interpreted by Spitzer (1948). I am anxious that these codes should not be lost sight of simply because they are incomplete varieties; they are comprehensible in terms of variety theory, and their potential importance is witnessed by the significance of the Balzacian code pinpointed by Barthes.

To sum up. The theory I am offering allows us to characterize and interpret texts in relation to their traditional coordinates: history, society, author, reader. 'Variety' and related concepts provide a realistic alternative to formalist description: the text is the material realization of a discourse conducted in the relevant varieties. A functional approach to linguistic variation entitles us to treat varieties as 'codes', as semantically motivated. Thus linguistic description leads to and involves interpretation, statements about the communicative function of the text in relation to its extra-textual coordinates. I regard such interpretation as potentially richer and less tenuous than traditional literary interpretation: partly because of the existence of established procedures for linguistic and sociolinguistic description, partly because the focus on sociolinguistic varieties locates the text in society and its history and therefore allows interpretations to be fed by and checked against the findings of other kinds of social and historical research.

At the present stage of development of the model, it is not possible to do much more than set out the beginnings of a programme. To bear out the claims I have made, we need the conclusions of a good number of descriptive projects. So far, only a handful of studies relying on sociolinguistic and functional principles have been published: for instance, the essays published here, and, independently, Kress, 1978, and Aers and Kress, 1978. No doubt some existing literary interpretations could be construed as compatible with this approach: e.g. Zumthor, 1971.

Finally, I regard this model of literature as social discourse, this programme of interpretative sociolinguistic description, as socially responsible and progressive, and educationally useful. By relocating literary texts within the semiotic resources of their society, the theory embodies an offer to remove certain barriers that have been erected around literature, and to return literature to the community. By emphasizing the communicative dimension of literature, the theory offers to relate texts to the experience of readers rather than, as at present, holding them up as objects for mere respectful contemplation. And the stress on sociolinguistic varieties in description and practical criticism allows literary study to be done in very much the same way as other studies of language in society. I should say that I am very much an advocate of a programme of native-language education in schools and universities which explores the varieties of language which pupils actually use and to which they are ordinarily exposed. For two reasons: first, to promote an analytic consciousness of how society and individual interrelate through language; second, to help people develop their own reading and writing (etc.) skills so that they can actively intervene in social practice as it is mediated through language.

The attitudes and methods sketched in this paper may facilitate the application of literature to such problems within the syllabus. And if taken seriously and sincerely, the programme should do more than just try to civilize the masses by graciously giving literature to them. The real aim is to change or even deconstruct the notion of literature so that a very wide range of discourses is actively used by individuals in their conscious engagements with ideology, experience and social organization.[7]

Notes

1. Posner's 'aesthetic communication' depends substantially on the notion of defamiliarization. I believe that it is very important and helpful to give defamiliarization a prominent place in any account of the conventions of productive and receptive behaviour relating to modern western literature (and modern and western uses of earlier and non-western literatures). My book *Linguistic Criticism* (forthcoming) takes as a central topic the relationships between defamiliarizing techniques and ideology. However, communication through literary texts has many other functions, including for instance speech play and verbal duelling, historical record and other reproductions of ideology, incantation, chant, etc. So defamiliarization ought not to be treated as necessary and sufficient in definitions of literary communication. Moreover, defamiliarization is a goal in other types of communication which would *not* be regarded as literary, e.g. criticism, political writing, some types of jokes and comic language.

2. Theories of literary communication which locate the process of communication within a social and historical rather than interpersonal framework are in fact gaining some currency; e.g. Schmidt, 1976: 241-2: 'literary study'

. . . should deal with the whole production i.e. genesis, transmission, receptive processing, and effects of 'texts' of language in a society, aiming at the discovery of inter-subjectively definable characteristics which allow for the sorting out of those texts and modes of dealing with them that can justifiably be called 'literary/poetic' . . . The field of inquiry of literary science is conceived as the total process of *literary communication* in its entirety, literary communication being regarded as a sub-system of the comprehensive system of verbal communication in society.

3. Some readers may be troubled by my unconventional transitions between the terms 'linguistics' and 'sociolinguistics'. When I mention 'sociolinguistics' I usually refer to extant work in that field, e.g. Labov, Ferguson, Gumperz, Hymes, Bernstein, in which correlations between linguistic forms and social structures are observed, but sometimes I refer to the stronger hypothesis that all linguistic form is socially motivated, i.e. that 'linguistics is sociolinguistics' (see Halliday; Fowler, Hodge, Kress and Trew, refs. above). This conception of linguistics is radically un-Chomskyan. I do not have the space here to relate my conception of linguistics point-by-point to more conventional modes, nor do I wish to complicate the argument by making constant explanatory gestures towards the dominant mode of linguistics.

4. Although a lot of offensive nonsense has been talked about this under the heading of 'verbal deficit'.

5. This sentence and the remainder of the paragraph are taken from Fowler, 1979a which compresses the same hypothesis in the context of a different argument.

6. This entails rejecting the transformationalist view of style as alternative realizations of the same meaning or deep structure: Ohmann, 1964; 1966; Jacobs and Rosenbaum, 1971; Fowler, 1972 are no longer tenable.

7. Discussions with Chris Hutchison, Gunther Kress and Tony Trew have greatly clarified many issues in social and linguistic theory explored in this paper; naturally, they should not be held responsible for my opinions or aims.

Further reading

This is a selection of books chosen to fill in the background to linguistic criticism and take the reader somewhat further in certain areas than the present volume goes. Note that I have included a good many 'classics' which have been of enormous value as I have formed my own conception of the field; I would now reject the positions and assumptions of most of the pioneers, but I admire their importance nevertheless. I also include all of the relevant introductory textbooks which I have come across; though some of them are unimpressive, all will give some basic guidance to newcomers to this field.

1. INTRODUCTORY TEXTBOOKS

R. Chapman, *Linguistics and Literature* London: Edward Arnold, 1973
A. Cluysenaar, *An Introduction to Literary Stylistics* London: Batsford, 1976
J. Culler, *Structuralist Poetics* London: Routledge and Kegan Paul, 1975
E.L. Epstein, *Language and Style* London: Methuen, 1978
R. Fowler, *Linguistic Criticism* Oxford: Oxford University Press, (forthcoming)
T. Hawkes, *Structuralism and Semiotics* London: Methuen, 1977
G.N. Leech, *A Linguistic Guide to English Poetry* London: Longmans, 1969
E.C. Traugott and M.L. Pratt *Linguistics for Students of Literature* New York: Harcourt Brace Jovanovich, 1980
G.W. Turner, *Stylistics* Harmondsworth: Penguin, 1973
H.G. Widdowson, *Stylistics and the Teaching of Literature* London: Longman, 1975

2 ANTHOLOGIES OF PAPERS IN STYLISTICS AND STRUCTURALISM

H.S. Babb, *Essays in Stylistic Analysis* New York: Harcourt, Brace, 1971
S. Chatman, *Approaches to Poetics* Ithaca, N.Y.: Cornell University Press, 1973
S. Chatman, *Literary Style: A Symposium* New York and London: Oxford University Press, 1971
S. Chatman and S.R. Levin, *Essays on the Language of Literature* Boston: Houghton-Mifflin, 1967
M.L. Ching *et al.*, *Linguistic Perspectives on Literature* London: Routledge and Kegan Paul, 1980
R. and F. DeGeorge, *The Structuralists* New York: Doubleday, 1972
T. Eaton, *Essays in Literary Semantics* Heidelberg: Julius Groos, 1978
R. Fowler, *Essays on Style and Language* London: Routledge and Kegan Paul, 1966
R. Fowler, *The Languages of Literature* London: Routledge and Kegan Paul, 1971
R. Fowler, *Style and Structure in Literature* Oxford: Blackwell, 1975
D.C. Freeman, *Linguistics and Literary Style* New York: Holt, Rinehart and Winston, 1970; revised edition forthcoming
P.L. Garvin, *A Prague School Reader on Esthetics, Literary Structure, and Style* Washington, D.C.: Georgetown University Press, 1964

Further reading

B.B. Kachru and F.W. Stahlke, *Current Trends in Stylistics* Edmonton, Alberta: Linguistic Research, Inc., 1972

L.T. Lemon and M.J. Reis, *Russian Formalist Criticism* Lincoln, Na.: University of Nebraska Press, 1965

G.A. Love and M. Payne, *Contemporary Essays on Style* New York: Scott, Foresman, 1969

L. Matejka and K. Pomorska, *Readings in Russian Poetics* Cambridge, Mass.: Massachusetts Institute of Technology Press, 1971

T.A. Sebeok, *Style in Language* Cambridge, Mass.: Massachusetts Institute of Technology Press, 1960

3. MORE SPECIALIZED STUDIES IN STYLISTICS, AND OTHER IMPORTANT WORKS

M. Bakhtin, *Problems of Dostoevsky's Poetics* Ann Arbor: Ardis, 1973

M. Bakhtin, *Rabelais and his World* Cambridge, Mass.: Massachusetts Institute of Technology Press, 1973

W.J.M. Bronzwaer, *Tense in the Novel* Groningen: Wolters-Noordhoff Publishing, 1970

C. Brooke-Rose, *A Grammar of Metaphor* London: Secker and Warburg, 1958

C. Brooke-Rose, *A Structural Analysis of Pound's Usura Canto* The Hague: Mouton, 1976

D. Burton, *Dialogue and Discourse* London: Routledge and Kegan Paul, 1980

S. Chatman, *The Later Style of Henry James* Oxford: Blackwell, 1973

S. Chatman, *Story and Discourse* Ithaca, N.Y.: Cornell University Press, 1978

S. Chatman, *A Linguistic Theory of English Meter* The Hague: Mouton, 1965

G.L. Dillon, *Language Processing and the Reading of Literature* Bloomington: Indiana University Press, 1978

U. Eco, *A Theory of Semiotics* London: Macmillan, 1977

R. Fowler, *Linguistics and the Novel* London: Methuen, 1977

M. Halle and S.J. Keyser, *English Stress: Its Form, its Growth, and its Role in Verse* Cambridge, Mass.: Massachusetts Institute of Technology Press, 1971

M.A.K. Halliday, 'Linguistic Function and Literary Style: An Inquiry into the Language of William Golding's *The Inheritors*', in Chatman, ed., *Literary Style*; see section 2 above

W.O. Hendricks, *Grammars of Style and Styles of Grammar* Amsterdam: North-Holland Publishing Co., 1976

W. Iser, *The Implied Reader* Baltimore: Johns Hopkins University Press, 1974

W. Iser, *The Act of Reading* Baltimore: Johns Hopkins University Press, 1978

R. Jakobson, 'Linguistics and Poetics,' in Sebeok, ed., *Style in Language*; see section 2 above.

R. Jakobson and C. Lévi-Strauss, 'Charles Baudelaire's "Les Chats"', in DeGeorge, ed., *The Structuralists*; see section 2 above.

G.N. Leech and M. Short, *Style in Fiction* London: Longman, 1981

S.R. Levin, *Linguistic Structures in Poetry* The Hague: Mouton, 1962

S.R. Levin, *The Semantics of Metaphor* Baltimore: Johns Hopkins University Press, 1977

J. Mukařovský, 'Standard Language and Poetic Language', in Garvin, ed., *A Prague School Reader*; see section 2 above.

A. Ortony, ed., *Metaphor and Thought* Cambridge University Press, 1979

N. Page, *Speech in the English Novel* London: Longmans, 1973

M.L. Pratt, *Toward a Speech Act Theory of Literary Discourse* Bloomington: Indiana University Press, 1977

V. Propp, *Morphology of the Folktale* Austin: University of Texas Press, 1968
M. Riffaterrre, *Essais de stylistique structurale* Paris: Flammarion, 1971
M. Riffaterre, *Semiotics of Poetry* Bloomington: Indiana University Press, 1978
V. Shklovsky, 'Art as Device', in Lemon and Reis, eds., *Russian Formalist Criticism*; see section 2 above.
L. Spitzer, *Linguistics and Literary History* Princeton, N.J.: Princeton University Press, 1948
J. Thompson, *The Founding of English Metre* New York: Columbia University Press, 1961
S. Ullmann. *Meaning and Style* Oxford: Blackwell, 1973
B.Uspensky, *A Poetics of Composition* Berkeley: University of California Press, 1973
W.K. Wimsatt, *Versification* New York: New York University Press, 1972

4. SUPPORTING LINGUISTICS

Stylistics, or linguistic criticism, has drawn on theory and methodology from a variety of distinct schools of general linguistics, and from specialized branches such as sociolinguistics and psycholinguistics. Therefore this list of recommendations is bound to include works of radically and perhaps confusingly different orientations. It could also be vast. I have restricted my recommendations to a couple of dozen books which are either exceptionally reliable introductions to various aspects of linguistics, or highly important works which are often cited in stylistics.

A. Akmajian and F. Heny, *An Introduction to the Principles of Transformational Syntax* Cambridge, Mass.: Massachusetts Institute of Technology Press, 1975
H.H. Clark and E.V. Clark, *Psychology and Language* New York: Harcourt, Brace Jovanovich, 1977
P. Cole and J.L. Morgan, eds., *Speech Acts* New York: Academic Press, 1975
M. Coulthard, *An Introduction to Discourse Analysis* London: Longman, 1977
R. Fowler, *Understanding Language* London: Routledge and Kegan Paul, 1974
R. Fowler, R. Hodge, G. Kress and T. Trew, *Language and Control* London: Routledge and Kegan Paul, 1979
P.P. Giglioli, ed., *Language and Social Context* Harmondsworth: Penguin, 1972
M.A.K. Halliday, *Language as Social Semiotic* London: Edward Arnold, 1978
M.A.K. Halliday and R. Hasan, *Cohesion in English* London: Longman, 1976
G.R. Kress, ed., *Halliday: System and Function in Language* London: Oxford University Press, 1976
W. Labov and D. Fanshel, *Therapeutic Discourse* New York: Academic Press, 1977
J. Lyons, *Introduction to Theoretical Linguistics* London: Cambridge University Press, 1968
J. Lyons, *Chomsky* London: Fontana, 2nd ed., 1977
R. Kempson, *Semantic Theory* Cambridge: Cambridge University Press, 1977
J.R. Searle, *Speech Acts* London: Cambridge University Press, 1969
N. Smith and D. Wilson, *Modern Linguistics* Harmondsworth: Penguin, 1979
E.C. Traugott and M.L. Pratt, *Linguistics for Students of Literature* New York: Harcourt Brace Jovanovich, 1980
P. Trudgill, *Sociolinguistics* Harmondsworth: Penguin, 1974

References

Several of the above papers cite references in the abbreviated form '(Abrams, 1953)'; the following list conflates the several separate listings of the original publications.

ABRAMS, M.H. 1953 *The Mirror and the Lamp* New York: Oxford University Press.

AERS, David, and KRESS, Gunther 1978 'Darke Texts Need Notes: Versions of Self in Donne's Verse Epistles', *Literature and History*, 8, 138-58.

AITCHISON, J., 1976 *The Articulate Mammal: An Introduction to Psycholinguistics* London: Hutchinson.

ALTHUSSER, Louis 1963 'Marxism and Humanism', in *For Marx*, trans. Ben Brewster (London, New Left Books.' 1977), pp. 219-47.

ARGYLE, Michael 1967 *The Psychology of Interpersonal Behaviour* Harmondsworth: Penguin.

ARGYLE, Michael, ed. 1973 *Social Encounters* Harmondsworth: Penguin.

AUSTIN, J.L. 1962 *How to Do Things With Words* London: Oxford University Press.

BABEL, I. 1960 *The Collected Stories*, ed. L. Trilling. Cleveland, Ohio: World Publishing Company.

BAKHTIN, M. 1963 1973 trans. R.W. Rotsel. *Problems of Dostoevsky's Poetics* Ann Arbor: Ardis.

BARTHES, Roland 1966 'Introduction to l'analyse structurale des récits', *Communications*, 8, 1-27.

BARTHES, Roland 1967 trans. A. Lavers and C. Smith, *Elements of Semiology* London: Jonathan Cape.

BARTHES, Roland 1970 *S/Z* Paris: Seuil.

BATESON, F.W. 1967 'Literature and linguistics', *Essays in Criticism*, 17, 322-47. reprinted in Fowler (1971), 54-64.

BAUMAN, Richard and SHERZER, Joel, eds. 1974 *Explorations in the Ethnography of Speaking* Cambridge: Cambridge University Press.

BENVENISTE, E. 1966 *Problèmes de linguistique générale* Paris: Gallimard.

BERGER, Peter L. and LUCKMANN, Thomas 1967 *The Social Construction of Reality* Harmondsworth: Penguin.

BERNSTEIN, Basil 1971 *Class, Codes, and Control*, Vol. I. London: Routledge and Kegan Paul.

BIERWISCH, M. 1970 'Poetics and Linguistics,' in D.C. Freeman, ed., *Linguistics and Literary Style* New York: Holt, Rinehart and Winston, 96-115.

BLOM, Jan-Petter and GUMPERZ, John J. 1972 'Social Meaning in Linguistic Structures: Code-Switching in Norway,' in Gumperz and Hymes, eds., 1972, pp.407-31.

BOOTH, Wayne C. 1961 *The Rhetoric of Fiction* Chicago: University of Chicago Press.

BRADBURY, M. and PALMER, D.J. (eds.) 1970 *Contemporary Criticism* London: Edward Arnold.

BRONZWAER, W.J.M. 1970 *Tense in the Novel* Groningen: Wolters-Noordhoff.
BROOKE-ROSE, Christine 1977 'Surface Structures in Narrative', *PTL*, 2, 516-62.
BROWN, R. 1973 *A First Language* London: Allen and Unwin.
BROWN, Roger, and FORD, Marguerite 1961 'Address in American English,' *JASP*, 62; 375-85; repr. in Dell Hymes, ed., *Language in Culture and Society* (New York: Harper and Row, 1964), pp.234-44.
BROWN, Roger, and GILMAN, Albert 1960 'The Pronouns of Power and Solidarity,' in T.A. Sebeok, ed., *Style in Language* Cambridge, Mass.: Massachusetts Institute of Technology Press, pp.253-76.
CAIRNS, H.S., and CAIRNS, C.E. 1976 *Psycholinguistics: A Cognitive View of Language* New York: Holt Rinehart and Winston.
CARR, E.H. 1964 *What is History?* London, Penguin.
CHATMAN, Seymour, ed. 1971 *Literary Style: A Symposium* New York and London: Oxford University Press.
CHATMAN, Seymour, ed. 1973 *Approaches to Poetics, Selected Papers from the English Institute, 1972* New York: Columbia University Press.
CHATMAN, S.B. 1975 'The Structure of narrative transmission', in Fowler, ed. (1975), 213-57.
CHATMAN, Seymour and LEVIN, S.R. eds 1967 *Essays on the Language of Literature* Boston: Houghton-Mifflin.
CHOMSKY, N. 1957 *Syntactic Structures* The Hague: Mouton.
CHOMSKY, N. 1964 *Current Issues in Linguistic Theory* The Hague: Mouton.
CHOMSKY, N. 1965 *Aspects of the Theory of Syntax* Cambridge, Mass.: MIT Press.
CHOMSKY, N. 1967 The Formal Nature of Language, in Lenneberg (1967), 397-442.
CHOMSKY, N. 1968 *Language and Mind* New York: Harcourt, Brace & World.
CLARK, H.H. and CLARK, E.V. 1977 *Psychology and Language* New York: Harcourt, Brace, Jovanovich.
CLUYSENAAR, Anne 1976 *Introduction to Literary Stylistics* London: Batsford.
COLE, P. and MORGAN, J.L. eds. 1975 *Syntax and Semantics Vol. 3: Speech Acts* New York: Academic Press.
COMMUNICATIONS 8 1966 Introduction à l'analyse structural des récits Paris: Seuil.
COULTHARD, Malcolm 1977 *An Introduction to Discourse Analysis* London: Longman.
COWARD, Rosalind and ELLIS, John 1977 *Language and Materialism* London: Routledge and Kegan Paul.
CROCE, B. 1941 *History as the Story of Liberty* London: Allen and Unwin.
CRYSTAL, David and DAVY, Derek 1969 *Investigating English Style* London: Longmans.
CULLER, Jonathan 1975 *Structuralist Poetics* London: Routledge and Kegan Paul.
DALE, P.S. 1976 *Language Development* New York: Holt, Rinehart and Winston.
DARNELL, Regna 1974 'Correlates of Cree Narrative Performance', in Bauman and Sherzer, eds., 1974, pp.315-36.
DeGEORGE, R. and F. DeGEORGE (eds.) 1972 *The Structuralists from Marx to Lévi-Strauss* New York: Doubleday Anchor.
DICKENS, Charles 1969 *Hard Times* (1854) Harmondsworth: Penguin.
van DIJK, T.A. 1971 'Some Problems of Generative Poetics', *Poetics* 2, 5-35.
van DIJK, Teun A. 1972 *Some Aspects of Text Grammars* The Hague; Mouton.
VAN DIJK, T.A. 1976 'Pragmatics and Poetics,' in van Dijk, ed., *Pragmatics of Language and Literature* Amsterdam: North-Holland Publishing Company, and New York: American Elsevier.
VAN DIJK, T.A. 1977 *Text and Context: Explorations in the Semantics and Pragmatics of Discourse* London: Longman.

References

VAN DIJK, T.A. (ed.) 1976 *Pragmatics of Language and Literature* Amsterdam: North Holland Publishing Co.

VAN DIJK, T.A. and PETÖFI, János S. eds., 1977 *Grammars and Descriptions* Berlin: De Gruyter.

DOLEZEL, Lubomír 1976 'Narrative Semantics,' *PTL*, 1, 129-51.

DITTMAR, Norbert 1976 trans. Peter Sand, Pieter A.M. Seuren and Kevin Whiteley, *Sociolinguistics* London: Edward Arnold.

DRESSLER, Wolfgang U. 1977 *Trends in Text linguistics* Berlin: De Gruyter.

DUCROT, O. et al. 1968 *Qu'est-ce que le structuralisme?* Paris: Seuil.

EAGLETON, Terry 1976 *Criticism and Ideology* London: New Left Books.

ECO, Umberto 1977 *A Theory of Semiotics* London: Macmillan.

EDWARDS, A.D. 1976 *Language in Culture and Class* London: Heinemann.

EHRMANN, J. (ed.) 1970 *Structuralism* New York: Doubleday Anchor.

ENKVIST, N.E. 1964 'On Defining Style' in Spencer and Gregory (eds) (1964: 3-56).
1971 'On the Place of Style in some Linguistic Theories' in Chatman (ed.) (1971: 47-61).

ERVIN—TRIPP, Susan 1972 'On Sociolinguistic Rules: Alternation and Co-occurrence,' in Gumperz and Hymes, eds., 1972, pp.213-50.

FERGUSON, Charles A. 1959 'Diglossia,' *Word*, 15, 325-40; repr. in Giglioli, ed., 1972, pp.232-51.

FIRTH, J.R. 1957 *Papers in Linguistics, 1934-1951* London: Oxford University Press.

FISH, S.E. 1979 'Literature in the Reader: Affective Stylistics', *New Literary History*, 2, 123-61.

FISH, S.E. 1972 *Self-Consuming Artifacts* Berkeley and Los Angeles: University of California Press.

FODOR, J.A. BEVER, T.G. and GARRETT, M.E. 1974 *The Psychology of Language* New York, McGraw-Hill.

FOWLER, Roger, 1965 'Sentence and Clause in English', *Linguistic* 14, 5-13.

FOWLER, Roger, 1966a 'Linguistics, Stylistics; Criticism?', *Lingua*, 16, 153-65; repr. in Fowler, 1971, pp.32-42.

FOWLER, Roger, 1966b Linguistic Theory and the Study of Literature', in Fowler, ed., *Essays on Style and Language* London: Routledge and Kegan Paul, pp.1-28.

FOWLER, Roger, 1966c 'Some Stylistic Features of the *Sermo Lupi*', *Journal of English and Germanic Philology* 65, 1-18, repr. in Fowler, 1971, pp.200-218.

FOWLER, Roger, 1967a 'Linguistics and the Analysis of Poetry', *Critical Survey* 3, 78-89, repr. in Fowler, 1971, pp.219-237.

FOWLER, Roger, 1967b 'Literature and Linguistics', *Essays in Criticism*, 17, 322-47; repr. in Fowler, 1971, pp.43-53.

FOWLER, Roger, 1968a 'Language and Literature', *Essays in Criticism*, 18, 164-82; repr. in Fowler, 1971, pp.65-74.

FOWLER, Roger, 1968b 'What is Metrical Analysis?' *Anglia* 86, 280-320, repr. in Fowler, 1971, pp.141-177.

FOWLER, Roger, 1970a 'Against Idealization: Some Speculations on the Theory of Linguistic Performance', *Linguistics* 63, 19-50.

FOWLER, Roger, 1970b 'The Structure of Criticism and the Languages of Poetry' in Bradbury and Palmer (eds.) (1970: 174-192), repr. in Fowler, 1971, pp.80-100.

FOWLER, Roger, 1971 *The Languages of Literature* London: Routledge and Kegan Paul.

FOWLER, Roger, 1972 'Style and the Concept of Deep Structure', *Journal of Literary Semantics*, 1, 5-24.

FOWLER, Roger, 1975 'Language and the Reader: Shakespeare's Sonnet 73', in Fowler, ed., *Style and Structure in Literature* Oxford: Basil Blackwell and Ithaca: Cornell University Press, pp.79-123.

References

FOWLER, Roger, 1977a *Linguistics and the Novel* London: Methuen.

FOWLER, Roger, 1977b 'Literature as Discourse,' in G. Vesey, ed., *Communication and Understanding*, Royal Institute of Philosophy Lectures, 10, Hassocks: Harvester pp.174-94; this vol. Ch.5

FOWLER, Roger, 1977c 'The Reader: A Linguistic View', *Cahiers roumains d'études littéraires*, 4, 47-60; this vol., Ch.7.

FOWLER, Roger, 1977d 'The Referential Code and Narrative Authority', *Language and Style*, 10, 129-61; this vol., Ch.6.

FOWLER, Roger, 1979a 'Anti-language in Fiction', *Style*, 13, 259-78; this vol., Ch.8.

FOWLER, Roger, 1979b 'Linguistics and, and versus, Poetics', *Journal of Literary Semantics*, 8, 3-21; this vol., Ch.9.

FOWLER, Roger ed. 1966 *Essays on Style and Language* London: Routledge and Kegan Paul.

FOWLER, Roger ed. 1973 *A Dictionary of Modern Critical Terms* London: Routledge and Kegan Paul.

FOWLER, Roger 1975 *Style and Structure in Literature* Oxford: Basil Blackwell.

FOWLER, Roger, HODGE, Robert, KRESS, Gunther and TREW, Tony 1979 *Language and Control* London: Routledge and Kegan Paul.

FOWLES, J. 1969 *The French Lieutenant's Woman* London: Cape.

FREEMAN, Donald C. (ed.) 1970 *Linguistics and Literary Style* New York: Holt, Rinehart and Winston.

FRIEDRICH, Paul 1972 'Social Context and Semantic Feature: The Russian Pronominal Usage', in Gumperz and Hymes, eds., 1972, pp.270-300.

FRYE, Northrop 1957 *Anatomy of Criticism* Princeton: Princeton University Press.

GARVIN, P. (ed.) 1964 *A Prague School Reader on Esthetics, Literary Structure and Style*, Washington: Georgetown University Press.

GENETTE, Gérard 1972 *Figures III* Paris: Seuil.

GIGLIOLI, P-P. (ed.) 1972 *Language and Social Context* Harmondsworth: Penguin.

GOFFMAN, Erving 1969 *The Presentation of Self in Everyday Life* Harmondsworth: Penguin.

GREENE, J. 1972 *Psycholinguistics: Chomsky and Psychology* Harmondsworth: Penguin.

GREIMAS, A.J. 1966 *Sémantique Structurale* Paris: Larousse.

GRICE, H.P. 1967 'Logic and Conversation', in Cole and Morgan, eds., *Syntax and Semantics, Vol. 3: Speech Acts* New York: Academic Press, 1975, pp.41-58.

GUMPERZ, John J. 1968 'The Speech Community', *International Encyclopedia of the Social Sciences* New York: Macmillan, pp.381-6; repr. in Giglioli, ed., 1972, pp.219-31.

GUMPERZ, John J. and HYMES, Dell (eds.) 1964 'The Ethnography of Communication', *American Anthropologist* 66, 6, pt. II.

GUMPERZ, John J. and HYMES, Dell (eds.) 1972 *Directions in Sociolinguistics* New York: Holt, Rinehart, and Winston.

HALLE, Morris and KEYSER, Samuel Jay 1971 *English Stress: Its Form, its Growth, and its Role in Verse* New York: Harper and Row.

HALLIDAY, M.A.K. 1961 'Categories of the Theory of Grammar', *Word* 17, 241-292.

HALLIDAY, M.A.K. 1964a 'Descriptive Linguistics in Literary Studies' in Freeman (ed.) (1970: 57-72).

HALLIDAY, M.A.K. 1964b 'The Linguistic Study of Literary Texts', in Lunt (ed.) (1964: 302-307).

HALLIDAY, M.A.K. 1967 'Notes on Transitivity and Theme in English, Part I', *Journal of Linguistics*, 3, 37-81.

HALLIDAY, M.A.K. 1970 'Language Structure and Language Function,' in J. Lyons. ed., *New Horizons in Linguistics* Harmondsworth: Penguin, pp.140-65.

References

HALLIDAY, M.A.K. 1971 'Linguistic Function and Literary Style', in S. Chatman, ed., *Literary Style: A Symposium* New York and London: Oxford University Press, pp.330-64.

HALLIDAY, M.A.K. 1973 *Explorations in the Functions of Language* London: Edward Arnold.

HALLIDAY, M.A.K. 1975 *Learning How to Mean* London: Edward Arnold.

HALLIDAY, M.A.K. 1976 ed. G.R. Kress, *System and Function in Language* London: Oxford University Press.

HALLIDAY, M.A.K. 1978 *Language as Social Semiotic* London: Edward Arnold.

HALLIDAY, M.A.K. and HASAN, Ruquaiya 1976 *Cohesion in English* London: Longman.

HALLIDAY, M.A.K., McINTOSH, Angus and STREVENS, Peter 1964 *The Linguistic Sciences and Language Teaching* London: Longmans.

HAMBURGER, K. 1968 *Die Logik der Dichtung* Stuttgart: Klett.

HARRIS, Z.S. 1952 'Discourse Analysis', *Language* 28, 1-30.

HASAN, R. 1968 *Grammatical Cohesion in Spoken and Written English I*. (Programme in Linguistics and English Teaching, Paper 7) London: Longmans.

HASAN, R. 1971 'Rime and Reason in Literature' in Chatman (ed.) (1971: 209-329).

HENDRICKS, W.O. 1967 'On the Notion "Beyond the Sentence"', *Linguistics* 37, 12-51.

HRUSHOVSKI, Benjamin 1976 'Poetics, Criticism, Science,' *PTL*, 1, iii-xxxv.

HYMES, Dell 1964 'Toward Ethnographies of Communication', in J.J. Gumperz and D. Hymes, eds., *The Ethnography of Communication* (Washington, D.C.: American Anthropological Association), 1-34.

HYMES, Dell 1977 *Foundations in Sociolinguistics* London: Tavistock Publications.

HYMES, Dell (ed.) 1964 *Language in Culture and Society* New York: Harper.

ISER, Wolfgang 1972 'The Reading Process: A Phenomenological Approach,' *New Literary History*, 3, 279-99.

ISER, Wolfgang 1974 *The Implied Reader* Baltimore: Johns Hopkins University Press.

ISER, Wolfgang 1975 'The Reality of Fiction: A Functionalist Approach to Literature,' *New Literary History*, 7, 7-38.

ISER, Wolfgang 1976 *Der Akt des Lesens* Munchen: W. Fink.

JACOBS, Roderick A. and ROSENBAUM, Peter S. 1971 *Transformations, Style and Meaning* Waltham, Mass.: Xerox College Publishing.

JAKOBSON, Roman 1960 'Closing Statement: Linguistics and Poetics,' in T.A. Sebeok, ed., *Style in Language* Cambridge, Mass.: MIT Press, pp.350-77.

JAKOBSON, Roman 1968 'Poetry of Grammar and Grammar of Poetry,' *Lingua*, 21, 597-609.

JAKOBSON, R. and JONES L. 1970 *Shakespeare's Verbal Art in 'Th'Expence of Spirit'* The Hague: Mouton.

JAKOBSON, R. and LEVI-STRAUSS, C. 1962 '*Les chats* de Charles Baudelaire', *L'Homme*, 2, 5-21.

JOOS, Martin 1961 *The Five Clocks* New York: Harcourt, Brace and World.

KACHRU, B.B. and STAHLKE, F.W. (eds.) 1972 *Current Trends in Stylistics* Edmonton, Alberta: Linguistic Research Inc.

KATZ, J.J. 1966 *The Philosophy of Language* New York: Harper and Row.

KEENAN, E.L. 1971 'Two Kinds of Presupposition in Natural Language', in C.J. Fillmore and D.T. Langendoen, eds., *Studies in Linguistic Semantics* New York: Holt, Rinehart and Winston, 45-52.

KERMODE, F. 1967 *The Sense of an Ending* New York and London: OUP.

KRESS, Gunther 1976 'You name it, sort of thing . . . : Some Syntactic Correlates of Code', *UEA Papers in Linguistics*, 2, 36-42.

KRESS, Gunther 1977 'Tense as Modality', *UEA Papers in Linguistics*, 5, 40-52.

KRESS, Gunther 1978 'Poetry as Anti-language: A Reconsideration of Donne's "Nocturnall upon S. Lucies Day"', *PTL*, 3, 327-44.

LABOV, William 1966 *The Social Stratification of English in New York City* Washington, D.C.: Center for Applied Linguistics.

LABOV, William 1972a *Language in the Inner City* Philadelphia: University of Pennsylvania Press.

LABOV, William 1972b *Sociolinguistic Patterns* Philadelphia: University of Pennsylvania Press.

LAVER, John and HUTCHESON, Sandy, eds. 1972 *Communication in Face-to-Face Interaction* Harmondsworth: Penguin.

LEECH, Geoffrey N. 1965 '"This Bread I Break" — Language and Interpretation', *A Review of English Literature* 6, 66-75; reprinted in Freeman (ed.) (1970: 119-128).

LEECH, Geoffrey N. 1966 *English in Advertising* London: Longmans.

LEECH, Geoffrey N. 1969 *A Linguistic Guide to English Poetry* London: Longman.

LEMON, L.T., and REIS, M.J. (eds.) 1965 *Russian Formalist Criticism* Lincoln, Nebraska: University of Nebraska Press.

LENNEBERG, E.H. 1967 *Biological Foundations of Language* New York: Wiley.

LEVIN, Samuel R. 1976 'Concerning What Kind of a Speech Act a Poem Is,' in Van Dijk, ed., 1976 pp.141-60.

LODGE, D. 1966 *Language of Fiction* London: Routledge and Kegan Paul).

LUNT, H.G. (ed.) 1964 *Proceedings of Ninth International Congress of Linguists* The Hague: Mouton.

LYONS, J. (ed.) 1970 *New Horizons in Linguistics* London: Penguin.

MACHEREY, Pierre 1966 trans. Geoffrey Wall, *A Theory of Literary Production* London: Routledge and Kegan Paul, 1978.

METZ, CHRISTIAN 1974 trans. Donna Jean Umiker-Sebeok, *Language and Cinema* The Hague: Mouton.

MINER, Earl 1976 'The Objective Fallacy,' *PTL*, 1, 11-31.

MORAVCSIK, J.M.E. 1975 *Understanding Language* The Hague: Mouton.

MUKAROVSKY, Jan 1932 'Standard Language and Poetic Language,' in Paul L. Garvin, ed., *A Prague School Reader on Esthetics, Literary Structure, and Style* Washington D.C.: Georgetown University Press, 1964, pp.17-30.

NOWOTTNY, Winifred 1962 *The Language Poets Use* London: Athlone Press.

OHMANN, Richard 1964 'Generative Grammars and the Concept of Literary Style', *Word*, 20, 424-39; repr. in Freeman, ed., 1970, 258-78.

OHMANN, Richard 1966 'Literature as Sentences', *College English*, 27, 261-7; repr. in Chatman and Levin, eds.., 1967, 231-40.

OHMANN, Richard 1971 'Speech, Action, and Style', in S. Chatman, ed., *Literary Style: A Symposium* New York and London: Oxford University Press), pp.241-54.

OHMANN, Richard 1972 'Instrumental style: notes on the theory of speech as action.' In Kachru and Stahlke (1972), 115-41.

OHMANN, Richard 1973 'Literature as Act', in S. Chatman, ed., 1973, pp.81-107.

OHMANN, Richard 1976 *English in America: A Radical View of the Profession* New York: Oxford U.P.

O'TOOLE, L.M. 1975 'Analytic and Synthetic Approaches to Narrative Structure', in Fowler, ed., *Style and Structure in Literature* Oxford: Basil Blackwell, and Ithaca: Cornell University Press, pp.143-76.

PAGE, Norman 1973 *Speech in the English Novel* London: Longman.

PALMER, D.J. 1965 *The Rise of English Studies* London: Oxford University Press.

POSNER, Roland 1976 'Poetic Communication vs. Literary Language,' *PTL*, 1, 1-10.

POSTAL, P.M. 1964 *Constituent Structure: A Study of Contemporary Models of*

References

Syntactic Description Bloomington, Ind.: Indiana University Publications in Folklore and Linguistics; The Hague: Mouton.

PRATT, Mary Louise 1976 *Toward a Speech Act Theory of Literary Discourse* Bloomington, Indiana: Indiana University Press.

PRIDE, J.B. and HOLMES, Janet, (eds.) 1972 *Sociolinguistics* Harmondsworth: Penguin.

PROPP, VLADIMIR 1928 trans. Louis A. Wagner and Alan Dundes (1968) *Morphology of the Folktale* Austin: University of Texas Press.

RICHARDS, I.A. 1924, 1926 *Principles of Literary Criticism* London: Routledge and Kegan Paul.

RIFFATERRE, M. 1959 'Criteria for Style Analysis', *Word* 15, 154-174.

RIFFATERRE, M. 1966 'Describing Poetic Structures: Two Approaches to Baudelaire's *Les Chats*' in Ehrmann (ed.) (1970: 188-230).

RIFFATERRE, M. 1971 *Essais de stylistique structurale*, trans. D. Delas Paris: Flammarion.

RIFFATERRE, M. 1973 'Interpretation and Descriptive Poetry: A Reading of Wordsworth's 'Yew Trees'', *New Literary History* 4, 229-256.

SACKS, H. 1972 'On the Analyzability of Stories by Children', in J.J. Gumperz and D. Hymes, eds., *Directions in Sociolinguistics* New York: Holt, Rinehart, and Winston, 325-45.

SADOCK, J.M. 1974 *Toward a Linguistic Theory of Speech Acts* New York: Academic Press.

SAPORTA, S. 1960 'The Application of Linguistics to the Study of Poetic Language' in Sebeok (ed.) (1960: 82-93).

SCHEGLOV, Yu. K., and ZHOLKOVSKY, A.K. 1971 trans. L.M. O'Toole, 1975 'Towards a "Theme — (Expression Devices) — Text" Model of Literary Structure,' *Russian Poetics in Translation*, Vol. I. University of Essex.

SCHMIDT, Siegfried J. 1976 'On a Theoretical Basis for a Rational Science of Literature,' *PTL*, 1, 239-264.

SEARLE, John R. 1969 *Speech Acts* London: Cambridge University Press.

SEARLE, John R. 1975 'The Logical Status of Fictional Discourse,' *New Literary History*, 6, 319-32.

SEARLE, John R. 1976 Review of N. Chomsky, *Reflections on Language*, in *TLS*, September 1976.

SEBEOK, T.A. (ed.) 1960 *Style in Language*. Cambridge, Mass.: MIT Press.

SEUREN, P.A.M. (ed.) 1974 *Semantic Syntax* London: Oxford University Press.

SHKLOVSKY, V. 1965; first published 1917 'Art as technique'. In Lemon and Reis (1965), 5-24.

SIMONIN-GRUMBACH, J. 1975 'Pour une typologie des discours', in J. Kristeva, et al., eds., *Langue, discours, société* Paris: Seuil, pp. 85-121.

SINCLAIR, J. McH. 1966 'Taking a Poem to Pieces' in Fowler (ed.) (1966a: 68-81).

SMITH, B.H. 1977 'Surfacing from the Deep', review of Fowler (1975), *PTL*, 2, 151-82.

SPENCER, J. and GREGORY M. (eds.) 1964 *Linguistics and Style* London: Oxford University Press.

SPITZER, Leo 1948 *Linguistics and Literary History* Princeton N.J.: Princeton University Press.

THORNE, J.P. 1965 'Stylistics and Generative Grammars', *Journal of Linguistics* 1, 49-59.

TILLYARD, E.M.W. 1958 *The Muse Unchained* London: Bowes.

TODOROV, Tzvetan 1966 'Les catégories du récit littéraire', *Communications*, 8, 125-51.

TODOROV, Tzvetan 1967 *Littérature et signification* Paris: Larousse.

References

TODOROV, Tzvetan 1968 'Poétique,' in F. Wahl, ed., *Qu'est-ce que le structuralisme?* Paris: Seuil, pp.99-166.

TODOROV, Tzvetan 1969 *Grammaire du Décaméron* The Hague: Mouton.

TODOROV, Tzvetan 1971 *Poétique de la prose* Paris: Seuil.

TODOROV, Tzvetan 1972 'Poétique,' in O. Ducrot and T. Todorov, eds., *Dictionnaire encyclopédique des sciences du langage* Paris: Seuil, pp.106-112.

TODOROV, Tzvetan 1973 'Structuralism and Literature,' in S. Chatman, ed., 1973, pp.153-68.

TODOROV, T. (ed. and trans.) 1965 *Théorie de la littérature. Textes des Formalistes russes* Paris: Seuil.

ULLMANN, S. 1964 *Language and Style* Oxford: Basil Blackwell.

USPENSKY, Boris 1973 trans. V. Zavarin and S. Wittig, *A Poetics of Composition* Berkeley: University of California Press.

VACHEK, Josef, (ed.) 1966 *The Linguistic School of Prague* Bloomington, Indiana: Indiana University Press.

VERSCHUEREN, J. 1976 *Speech Act Theory: A Provisional Bibliography with a Terminological Guide* Indiana University Linguistics Club.

VOLOŠINOV, V.N. 1973 *Marxism and the Philosophy of Language*. Trans. L. Matejka and I.R. Titunik New York: Seminar Press.

WEINRICH, H. 1964 *Tempus: besprochene und erzahlte Welt* Stuttgart: Kohlhammer.

WELLEK, René 1970 'The Name and Nature of Comparative Literature,' in *Discriminations* New Haven: Yale University Press, pp.1-36.

WELLEK, René 1971 'Stylistics, Poetics, and Criticism' in Chatman (ed.) (1971: 65-76).

WELLEK, René, and WARREN, Austin 1949 *Theory of Literature*, 3rd ed., 1963 Harmondsworth: Penguin

WILLIAMS, Raymond 1976 *Keywords* London: Fontana/Croom Helm.

WILLIAMS, Raymond 1977 *Marxism and Literature* Oxford: Oxford University Press.

WIMSATT, W.K., Jr., and BEARDSLEY, M.C. 1946 'The Intentional Fallacy,' *Sewanee Review*, 17; repr. in Wimsatt, *The Verbal Icon*, Lexington, Ky.: University of Kentucky Press, 1954, pp.3-18.

WIMSATT, W.K., Jr., and BEARDSLEY, M.C. 1949 'The Affective Fallacy', *Sewanee Review*, 13; repr. in Wimsatt, *The Verbal Icon*, Lexington, Ky.: University of Kentucky Press, 1954, pp.21-39.

WOLLHEIM, Richard 1968 *Art and Its Objects* New York: Harper and Row.

ZUMTHOR, Paul 1963 *Langue et techniques poétiques à l'époque romance (XIᵉ-XIIIᵉ siècles)* Paris: Klincksieck.

ZUMTHOR, Paul 1971 'Style and Expressive Register in Medieval Poetry', in S. Chatman, ed., 1971, pp.263-77.

ZUMTHOR, Paul 1972 *Essai de poétique médiévale* Paris: Seuil.

Index of Names

All names in the text and footnotes are indexed, but not those already appearing in the
Further Reading (pp. 201-203) or *References* (pp. 204-211).

Index of Names